INTERNATIONAL
RELATIONS

INTERNATIONAL
RELATIONS

A GENERAL THEORY

J. W. BURTON

Senior Lecturer in International Relations
University College London

CAMBRIDGE

AT THE UNIVERSITY PRESS

1965

141374

PUBLISHED BY
THE SYNDICS OF THE CAMBRIDGE UNIVERSITY PRESS

Bentley House, 200 Euston Road, London, N.W. 1
American Branch: 32 East 57th Street, New York, N.Y. 10022
West African Office: P.O. Box 33, Ibadan, Nigeria

©

CAMBRIDGE UNIVERSITY PRESS

1965

*Library of Congress Catalogue
Card Number: 65-14857*

*Printed in Great Britain by
Willmer Brothers Limited, Birkenhead*

CONTENTS

ACKNOWLEDGMENTS

It is with appreciation that I acknowledge the support of the Rockefeller Foundation of the United States, and the Joseph Rowntree Trust of Great Britain, both of which made available grants for this study, and in particular to those within these administrations whose imagination and understanding of current international affairs have led them to encourage such exploratory studies as this. I am indebted for the same reason to Professor Sir John Crawford, the Director of the School of Pacific Studies at the Australian National University, who made it possible for me to commence this line of enquiry, and to Professor Georg Schwarzenberger at the University College London, whose assistance I had while completing the manuscript.

It was possible for me to revisit Indonesia, Malaya, India, Egypt, Yugoslavia and the United Nations in connection with this study, and my special thanks are due to many Australian representatives, and to those political leaders, press editors and academics who were prepared to give their time to discussion of their national policies.

I wish to acknowledge the value of discussions at the Ninth and Tenth Pugwash Conferences held at Cambridge and London in August and September 1962, at the Eleventh Conference held in September 1963 at Dubrovnik, and at the Fourth International Conference on World Politics held in Athens in September 1962. Discussions with F. H. Hinsley at Cambridge, with my colleagues and students at the University College London and the London School of Economics, have been most stimulating. The text will show how greatly I am indebted to the published works of many scholars whose discontent has led them to demonstrate that much of our thinking in relation to International Relations was always misled, and in the nuclear age, is more clearly so. Many of my friends have generously contributed to this study, and I am grateful. In particular, thanks to Mrs Olive Currie who prepared the index.

The Editors of several journals have given permission for the use of material previously published, and these include

Acknowledgments

the Editors of *Disarmament and Arms Control, Australian Outlook,* and *Conflict Resolution.* The Editors of *The Natural History of Aggression,* at the Institute of Biology, have also accorded permission to use material contained in my paper.

J. W. B.

UNIVERSITY COLLEGE LONDON

PREFACE

A power approach to International Relations is traditional; historians and students of International Relations most usually have been concerned with recording and describing power balances and alterations in them, and the operations of power politics as they have been revealed by events. The various means by which power is exercised by States, and the international regulation of power, have been the central subject-matters of the majority of international histories and studies of International Relations.

Power in the form of force or the threat of force now plays a less important role than it did before 1945, due to restraints imposed on nuclear States by mutual deterrence, and on all States by an altered political environment. Power in the form of economic or political pressure is also restrained because in practice there can be no clear dividing line between the effective employment of such power, and the threat or use of force. Even the Great Powers have been obliged to make inconvenient economic and political adjustments to circumstances, such as social revolution in small States, which once they could and did prevent occurring. Furthermore, there are segments of the world society in which force, and economic and political power, seem not to be of fundamental importance in relationships. These have increased in size and influence during this century, and especially since World War II; for instance force and power is not significant in the relationship of the British Commonwealth, or of the nonaligned States. In other groups, for instance the Western European States, the States of Africa and of Latin America, power is in evidence, but it is tempered by considerations of co-operation in the pursuit of mutual interests, and by types of authority and influence which do not necessarily rest even ultimately upon force, the threat of force or power.

The purpose of this study is to suggest:

(i) the nature and significance of International Relations, its methods, the current trends in thought, and its present condition (Part I);

(ii) that orthodox power theory is based on several assumptions that cannot be substantiated; and that it has led to policy conclusions that are both self-perpetuating and self-defeating in terms of peace and security (Part II);

(iii) that the altered strategic and political conditions of the nuclear age have imposed significant restraints on the employment of force, and on the exercise of economic and political power; that States are being obliged to break from reliance on alliances and forms of collective security, and to pursue their own independent strategic and political policies; that these trends which seem to be strengthened by current strategic and political conditions are part of a long-term continuum toward increased nationalism associated with the growth of the modern State; that the world society is one in which there is an increasing independence of each of its units, each co-operating in regional and functional arrangements, and in an international organization that has no enforcement capability (Part III);

(iv) that accompanying the decrease in the role of force and of power, there is an increase in the role of decision-making, which implies an increased interest, within each State, in the responses of other States to its policies, in processes of change, in goal-changing, and in national adjustment to change elsewhere; that to understand these aspects of relations between States, concepts, systems and models are required which relate to steering, to communication, to feed-back and to other aspects of decision-making (Part IV);

(v) that nonalignment, looked at in this perspective, is a relevant response to the conditions of the nuclear age; and that there are trends in relations between other States toward a world society of independent States that does not rest on, however much it is influenced by, power relations; that these trends can be explained by reference to the theory of non-alignment (Part V); and

(vi) that under pressure of nuclear and political circumstances a system not dependent upon power is emerging, comprising independent States, each pursuing policies designed to avoid involvement in the affairs of others; and that the theoretical basis of this sytem is non-discrimination in political as well as economic relations (Part VI).

PART I

THE PRESENT STATE OF INTERNATIONAL RELATIONS

1

THE NATURE AND SIGNIFICANCE OF
INTERNATIONAL RELATIONS

I. SOLUTIONS AND GOALS

International Relations as a science is concerned with observation and analysis, and with theorizing in order to explain and to predict. As such it does not seek solutions to problems of peace and security; but in so far as observation, analysis and theorizing succeed in exposing and explaining the operations and processes of relations between States, and of the world system as a whole, politicians and administrators may be in a position to determine policies which reliably achieve their national or international goals.

The distinction between analysis and policy is not always made; many theoretical treatments of international relations conclude with a chapter in which some policy or remedy is advocated, such as 'one-world' or some variation of collective security. International Relations as a science which can contribute to problem-solving has been slow to develop and to achieve results, largely because of such unscientific excursions into policy, and the advocacy of single solutions. International Relations has been further impeded by a confusion with analysis of policy problems: disarmament, arms control and collective security, are some of these. The 'theories' or 'solutions' advanced in respect of these problems are quite separate from general International Relations theory, which is concerned with the revealing and explaining of relations between States in any given set of circumstances.

Nor is the science concerned with goals: world government, democracy, peace, national survival, world domination, are amongst goals that might be sought by States. International Relations can merely suggest that if certain events take place, certain results are likely to follow, that certain policies are likely to produce certain consequences; it can state alternative goals, but their selection is a matter of policy.

One elaboration of this last statement is required. Economics is the study of how best to use scarce resources; there is an implicit goal due to the presumption that there is a universal desire or need or wisdom to be satisfied in determining the most efficient use and distribution of all available resources in the satisfaction of wants—however these latter are determined. This does not prevent the science Economics being employed by those who might have other goals, for example, the prevention of an international division of labour which in producing efficient use of resources would adversely affect some States. So, too, in International Relations; there is the presumption that there is a universal desire or need or wisdom to be satisfied in determining means by which relations between States might be peaceful. In this limited respect International Relations has the goal of peace. This does not prevent International Relations from being employed by those who have a different order of priorities.

It will be at once apparent that 'peace' is used here in two senses. The first describes a 'non-war' condition; strategy, armaments, alliances and collective security arrangements are designed to prevent war, to maintain a non-war or a 'neither-peace-nor-war' situation. Traditional eighteenth- and nine-teenth-century theories concerning alliances and power-balances were of this nature; the twentieth-century treatment of the non-war approach is in respect of nuclear deterrence, and nuclear strategy generally. In the 1958 edition of *The Year Book of World Affairs*, H. D. Lasswell reviewed recent developments in 'The Scientific Study of International Relations'. He noted an increase in theories of international equilibrium, and of military, diplomatic, ideological and economic strategy. He was reviewing work stimulated by the sudden appearance of nuclear deterrence; it was carried out within the accepted and traditional framework of power-balances. Since his review, a vast literature has developed around nuclear strategy, including the application of game-theory, studies of deterrence, of disarmament and its politics. All of this literature is within the broad field of relations amongst States, but it is peripheral to International Relations theory. The fact of nuclear weapons, and academic consideration of strategy and consequences of nuclear weapons, are relevant to International Relations theory only in so far as they provide some of the data, and have prompted re-thinking of many generally accepted propositions.

The second meaning of 'peace' as a goal in International Relations theory relates to those processes of the system which do not rest upon deterrence or enforcement by any agent. Theory, in this context, is particularly concerned with descriptions and analysis of processes that promote a self-supporting international relationship. The characteristic of recent developments in International Relations is a shift of interest from classical concern with a condition of non-war maintained by alliance and collective security and other power threats, to the operations and processes of relations between States, many of which are hidden or suppressed in a non-war condition maintained by power.

It is only as the world environment changes that assumptions and theories about relations between States are re-examined by political scientists; world events, and not intellectual activity, were responsible for the shift in academic interest from conditions of non-war to conditions of peace. First and foremost was the development of thermo-nuclear weapons and their means of delivery which destroyed major war as a useful instrument of policy, and as a means of preventing or promoting change. Accompanying the nuclear development there have been political changes, including the creation of new States, the establishment of a world forum from which they could express themselves, improved means of communication and the further democratization both nationally and internationally of decision-making, the rise to a competitive position of a new ideology, and generally an alternation in values, including values attached to independence and sovereignty. Demands for opportunities for economic and social development, and movements seeking independence had little influence in a non-war system preserved by force; however, once wartime circumstances enabled them to find expression, once they attracted attention and support to the extent that even the most powerful States were obliged to acknowledge them, these demands became important academically as well as politically. As a consequence, a second literature has flourished, dealing with economic development, the politics of economic and technical aid, and the consequences of population increases. The world review edited by Morton Kaplan in 1963, *The Revolution in World Politics,* is not only a most valuable contribution to understanding, but also striking evidence that problems of change are being perceived as central to International Relations—whereas in a power-dominated world they had less relevance. These studies are revealing aspects of relations between States which could not readily emerge within the former power structure, and which are important in the power relations of major States. Parkinson observed in an article in 1960 that 'There was a time when underdeveloped countries were objects rather than subjects of international relations'. This meant propping up whatever regime was in power; but with the advent of political and social upheavals within underdeveloped countries, 'persistence in backing social forces inimical to development must result in placing groups of Great Powers at a decisive diplomatic disadvantage *vis-à-vis* rival groups adopting the opposite course'.[1]

The shift in academic interest from non-war structure to a condition of peace has been further promoted by a realization outside academic institutions that collective security has been a failure, the League and the United Nations both providing evidence of this. In so far as policies of alliances and collective security persist, it is because there is nothing to take their place. Inis Claude in 1963 gathered together the criticisms that have for a long time been made of 'the continuum', as he termed it, of alliances, collective security and world government, and reconsideration of our traditional power concepts is now required.[2] Power in one sense is merely the ability not to have to change, to adjust to change or to tolerate change. Relative power is an explanation of only some aspects of relations between States, especially aspects of relations amongst powerful States, and between powerful and powerless States. The relationships which exist amongst powerless States—of which there are now many—and underlying relationships that exist amongst and with powerful States, and which have been overshadowed by organized power relationships, are not suitably revealed or wholly explained by theories based on power-balances.

There are also developments in other sciences that have helped to promote the shift in interest from non-war conditions, to conditions of peace. Other sciences have provided models

[1] F. Parkinson, 'Social Dynamics of Underdeveloped Countries', *14th Year Book of World Affairs*, 1960, p.207.
[2] I. Claude, *Power and International Relations*, 1962. See pp. 56 ff. below for discussion of balance-of-power and collective security.

and concepts whereby relations between States can better be understood. Deutsch in *The Nerves of Government* demonstrated how breakthrough in any science promotes advances in others, and in particular he showed how cybernetics can help in an understanding of international politics.

Mechanical, organismic, and historical models were based, substantially, on experiences and operations known before 1850, even though many of their implications were worked out more fully only later. A major change in this situation began in the 1940's. Its basis was in the new development of communications engineering with its extensive use of self-monitoring, self-controlling, and self-steering automatic processes. By making equipment that fulfils the functions of communications, organisation and control, significant opportunities were gained for a clear understanding of the functions themselves.[1]

The introduction of cybernetics as a basic model instead of, or in addition to, a power-balancing model, is evidence of the shift of interest to processes underlying relations between States, and of an interest in consideration of a self-supporting condition of peace; it was a shift provoked by circumstances and made possible by the availability of new concepts.

In its present phase International Relations is becoming both narrower and broader: narrower in the sense that it excludes many aspects of relations between States that are now dealt with by specialists in institutions, disarmament and strategic studies; and broader in the sense that it includes features of domestic and international politics, behavioural responses, demands for change, processes of decision-making, which have not in the past featured in the standard texts of International Relations. International Relations is concerned with all national policies that affect other States. Options that governments have include the exercise of military power to preserve a market, and, on the other hand, domestic subsidies or shifts of labour in order not to have to exercise this power; the one is no more or no less in the area of International Relations than the other.

II. METHODS

In few disciplines are problems of method more difficult, and it is clear that personal endeavours to be objective are easily defeated by the adoption of unscientific methods.

[1] K. Deutsch, *The Nerves of Government*, 1963, p.75.

International Relations is concerned, amongst other things, with all events and situations affecting more than one State. In a deductive approach to politics it is customary to make references to past events and situations by way of example, and in an inductive approach, by way of support for a theory. In either case there is reference to history and to current affairs. In both cases the reference has value only if, first, the record of events is exact, and, second, there is agreement on the interpretation of the record.

Herein lies one of the major obstacles to a consensus in International Relations. It is not difficult to give examples in support of a preconceived theory, no matter how improbable, and it is easy to extract from the record sufficient evidence on which to build any theory. Even the most objective and scientific of students will be misled by reference to the historical or current record of particular events. In one's own experience there are many situations, in which one has had direct participation, and about the details of which one believes one is clear; yet the press and the texts report quite differently. The latter may be correct—they may reflect a better perspective than an actor could have; but one questions the usefulness of references to particular happenings to demonstrate or to support a theory when widely differing recordings and interpretation of fact are possible. One may take aspects of the Suez, Cuban, or Dutch-Indonesian disputes to prove almost any proposition one wishes to argue; the facts and their interpretation can be arranged accordingly. It is still more misleading, probably, to take events and situations that are beyond living memory. Furthermore, apart from difficulties of fact and interpretation related to a particular situation, there is an infinite number of cases in the history of man from which to select, and reference to a small number of them cannot be regarded as a reliable basis for generalization.

Two uses of history and of particular events are less open to criticism. First, there are observable long-term trends which appear consistent, and on which one might reliably predict. Population growth, improvement in communications, decreasing illiteracy, increasing destructive power of weapons, and the progressive development of the modern State towards centralization, and less certainly, increasing nationalism and resistance to foreign domination, may be regarded as trends. Historic studies such as Hinsley's *Power and the Pursuit of Peace* are useful in revealing some of these.

Second, it is useful, in order to provide colour and interest, to refer to real situations, provided the circumstances to which reference is made are first described in detail, and no value is attached to the reference outside analogy or allegory. The selection of the example is based upon the prior observation of a long-term trend. Even in this case, it is desirable to argue on the basis of a hypothetical situation using symbols for States, and stating the circumstances, and then placing in brackets, as it were, the type of real situation one has in mind. One example used in this study on several occasions is that of Japan, and the way in which it was forced to seek by war the markets and raw materials denied to it by Western policies. This interpretation of history may be quite distorted; but it is useful to refer to the 'case of Japan' after having earlier stated that if a State A is prevented from acquiring its marketing needs by the discriminating policies of States B, C and D, it will react in certain ways because of certain influences. Similarly, it is often useful to refer to 'revolutionary' and *status quo* States, thus abstracting particular features of policies, even though one is aware that in the real world every State is in some respects in support of change, and in others in support of existing structures.

This neutral method of exposition has a practical value. There can be no meeting of scientific minds across the borders of opposing States if argument is tied to cases on which there is no common agreement as to facts or interpretation. In physics and related subjects there is a common language and there are common reference points, and this has already been demonstrated in international scientific discussions;[1] in sociology and political science there are, as yet, few common concepts, and clearly there could not be widespread agreement on situation analysis. Useful discussion is possible, however, once language and concepts are neutralized, and once the analogous situations under discussion are broken down into their essential and agreed elements.[2]

[1] The outstanding example of East–West discussion is the series of Conferences on Science and World Affairs popularly known as 'Pugwash' Conferences after the name of the town in which the first one was held.

[2] In 1964 it was agreed between political scientists and sociologists from East and West to establish an International Peace Research Association to operate on the Pugwash pattern.

More recently another methodological difficulty has arisen. It was in the fifties—during the 'theory decade'[1]—that International Relations evolved as a discipline in which students could be taught and which could produce its own teachers; previously it relied on scientists from other disciplines such as history, economics and politics. Simultaneously and seemingly in contradiction, International Relations became a field to be worked in, not only by these scientists but also by psychologists, sociologists, and natural scientists, all of whom can claim an interest in relations between States, which clearly touch on aspects of every facet of Man's environment and nature. A philosophic phase in any science is likely to be also an inter-disciplinary one.

This inter-disciplinary interest in International Relations should not be confused with the study of it as a separate discipline. Fox has observed that 'sociology (psychology, etc.) in general, does not contribute to international relations in general. Specific sociological (psychological, etc.) insights may provide practical and sometimes direct assistance to the policy-maker. They also become, like other records of human action, data of possible relevance to the international theorist.'[2] There is not necessarily any direct application of one discipline to relations between States: the existence of aggression in animals and in Man does not prove the existence of aggressiveness in relations between States; seemingly abnormal behaviour by a head-of-State may not be explicable in terms of abnormal psychology or psychiatry; examination of the organizing forces within a provincial community may not help to explain the nature of the international society; no continuity can be assumed which would give reason for assuming some natural growth from the family, to the tribe, to the provincial State, to an international community. International Relations is a separate discipline in the sense that economists, psychologists and others can make a contribution only as International Relations scientists, evolving whatever terminology and concepts are required to describe and to explain the international system and its

---

[1] See W. T. R. Fox's Introduction to *Theoretical Aspects of International Relations*, 1959, p. 11.
[2] *Ibid.* p. 43.

processes.[1] Once the philosophic phase has passed, once concepts and terminology are more generally accepted, International Relations will have benefited greatly from the interest of other sciences; but its concepts and terminology will be meaningful only in relation to this discipline. Ultimately it will evolve its own interdisciplinary structure, comprising specialist studies of the behaviour of States, and these may draw very little upon the existing specializations dealing with Man and men in societies.

[1] See pp. 35 ff. below for an elaboration of the view that conclusions from studies within the provincial community cannot be applied to international society.

2

CURRENT TRENDS IN
INTERNATIONAL RELATIONS

There is not yet any theory of International Relations that provides clear policy-leads for the national or international conduct of international affairs. The official adviser on foreign policy has no references or texts to which to refer, similar to those available to advisers on economic and financial policy. Many political scientists have been attracted by the political realism of theories of power politics; they have not, however, been satisfied that they can explain and predict on this basis, and they have not been able to suggest alternatives to the fatalistic conclusions to which they are usually led. Governments continue to pursue policies based upon power-bargaining and alliances, though politicians and their advisers have no conviction that this power approach will achieve the goals of peace and security that they seek. Indeed, these policies continue to be acceptable despite repeated experiences which suggest that they have self-defeating features. Their legitimacy is indebted to the absence of any credible alternative.

In the period immediately prior to the 1914 war there was a body of thought concerned with politics, with balances-of-power, with limitations of sovereignty and with world government, little changed, except in manner of exposition, since the seventeenth century. Much of this thinking was incorporated in the League of Nations. It persisted throughout the between war period, and was the fundamental basis of the United Nations. President Wilson adopted the view that if the League would not work it must be made to work. Then, and again in 1945 at San Francisco, those who advocated schemes for collective security and international order had no real conviction that they were on the track pointing to lasting peace and security; they argued merely that the consequences of war are such that the sought-for goal *must* be found, and, because there was no other, it must be found on this particular track as though some natural law of human survival would ensure this.

Peace or, more accurately, the absence of major-war, is thought to rest at present upon a condition of mutual terror; if so, it could be destroyed at any moment by accident or by mistake in judgement, or in the future by the deliberate policies of Chinese, Asians, Africans or Latin Americans, whose frustrations might one day seem to counsel the risks involved in warfare with other Powers. This view is an admission that if peace or the absence of war continues, it will be due to the greatly increased deterrence which results from the greater efficiency of warfare, and not to any increased understanding of international relationships or of the origins and nature of conflict. There have been 244 significant wars since 1550, and 15 of these have involved at least one of the greatest powers of the day.[1] Over the years the tendency has been strongly in the direction of more State-participants, and greater total destruction. We are now in the nuclear age; but in terms of policies there has been little evidence of any learning process—we still base foreign and strategic policies on the final use of war, and employ the threat of war. If there were nuclear war now, and if there were a remnant of civilization remaining, it would presumably pursue the same policies; Man would once again develop power relationships, and manage them in ways which he would have once again learned by experience were self-defeating.

Furthermore, there is not any widely accepted alternative to orthodox power theories which helps us even to determine the main factors on which research should concentrate. Hinsley pointed out in 1963 that we were still following the specific proposals of the seventeenth century, despite the differences of the modern world. 'That a civilisation which has broken through immense barriers in almost every other direction, and which has surpassed all its predecessors on innumerable fronts, should still hold views and pursue programmes in international politics that it held and pursued when it was young—this is the outstanding failure of recent times.'[2] We have recorded wars, and analysed the thinking of the philosophers of the day; we have had few suggestions to offer which have not been debated for hundreds of years. Until recently it has been difficult to point to any twentieth-century observations which cannot be

---

[1] Hinsley, p. 278.   [2] Hinsley, p. 3.

found, debated and mostly rejected, by Dante, Grotius, Crucé, Sully, Saint Pierre, Rousseau, Kant, Bentham, James Mill and many others who, before and since, recognized the issue of war and peace as the major problem in the future of Man.

In the last five years, however, there have been most significant contributions to International Relations. In the publisher's frontispiece of Rosenau's *International Politics and Foreign Policy* it was claimed that 'The frontiers of research in international politics are currently alive with activity. Recent articles and books have revitalized the field by challenging and re-examining long-established concepts'. Deutsch has observed: 'The history of many fields of science shows a characteristic pattern. There is a time in which the science goes through a philosophic stage in its development; the emphasis is on theory, on general concepts, and on the questioning of the fundamental assumptions and methods by which knowledge has been accumulated.'[1] This describes the current lively stage of the discipline International Relations.

Some of the more recent contributions are negative in the sense that they are destructive of traditionally held notions, and others are positive in the sense that they provide additional insight into the nature of international society. None has provided a break-through in the sense of a general theory, for each has been concerned with a particular aspect of International Relations. All, however, reflect a shifting interest from international balances and structures, to the processes of relations between States, from *form* of institutions to *processes* of politics.[2] It is my present view that the break-through, the absence of which Hinsley has deplored, will at least be in sight once these separate contributions are fused into a general understanding.

This study rests heavily upon many recent publications, and a concentrated review of current trends in theory will help to introduce it. Recent trends include a challenge to certain assumptions that are important to much of the thinking of the past, in particular to the assumption that Man is by nature aggressive, one that has pervaded thought on relations between States since the problems of peace and war were first considered.

---

[1] Deutsch, p. 3.

[2] This terminology is from W. T. R. Fox in his own article in the book edited by him: *Theoretical Aspects of International Relations*, 1959.

After considering the contributions of past thinkers, Waltz describes one important stream of thought thus: 'Wars result from selfishness, from misdirected aggressive impulses, from stupidity. Other causes are secondary and have to be interpreted in the light of these factors'.[1] St Augustine and Spinoza have their modern disciples in Niebuhr and Morgenthau. Morgenthau believes that we are dealing with 'those elemental biopsychological drives by which in turn society is created'. The starting point has been that 'the struggle for power is universal in time and space and is an undeniable fact of experience'. 'International politics, like all politics, is a struggle for power. Whatever the ultimate aims of international politics, power is always the immediate aim.'[2] Kennan refers to 'man's' irrational nature, his selfishness, his obstinacy, his tendency to violence' as basic to the conduct of international affairs.[3]

Marx and Kant amongst others in the nineteenth century, and President Wilson and most politicians later, were prepared, for different reasons, to attribute war to the existence of the State, or certain types of States. Sometimes the State was regarded as a cause because it reflected the nature of Man, and sometimes the State in itself was regarded as a source of aggression. It is of great importance to International Relations theory to determine the validity of the assumption that the origin of international conflict is in the nature of Man or State. If valid, policy is anchored to power, and to the establishment of balances or deterrence. On the assumption that aggressiveness is a prime motivation, it is difficult to see what 'breakthrough' is possible: some form of world imperialism or international enforcement would seem to be necessary on the analogy of a provincial government with central enforcement powers. But this analogy is misleading; the international society is decentralized and based on independent sovereign States. There is historic evidence of a progressively increasing value being attached to independence and sovereignty,[4] and there are sociological explanations of this trend.[5] Sovereign States will not accept control by any super-State. It is this

[1] K. N. Waltz, *Man, the State and War,* 1959, p. 16.
[2] H. J. Morgenthau, *Politics among Nations,* 1960 ed., Chapter 3.
[3] See Waltz, p. 16.
[4] See in particular Hinsley, and pp. 67 ff. below.
[5] See in particular J. W. Burton, *Peace Theory,* 1962.

dilemma which has been central to studies in International Relations. The need to break from power-politics and power-politics in disguise is acknowledged; but any clear-cut alternatives, such as the universal federal pattern, seem politically unrealistic.[1] If, on the other hand, aggressiveness is not a prime factor, and is the consequence of lack of alternative processes of change, then this dilemma is avoidable. Reasonably, in the nuclear era, a great deal of attention has been given to the nature of Man, the State and processes of change.

Aggression has been examined from several points of view. Waltz, in his most usefully destructive book *Man, the State and War,*[2] demonstrated that neither Man nor State—any type of State—could alone be held responsible for the origins of the situations which have led to war. More fundamentally, aggressiveness in animals and in Man is being re-examined; it is not usually described as a prime motivation. Biologists, sociologists and medical scientists have arrived at no clear conclusions. 'Aggressiveness' may not be an appropriate term to use in describing relations between States. One of the more thorough examinations of aggression was recently made at a symposium on the Natural History of Aggression.[3] In any case—and this is the more important consideration—aggressiveness in Man does not demonstrate aggressiveness in the State. Wolfers has on several occasions pointed out the difference between Man in society and the actors on the international stage.[4] The State is an institution with machinery of government and decision-making processes which make any direct application of human studies quite misleading.

Attempts to bring about change raise issues of justice in relation to the proposed alterations, and attention has been directed both to justice and to peaceful change. A non-war system can be stable over numbers of years by reason of restraints, exercised by those States that have a predominance of military power, on others that might wish to bring about changes in international relationships. This is the power-based model which thinkers and decision-makers have traditionally

---

[1] See in particular G. Schwarzenberger, *Power Politics,* 3rd ed., pp. 527-33.

[2] See also pp. 34 ff. below for discussion of 'aggression'.

[3] J. D. Carthy and F. J. Ebling (editors), *The Natural History of Aggression,* The London Institute of Biology, 1964.

[4] A. Wolfers, *Discord and Collaboration,* 1962.

employed. In his review of previous thinking, Waltz observes: 'The optimists see a possibility of turning the wicked into good and ending the wars that result from present balance-of-power politics. The pessimists, while accepting the derivation of the balance-of-power and war from human nature, see little if any possibility of Man righting himself.'[1] In any non-war or enforced-peace relationship, stability is the important consideration, except in so far as those States which exercise the restraint themselves want to change, in their favour, their relations with others. In these circumstances, wars are politically judged 'just' or 'unjust'—to use terminology employed by Grotius and many others since—according to the standpoint of the State making the judgement. A *status quo* Power would presumably judge as 'unjust' any war which sought to upset the existing relationship. From terminology of this subjective kind has developed concepts of 'defence' and 'aggression' according to the national viewpoint from which the judgements are made. But war being a legitimate instrument of policy, war to change the *status quo*, often depicted as 'aggression', must also be regarded—as it often was in the classic period of the balance-of-power—as legitimate and unavoidable in the absence of means of peaceful change.[2]

Once processes of change without war become important to relations between States, attention comes to be focused upon national policies rather than upon international structures. Once it is acknowledged that a condition of peace can rest only upon the satisfaction of sovereign States with their opportunities to pursue their interests by peaceful means, once it is acknowledged that even nuclear States cannot prevent change and demands for change, then attention becomes focused on processes of change, adjustment to change, on all the relevant detailed processes such as re-training of labour, and on internal reorganization of social, political, and economic life to make them relevant to altered circumstances. Foreign policy, which is designed to pursue national interests, is in the nuclear age turned inwards, and alteration in goals and values is inevitable. The relevant academic exposition is by use of the concept 'nationalist universalism' of Hans Morgenthau[3] taken up by Herz in *International Politics in the Atomic Age*. In the nuclear age,

[1] Waltz, p. 20.
[2] See in particular R. W. Tucker, *The Just War*, 1960. See also pp. 71 ff. below.
[3] Morgenthau, *Politics among Nations*, 3rd ed., 1960.

to a far greater extent than ever before, each State is bound to pursue its national interests in ways which are compatible with the universal interest; otherwise, there could be conflict and the total destruction of national interest.

Thus it is that decision-making has recently received perhaps the main attention of International Relations theorists; and decision-making is being studied from a 'peace' rather than from a 'non-war' point of view. Deutsch explains his 1963 study:

This book suggests that it might be profitable to look upon government somewhat less as a problem of power and somewhat more as a problem of steering; and it tries to show that steering is decisively a matter of communication. It tries to suggest some of the implications of this viewpoint for the analysis of governmental institutions, of politicial behaviour, and of political ideas, and it points to some areas of empirical research on politics that might deserve a higher priority of attention than they have often received in the past.[1]

Snyder, Bruck and Sapin published in 1962 *Foreign Policy Decision-Making* as 'An Approach to the Study of International Politics'. In their view, 'to create an applicable scheme of analysis, it is necessary to draw upon works and methods of scholars outside the field of Political Science', and they found 'one possible solution through a study of decision-making, showing how this technique may be applied to international politics as well as to the individual involved'.

A communications or steering model will be acceptable academically as evidence increases that circumstances are forcing States away from the application of power, and it will be acceptable politically if it points to alternative policies that are practical alternatives. In this connection, the study of the relations of small States which rest on communications rather than power is of special interest. Amongst these States are those that avoid alliances—the nonaligned States. The first serious study of nonalignment, outside articles in journals, was contained in *Neutralism and Nonalignment* edited by L. W. Martin, and contributed to by eight others, all of whom were associated with The Washington Center of Foreign Policy Research. This was written largely from the point of view of United States' strategic interests. In 1963, Lyon published *Neutralism* and endeavoured to be more descriptive and comprehensive.

[1] Deutsch, p. 9.

Analytical and descriptive studies of decision-making are to be expected in this altering international background. In 1963, J. Frankel gave the subtitle 'An Analysis of Decision-Making' to his book *The Making of Foreign Policy*. The new interests of International Relations are at once apparent in the subtitle, and the treatment is not just a formal description of foreign offices and of diplomacy as included in former texts.

The new interest in processes of decision-making has not eliminated interest in international organization; on the contrary, there is a consequent new interest in types of structures which do not pre-suppose enforcement, and which facilitate cybernetic processes in relations between States. After a warning that functionalism and regionalism depend on, rather than determine, political climate, Claude observes, 'In the long run, however, it may be that the economic and social work of international organization will prove to be one of the means of developing a system whereby Man can control his political climate'.[1] The description of ECAFE given in 1963 by David Wightman supplies some practical evidence of the way in which functional co-operation tends to lead into political co-operation.[2]

This description of recent trends in International Relations theory should not be interpreted as implying that descriptions of relations between States that are based on power have now lost their relevance, or that policies relying on power will necessarily give place to others. On the contrary, once a power situation occurs, it tends to be self-perpetuating and cumulative. Take, for example, South African racial policies; no adjustment process, or gradual goal-changing takes place for fear that the national objectives will be prejudiced; any co-operation or improved contact with excluded races is in any event regarded as weakness or appeasement. South Africa relies on repressive legislation backed by force. Feed-back, knowledge of local and world reactions, assessments of likely future responses, are deliberately excluded from decision-making processes, if not employed to justify even greater efforts to defend existing policies. Such a situation is finally resolved by power. We are likely to see an increase in the number of power situations,

---

[1] I. Claude, *Swords into Plowshares*, 1959, p. 402.
[2] D. Wightman, *Toward Economic Co-operation in Asia*, 1963.

especially in the developing areas and where racial conflicts occur.

Even in relations between thermonuclear States, which cannot sensibly employ the destructive power at their disposal, the power relationship will continue to dominate; like a gold reserve it is in the background, and has a real function even though not used.[1] But despite these continuing realities of power, and because of the deterrence to its employment, trends in theory which reflect trends in events, are inviting more attention to goal-changing, and processes of adjustment generally.

It follows that options and values are now important to International Relations. Nitze asks, 'What are the central values which comprise the ultimate, non-contingent values of the group? One of these is probably survival of the group as a group. But related to this is the problem of the essential character of the group, to change which would be in essence tantamount to non-survival of the group.'[2] Two out of five Canadians recently indicated that they thought 'The West should take all steps to defeat Communism, even if it means risking nuclear war'.[3] International Relations is now far more interested, than was the case even in the late fifties, in the processes by which these options are presented and chosen. A power model describes the resultant of decision-making processes. The significance of the new model is that it is explaining how decisions are made.

These are features of International Relations which in the nuclear age are becoming of far greater importance. The historian will be impressed with continuity of thought, with continuous threads that weave through the fabric of theory; anyone reviewing trends in theory which appear to be recent will be impressed with the manner in which insight and theory in International Relations have been stimulated, not by intellectual effort, but by changing world circumstances.

In 1962, Snyder and colleagues summarized recent trends thus:

A bird's eye view of thirty years of intellectual development in the field of international politics reveals obvious trends aside from the one toward more systematic analysis. First, there has been a notice-

---

[1] See pp. 105 ff. and also Part VI below for discussion of these issues.
[2] Fox, p. 6.
[3] See J. Paul and J. Laulicht, *In Your Opinion* (Canadian Peace Research Institute), 1963, p. 21.

able tendency to balance the earlier institutional approach with the more recent behavioral approach. Second, interest has broadened from simply the interaction of States to include the analysis of the 'why' of patterns of interaction. This requires inquiry into policy-formation. Third, an effort is being made to break the confining effects of the realist-idealist polarity which in turn has grown out of a reaction to idealistic reformism in the 1930's and to the power emphasis of the 1940's.[1]

[1] Snyder, Bruck and Sapin, p. 55.

3

THE SEARCH FOR A
RELEVANT RESPONSE

Thanks to thermonuclear weapons, far greater attention is now being focused on the intellectually unsatisfactory state of International Relations. At the time of writing there is widespread public comment in England about housing conditions, and the need to prevent the landlord rackets. Uncivilized housing conditions have been known for years to exist, but no earnest public attention was given to the problem until there was a political scandal in the course of which, and as an incidental, housing rackets were exposed. The thermonuclear invention and effective means of delivery of warheads may be the public scandal which will direct increased attention to problems we have lived with for hundreds, if not thousands, of years.

Increased attention, however, is not sufficient; a score of philosophers have failed to make a break-through in this area of human relationships. Re-phrasing and re-statement of earlier thinking, and comparison of similarities and differences in the conclusions reached, are exercises which have been productive of great works, but not of increased insights. More social imagination than this is required; and for there to be imagination, new stimuli are usually needed.

It is in this that currently our opportunity lies. Three international revolutions have taken place in the post-war period: the availability of weapons of mass destruction, and their means of delivery from any point on the globe to any other point; the emergence of Communism as a viable system of government at a time at which the former system of private enterprise is still adapting and strengthening its institutions; and the creation of many new States out of former colonial or dependent areas. These three world revolutions have taken place in a world environment which was already being revolutionized; the age of exploitation and colonization, the age of *laissez-faire* international trading competition, had given place to an age of social revolution in which the nature of international rivalries had changed. A feature of this altering environment is what Morton Kaplan describes as the discontent and disenchantment of sections of politically-aware populations in the face of world changes and failure to adapt to them.[1] Apart from this common background, these three world revolutions were as unrelated in their origins as any revolutions taking place in the one civilization at the same time could be; there is no obvious relationship between the introduction of Communism and the technological advances which led to the discovery of nuclear energy, nor is there necessarily any causal connection between either of these and the successful wartime and post-war demands for independence made by formerly dependent peoples. If there is a common factor it is only one which has hastened these developments, and that is World War II. If there is a common factor which continues to promote them it is the prospect of World War III. Each is a revolution in its own right. But while Communism, technological developments in armaments, and the creation of new States may have had little causal connection, they have inter-acted and their effects are inter-twined in International Relations. All three have brought about modifications in the structure of world society, and in the traditional policies of the older States.

Each one of these three world revolutions, and the background in which it has taken place, seriously challenges pre-war assumptions and analysis, necessitating a fundamental re-thinking of some concepts that have been current since sovereign States commenced to be in contact with one another. Traditionalism is the practice of re-stating old arguments so that they appear to include the changed circumstances of the day; but in the post-war world the re-statement required is so different that less confusion in thought might be created by new statements. We have always had a deterrent, this was the nature of national arms; but a concept which applied to bows and arrows has differences from the concept of a nuclear deterrent so great that new terminology and treatment is required. A multilateral balance-of-power structure in a world in which there are many more-or-less equally powerful nations is so utterly different from the bilateral balance now created by the existence of two

---

[1] Kaplan, *The Revolution in World Politics,* 1963, p. 14.

giant thermonuclear powers, that a new description of balances, and not a re-statement, is required.

International Relations as a study has been orthodox-bound for a long time, perhaps because many of those engaged in it—East and West—have been culturally bound, and have tended to reject new approaches put forward in other countries for fear that these might prejudice the interests of their own nation. But re-thinking and re-statement is now taking place under the pressure of these revolutions. Political scientists, strategists, international lawyers and others engaged in disciplines normally regarded as being distinctively outside that area of studies described as International Relations, have begun to show dissatisfaction with and anxiety about the state of our thinking in relation to peace and war. Most are toying with the concept of power, but trying to break away from this age-old welder of social organization whose increased potential is now capable of destroying the modern civilization which it helped to create, and trying to do this in a way which is politically and academically credible.

When events require fundamental changes in thinking, then this is evidence that thinking had not been sufficiently fundamental. The rise of a new political system, the creation of new States, the intervention of powerful weapons of destruction are all revolutions which have occurred independently as I have suggested; but each has a history which makes each credible, for each forms part of the normal and predictable development of social organization and technological progress. The possibility of nuclear energy was known to the fathers of the generation that constructed the bomb. There was something inadequate about classical and pre-war thinking if each of these revolutions has upset this thinking, and necessitated a reassessment of assumptions and values. The probability is that, if by reason of re-thinking in the light of these post-war developments we can explain warfare in the past, we will find an explanation of warfare now; if we find an adequate explanation of warfare in this age, it will also explain warfare in the past.

The solution to the problems of war and peace will not be found in the invention of new structures and systems, or in ingenious strategic devices, or in legal or institutional gimmicks designed to enforce conformity with some stated principles. If the critical problems in International Relations are finally solved, it will be through an understanding of developments taking place within the international system. The political scientist cannot produce new devices or solutions; he can observe and explain only, and thus make possible policies which reliably achieve the objectives sought.

When policy and theory persist only because nothing more satisfactory is taking their place, and because effective policies must emerge within the general flow of international life, it would be folly on a practical plane, and unscientific on an academic plane, not to examine all innovations in policy and all unorthodox theories as they develop. One of three world revolutions, the development of weapons of mass destruction, being technological, can do no more than underline the seriousness of the problem of peace and war, and bring to attention the failings of systems based on power, and which include warfare as an instrument of national policy. The other two revolutions represent new thinking, and new approaches to International Relations. Marxism appears to provide no clear theory of International Relations, despite the claim that international conflict arises out of class struggle and would be eliminated if all States were communist States; steps toward the goal of universal socialism must still be taken within the framework of power politics, thus making the ideological clash itself part of the operation of power-politics. In the nuclear age an ideological issue of this order could not sensibly be resolved within the framework of power politics.

Interest shifts, therefore, to the third revolution, that is, the rise of new nations, and in particular to the policies of independence and nonalignment which they have pursued. Nonalignment and its theoretical justification are an important part of this study because it is an innovation, and, as such, may provide some pointers toward an understanding of relations between States generally. The theory of nonalignment stems from the defects of balance-of-power, and collective security and world government. It appears to be a relevant response of States not possessing significant power in the circumstances of the nuclear age, in which there is a surplus of power which destroys any idea of balance; and particularly revelant when there is a great number of independent sovereign States many of which act and exercise power independently, and all of which together exercise an influence upon far more powerful nations.

Nonalignment is only part of the protest against academic and political orthodoxy. It is a practical response to circumstances, though in some cases by leaders brought up in the Western intellectual tradition. The academic protest against orthodox theory is to be found in what has come to be termed 'Peace Research', and developed on the initiative of social and natural scientists not primarily concerned with the discipline of International Relations. But so far Peace Research has been concerned with aspects of peace somewhat remote from immediate political realities, such as conflict resolution in small groups, and frequently has not been related to the body of theory surrounding International Relations.

We have already noted the work of a great many political scientists who have been thinking around aspects of the general problem of peace and security. Certain trends in thought, stimulated by the altered political and strategic conditions of the nuclear era, are observable. Each has made a special contribution. Not infrequently, however, the political scientist is so pre-occupied with one idea, that others are regarded as conflicting or falsely valued. Personal antagonisms are not unknown in this otherwise scientific endeavour to ascertain the nature of International Relations. The task ahead is to feed all these ideas through a computer, and in this case it must be a human computer. Unless a current stream of thought is organized from time to time, direction is absent. It is for this reason that one must attach value to the many conferences and discussions that are in the sixties taking place nationally and internationally in the field of Conflict Research and International Relations generally.

In the Parts of this study that follow we will examine the failure of orthodoxy, the altering world environment, the new models and concepts which seem to be required to explain relations between States, nonalignment as a working model, and the international system which appears to be evolving under pressure of altering circumstances.

PART II

CHALLENGE TO ORTHODOXY

4

FALLACIES REGARDING MAN AND THE STATE

A challenge to orthodoxy is still required in a general theory of International Relations; relations between States are still widely regarded as being concerned primarily and fundamentally with alliances, power balances, collective security, international enforcement institutions, diplomacy, the prospects of international law, and the threatened or actual use of military power. In more recent theoretical studies most of these aspects have receded into the background; but there still exists a great gulf between the 'frontiersmen',[1] on the one hand, and teachers and students of International Relations, on the other. For fifteen years trends of thought have been strongly against the traditional approach to relations between States. Current frontiersmen thinking may be a passing phase, existing only until World War III; the challenge to orthodoxy may not finally succeed. The nature of the challenge is, however, not yet widely known, and it is not possible to follow developments in theory without knowledge of criticisms made of previous thinking.

The world international system is one comprising sovereign States, each having laws which have no validity outside its territories, each safeguarding its own interests by whatever means are within its capabilities, and each basing its foreign and strategic policies on the expectation that in the pursuit of their interests other States will employ whatever means are within their powers. The international system throughout recorded history has rested upon the national expectation of violence, and consequently upon national policies of defence and of power-politics. The great question of all times has been whether power could be managed so as to eliminate or to confine conflict, and if so, how.

---

[1] 'Frontiersmen' is the term Rosenau used to describe theorists in his Introduction to *International Politics and Foreign Policy* which he edited (p. 1).

Orthodox theory which developed in relation to this power-politics system of International Relations, continued to accept the assumptions on which it was traditionally based, assumptions regarding the nature of Man and the State. Indeed, philosophers in all ages have, with few exceptions, so taken for granted the aggressiveness of Man and the State that no alternative to national policies, based on the exercise of whatever power is possessed, has seemed expedient.

In the nuclear age we are confronted with a stalemate position; there appear to be no alternative theories or policies to those which rest upon power-politics and the use of war as an instrument of policy, yet the obvious consequences of these theories and policies in the nuclear age would seem to make them impractical. This intellectual stalemate position is acceptable only by reason of the strategic stalemate position which nuclear weapons have created. It is, nevertheless, an intellectually untenable position; the nuclear stalemate is not theoretically a stable situation, and it should not be permitted to disguise the unsolved dilemmas inherent in orthodox theory.

Objections to aspects of orthodox theory of International Relations can be sustained either by examining assumptions made regarding the sources of international conflict, which we do in this chapter, or by an analysis of the structures that are put forward on the basis of these assumptions, which will be made in the next chapter.

I. THE NATURE OF MAN

The source of war, along with other evils, has most commonly been held to be in the nature of Man. Spinoza, St Augustine, Niebuhr, most political scientists to the present day, and 'the man in the street' of all ages, have nominated Man as the cause of war, because of his selfishness, greed, aggressiveness, the drive for self-preservation, ignorance, and lack of insight and spiritual guidance. With Man as the cause of war, certain remedies immediately suggested themselves. It is at once clear that if selfishness, greed and aggressiveness are the cause of war, the remedies are those such as advocated by psychologists, psychiatrists and adherents of religions which believe Man can be 'saved'; but these are long-term processes, not particularly relevant to a world situation in which the threat of war is constant and immediate. Education, even the education of élites, must also be eliminated as a remedy on these grounds. The more practical, and the more usual remedies that have been advocated, based on the assumption that Man's nature is the source of conflict, are those that take his nature as static, and seek to contain or to inhibit evil or anti-social tendencies; alliances, balance-of-power, and collective security are some of these, and all seek the organization of aggressiveness to deter aggressiveness.

Balance-of-power and related devices can be criticized as structures, quite apart from the assumptions regarding Man which seem to have called them into existence. We will later proceed to do this. If, however, these basic assumptions remain unchallenged and untested, all alternatives to these devices based on them may prove no more successful. It is not sensible to destroy a structure, and then to build another on the same basis, if that basis is itself false.

A distinction is required between the nature of Man as such, that is the instinctive or other attributes associated with the individual, and Man living in society. Rousseau seemed to be confident that when each primitive individual provided for his own requirements there was no conflict; but when men began to depend upon each other conflict arose. This distinction between Man as an individual, and Man in society is an important one which seems to have been missed by many writers. Having observed that Man in society is aggressive, they have assumed this aggressiveness is an individual and fundamental character-istic. Thus Morgenthau and others have argued that men and States, being fundamentally aggressive, must be deterred by the aggressiveness of others, or by some other balancing device. It could be that the introduction of this deterrence may have been the prime provocation of aggressiveness in an otherwise non-aggressive individual. Clearly, an expectation of aggression or greed can promote responses which will ensure aggression and greed; and remedies based on the assumption of Man's aggressive nature, such as balance-of-power, can establish conditions in which that balance-of-power would seem to be required, even though there were no original aggressiveness. One suspects that much of Man's history could be written in these terms of self-defeating and erroneously based policies.

The assumption of aggressiveness deserves more serious

attention than early philosophers and orthodox theorists have given it. If one answers the question what is orthodox theory in International Relations about, the uncomplicated answer must be, how to manage the normal and to-be-expected aggressiveness of sovereign States. Experience is that States have been aggressive; but whether this aggressiveness is a primary urge which would justify precautionary measures, or merely a secondary condition which could be partly brought about by such measures, is an issue at the heart of orthodox approaches which has not been determined. At the risk of seeming to labour the point, and because this must be the starting point of any enquiry into relations between States, let us turn to consider aggressiveness.

II. THE NATURE OF AGGRESSIVENESS

The notion of aggressiveness in animals may finally be shown to be valid; however, it should not escape attention that in the present state of our knowledge we have no conclusive evidence of this. The pecking hen is a most contented bird once placed in a single cage from which it can enjoy the company of other female machines without fearing them, and the aggressive cow in the milking yard undergoes what appears to be a change in character once it is polled. But even though biologists can show aggressiveness in lower forms of life to be a prime motivation, human aggressiveness is not thereby established. There may be a continuum in cortical evolution, but this does not argue against the possibility of effective cortical dominance of behaviour at a certain stage. Indeed, whatever may be the case with animals, psychologists seem generally to agree that 'there is no direct physiological basis for aggression, although the blocked frustrated or deprived organism can be counted on to show the physiological changes accompanying emotion. . . . One cannot cite man's inherent aggressiveness as a factor that makes war inevitable.'[1] Aggressiveness is described and understood by psychologists in terms of frustration, fear, displacement, scape-goating, rationalization, projection, compensation, identification, and a host of other relevant concepts, and this seems to indicate that aggressiveness is regarded as an emergent or dependent state of mind.

[1] F. H. Sandford, *Psychology—A Scientific Study of Man*, 1961, p. 212.

This academic conception of aggression as a secondary or derived motivation does not prevent aggressiveness being treated by law, and by society generally, as a primary one for which the individual himself is responsible. We still endeavour to control and to suppress aggression by the individual without regard to environmental causation. Just as vagabonds were once hounded as lazy people, and not considered to be the product of a system which included unemployment, so aggressive people are still an object of social condemnation, and subject to laws designed to suppress them.

This gap between academic theory and social practice, which exists within a provincial society, is even more in evidence in the international society. We in the West did not consider the degree to which Western nations were directly and indirectly responsible for Italian, German and Japanese aggressions. Not only is the gap between theory and practice greater in our approach to international aggression, but the consequences are greater. The gaoling or execution of the aggressive individual does not destroy society. But in the international field in the nuclear age, any attempt to repress apparent aggressiveness, as an alternative to the removal at an early stage of the underlying causes of the so-called aggression, is of concern to the whole of civilization. We have been prepared, however, to leave this gap unbridged; it has been more expedient in a system of power politics for a State to create an image of unprovoked aggression than to indulge in analysis of its own policies. The nuclear deterrent may be changing this complacency.

Even though the popular notion of aggressiveness in the individual as a prime motivation were valid, it still could not logically be argued that States were aggressive. While certain behavioural aspects of international affairs are obvious, there is not necessarily any valid application of terms and concepts developed in a closed society to relations between States. In recent years there have been many bold and questionable extensions into the international society of concepts developed in the closed society. International affairs have come to be attractive as an 'interdisciplinary' study. Terminology which is precise in, and relevant to, a particular discipline, has been injected into discussion of international affairs; according to their interests, psychologists, psychiatrists, educationalists, biologists, physicists and others, have their own images of the world. Hoffmann, who regards decentralization and the fragmentation of power as the chief characteristic of the study of International Relations, issues a warning to sociologists. 'If we look at the two social sciences whose contributions have been most vital for the development of International Relations— political science and sociology—we see that these disciplines use as a model the image of the integrated community.' He goes on,

Now, whatever else the nature of International Relations may be, it is not an integrated system. It would be very dangerous in the long run to continue to work in our field with a model that does not fit. Many of the mistakes of contemporary theoretical attempts in International Relations and International Law come from the systematic misapplication of the model of the integrated *Rechtsstaat*— the modern State characterized by a sense of common purpose, a rational organization of power, a bureaucracy and the rule of law— to the decentralized international milieu, either as a norm for analysis or as a goal.[1]

One of the most common images is that of an international society in which States each have the attributes of persons within a community. Abnormal psychology, game-theory, value judgements and moral responses then appear to be immediately relevant to international studies. In reality the nation-State is not of this order; if there must be an analogy then it would be at least as appropriate to use mechanics or electronics as sociology. It is only by describing the world system as it operates that there can be any understanding of it: and then it becomes clear why mentally healthy leaders sometimes appear to respond abnormally in the international system, why seemingly moral men take seemingly immoral decisions, why mild and humble members of the leading élite appear aggressive. It is true that nations are led by humans, and that these people are subject to certain pressures from other humans, and it is therefore true that there are important problems associated with perception and understanding of the policies and motives of others; but to argue some continuum in the development from a family, to a tribe, to a community, to an international society, is false. Families may have some characteristics and responses which can be described in terms appropriate to its members, but the State and

[1] S. Hoffmann (ed.), *Contemporary Theory in International Relations*, 1960, p. 3.

its machinery of government cannot be given these same psychological attributes. It is as misleading to adopt a Man-as-actor approach as it is to adopt an unqualified State-as-actor approach to International Relations.

Any theory which postulates the continuous development of social organization from primitive forms to an international society, leads logically to world government as a final policy to be sought. If in fact there is no continuum, the goal may be unattainable, even in theory; energies will have been wrongly directed, leading to failure and disaster, in addition to academic and popular disillusionment and desperation. Indeed the dangers of a false approach are greater than mere disillusionment. When the biologists and the psychologists assert that there are aggressive tendencies amongst individuals within nations, and imply that for this reason nation-States tend to act aggressively, then they are encouraging every State to have an expectation of aggression, even though there is no discernible enemy. The defence policy of the State will tend to produce just the results it seeks to avoid—and the ultimate responsibility for this could be that of the intellectual in society. One wonders to what extent the philosophers of the past have been directly responsible for peace-through-strength ideas, and for the whole notion of national independence being a function of defence capability. The extension of the findings of biology and psychology into the international relationship is probably false; but as an analogy it could be useful to point out that in animals and in Man, aggressiveness is frequently a non-passive response to the perception of a threat, or to the experience of a frustration. Political leaders of States who accuse other States of being aggressive, would then know where the responsibility for aggression frequently lies.

It is difficult even for the academic to divorce himself from popular notions. Hans Morgenthau, despite references in one passage to the elements of fear and frustration in aggression, has difficulty in bridging this gap between scientific and popular conceptions of aggression. He is prepared to assert that it is possible to predict on the basis of the past because of 'those elemental bio-psychological drives by which in turn society is created'. He continues, 'The essence of international politics is identical with its domestic counterpart'.[1] On this basis every

[1] Morgenthau, *Politics among Nations,* 1960, pp. 33, 34.

responsible government would be fully justified even in the most peaceful circumstances in taking extreme and provocative defence measures. Waltz, in *Man, the State and War*, set out to demolish several of these pre-conceived notions, in particular the single-cause approaches which suggest that Man or the State is responsible for war. Claude,[1] by careful analysis, destroyed any reason for counting upon power-balances, collective security, or world government, as our haven. One suspects that if more work were done along the same lines it would be found that modern political thought, East and West, is full of implied assumptions, false premises and causes and cures derived from folk-lore of the past, which have been handed down without much question for hundreds of years.

The circumstances of the post-war world seem to be exposing the nature of conflict more clearly than has been the case ever before. In the days of conventional weapons, situations of apparent aggression tended to develop quickly and to promote immediate political and military responses, and consequently their causes could not currently be analysed. History is liberally scattered with records of wars which commenced with what appeared at the time to be unprovoked aggression. In our memory are the aggressions of Italy, Germany and Japan. What led to aggression was not clearly perceived at the time; and in any event it would not have been politically expedient to contradict official and popular explanations which accompanied one's country's war effort.

In the nuclear age, in which firstly there is an overwhelming power of destruction the use of which no State can readily contemplate, and in which secondly, there is a world forum at which large numbers of independent peoples can freely express themselves, time and opportunity are available for analysis of situations of aggression as they develop. In the pre-SEATO days of disturbance in the territories which were formerly French Indo-China, the United States had a virtual monopoly of nuclear weapons. In 1953 Mr Dulles threatened over-whelming force at a time and place of American choosing if communist aggression continued. He was employing the ortho-dox tactics of power politics of the pre-nuclear age, but with nuclear weapons. There was a widespread reaction even in the United States, and hesitation in implementing such a grave

---

[1] Claude, *Power and International Relations*.

threat gave opportunity for some objective assessments of Nationalism in South-East Asia as a movement quite separate from Communism. Once thoughtful discussion and debate had taken place in press, parliaments and on popular platforms, the threat could not be implemented, at least without inviting the active hostility of Asian, African and important sections of Western public opinion. The restraint was not due just to the consequences of the use of nuclear weapons—far more importantly it was due to the grave doubts raised about the merits of the United States case. The prolonged tug-of-war between existing and opposing regimes in South-East Asia has continued ever since, and there are now appearing, after some ten years of public debate, grave doubts in Western circles as to the wisdom and justice of supporting unpopular and repressive regimes, and blaming local opposition to them upon 'communist aggression'. If it had not been for the power of modern weapons, and the hesitation which enabled debate, Mr Dulles might have been able to act, China would have been destroyed, and movements dubbed communist would have been repressed in South-East Asia; history would have recorded the episode as another example of meeting aggression—whereas thanks to nuclear weapons and to world public debate, the accused was not executed, and there were subsequently at least some doubts about his guilt.

This was the position when the United States had a virtual monopoly of nuclear power. The development of a mutual deterrence now causes even greater hesitation, and occasions even more important delays, thus giving opportunities for world assessment of complicated situations. Perhaps Suez will mark for the historian a turning point in world affairs as important as Cuba; in such cases in the pre-nuclear age, invasion would have been completed quickly and effectively by the Power whose interests seemed to be threatened. The mutual deterrent of the thermonuclear age has provided opportunity for reflection, just at a time when the interests and opinions of smaller nations are a matter of great relevance in the struggle between the great nations. Law, justice, strategic interests, morality, the role of vested interests, are all matters now widely debated in respect of any crisis situation.

The consequence is that a clearer vision as to what constitutes aggression is now being obtained. What is being revealed by this nuclear-age slow-motion picture of aggression appears to be quite different from the orthodox and popular notion. In the area of Asia traditional expectations of aggression have led to policies which have appeared to be aggressive to both Communist and Western leadership. There have been actual confrontations, and expectations of aggression have become self-supporting. In Vietnam and Laos, in Formosa and Korea, Western support for unpopular and sometimes repressive regimes has had the appearance to the Chinese of a deliberate encirclement, and aggressive intents have been deduced from frequent, though unofficial and irresponsible, statements coming out of the United States. Chinese responses in each of these areas have in turn appeared to be aggressive, and have seemed to justify Western policies.

Once unpopular governments are maintained by foreign support in the context of the United States confrontation with Communism, any local oppositions, even genuine ones, can conveniently be labelled subversive, and dealt with as such. This has happened both in Communist and in Western-dominated nations. It is by this process that there has developed the appearance of active communist aggression in South-East Asia, even when there is no tangible evidence of aggression. Admittedly the existence of internal unrest due to a feudal land-tenure system, and to extremes of privilege, does not prove that foreign subversion is absent; but it can be assumed that any government which lacks popular support, and whose continuation in office is of strategic value to a major Power, will attempt to attribute internal threats to its security to a foreign Power. It can also be assumed that intervention by a foreign Power will be interpreted by a nation in the opposing power-bloc as aggressive in intent. It is the duty of any government in a system of power politics to prepare for the worst, and to take counter-measures against the type of military encirclement which the West has imposed on China.

The element of fear in Chinese policies is understandable— many countries in the area, for diverse reasons, seem to wish to contain if not to damage China. After ten years of isolation from world councils, the element of frustration is also inevitable. China, like Japan before the war, having tried every means of breaking through the barriers to normal political and economic intercourse, will, if the isolation is maintained, have little option but to aggress; but this will not necessarily prove that the Chinese Government is aggressive, or has been forced by population pressures to expand, or has been brought into conflict by revolutionary leadership. It will only suggest that Western responses to change in China have promoted fear and frustration in China.

Support for the view that aggression is not a prime motivation in international relationships has emerged as an unintended effect of nonalignment. The nonaligned nations comprise a variety of political systems including capitalist, feudal and communist. Some, like Burma and Cambodia, happen to be on or near the borders of China, yet they seem to consider themselves more secure in relation to China than in relation to some of their non-communist neighbours. Thailand and Vietnam, on the other hand, even though not as close to China, are aligned with a great Power, and allow that Power to establish bases, and depend upon it for their security. They fear Chinese aggression more than do the nonaligned States of Burma and Cambodia. Nonalignment seems to be demonstrating that security may be possible, even for a small country on the border of a major Power, provided firstly that it has internal political support, and secondly that there is no threat from it to that neighbouring Power by reason of foreign bases for use by an opposing major Power. In this way nonalignment seems to have shown that what appear to be aggressive policies arise out of false perception, and fear of aggression, and not out of some innate or inevitable aggressive instinct or desire for power on the part of sovereign States. It seems to show, moreover, that the type of system, whether it be communist or capitalist, is not an important consideration: a State is not aggressive in a primary sense, regardless of its internal institutions. The avoidance of military alliances may be a strategic policy more in accord both with political reality and with our academic knowledge of the nature of aggression, than the traditional policies of alliances which consistently throughout history have ultimately produced the results they sought to avoid.

The term 'aggression' is one which has no useful place in a description of relations between States. In the balance-of-power system of the nineteenth century, change was brought about by attempts to challenge the existing balance. The State making the attempt was not more an aggressor than were those

States which sought to preserve their interests in an existing structure. Wars were neither just nor unjust. However, once objectives other than power-balancing guide policy, subjective judgements become important, and terms such as 'aggressor' are given a new meaning; they no longer accurately describe relations between States, and reflect only the image one State has of another. 'Aggression' in international relations has little if any relationship with the aggressiveness of Man; it is the institutionalization of conflict in circumstances in which organized social groups compete for possessions which cannot be shared, which neither would share, or which some wish to deny to others, and in circumstances in which inequality of power and inequality of strength of desire for these possessions leads to differing judgements as to the pay-off from the use of force. Up to a certain stage in the development of the modern State, and the sharing of world resources and opportunities between States, this competition was to be expected —quite apart from any consideration of Man as aggressive or not.

Confusion between the use of force because of Man's aggressiveness, and its use as a social or international institution, has clouded thinking in most ages—the nineteenth century being to some extent a period of greater clarity in this respect. A second confusion has resulted from a failure to differentiate different stages in the development of 'aggression' or in the use of force as a social institution. The ritual fighting of tribes, ending in a drinking bout, has features somewhat different from wars between modern States. Conflicts between neighbouring groups in the development of the modern State, and between States in the distribution of world territories and resources, were in motivation different from wars to hold trading advantages and to preserve strategic bases. The changing role of imperialism from exploration, to colonization, to trade, to strategy, to promotion or defence of political institutions and social values reflects a change in the nature of and drives behind so-called aggressiveness, though fighting when it occurred in all cases has been called 'war'. Political conflict, the threatened use of force, and the use of force, are different in character and in motivation in different times and in different places and circumstances. Lumping all the various types of activities together under aggression, conflict, or warfare, is seriously misleading in a description or explanation of relations between States.

III. THE STATE AS CAUSE OF WAR

The general proposition that it is the internal political institutions and organizations of States that explain their external aggressiveness has had wide support throughout all modern times. It is not clear which types of States are apt to be more aggressive, though it is clear that the type of State in which any writer happens to be living is far less apt to be aggressive than any other. Currently capitalist States regard socialist dictatorships as the main cause of war, and communist theory seems to argue that there may be peace only when all States are socialist. Even nonaligned States are seen by others as a cause of international tensions because of their own internal weaknesses. Communists can claim theoretical support for their position, but it is not clear whether the requirement is that all States be socialist States, that is, that capitalist States must be eliminated in order to obtain peace, or whether all States must be abolished, capitalist and others. Non-communists have been content merely to assert a distinction between peaceful and aggressive States, democracies of the Western type being peaceful. This was the broad viewpoint of Woodrow Wilson after the First World War, and has not altered materially since. Many writers in the West agree with Richard Nixon, 'If it were not for the communist threat the free world would live in peace'.[1]

There are many objections to regarding the State as the cause of war. There is no reason for believing that, in any particular world situation, the removal by one side of 'bad States' would lead to perpetual peace. On the contrary, experience is that wars which have been fought to end all wars by the removal of offending States have not achieved this end. Apart, however, from the obvious fallacies in the argument, there are some practical objections. If the nature of the State is the cause of war, then there must be a universal perfection in all States for peace to be assured. The possibility of any agreement on the nature of a perfect State, even amongst States with similar institutions, is quite remote. The possibility of agreement amongst States with different institutions, on what changes should be made within them in order to promote peace, does not exist.

Whether valid or not this approach is no more useful in the

---

[1] *New York Times,* 19 November 1953, p. 1.

conditions of the modern world than the approach which endeavours to reform the nature of Man. Capitalist, communist and other States are currently required to live in the same world, and will be so required, for many decades to come. It is not reassuring to assert that in the meantime peace may be possible only if the Communist States, which are peace-orientated, are powerful enough to deter aggressiveness in capitalist States pending their collapse; or to assert the opposite proposition that peace may be possible only if the capitalist States maintain a predominance of power. Indeed, on this theory, war could be expected, even thermonuclear war, initiated by whichever group of States regarded themselves as being about to be defeated by the other group in non-war competition.

It could be argued that, as with Man, it is not necessarily the State as such which is the source of conflict, but the processes which occur once one State is in a relationship with another. In other words, while those that attribute war to States believe that peace will flow from the perfection of States, there are those who assert that the nature of the State is determined to some degree by its relations with others. This would appear to be the position of Machiavelli, Hobbes and Rousseau. It is a view in sharp distinction from that held by Cobden, Wilson, and by politicians who are bound to take the prejudiced view that it is the nature of *other* States which is the source of tensions.

The view that it is the response of States to the actions of other States that is the cause of war, rather than the internal organization of States, appears to be based on the view expressed by Rousseau that conflict is inevitable because the relationship is based and maintained on nothing better than chance. Wars occur, firstly, because there is no control or order in relations between States, and secondly, because there is nothing to prevent them. States are not by nature aggressive; but their relationships are ones in which power and conflict are inherent. On this thesis wars are likely to occur between identical States, each having a high degree of perfection in internal organization, whatever type of internal organization might be postulated. The argument is not necessarily that States are aggressive, but that in the absence of world order or world government, they will come into conflict.

There is a weakness in this approach. Rousseau seemed to argue that the cause of war is located in the fact that States live in an accidental relationship with other States; but even an accidental relationship leads to experience, conventions or order in relationships. The cause of war would better be attributed to the absence of experience. The remedies suggested, that is, voluntary federations or a far tighter world government, would follow only if this were the only type of order which is possible amongst States. But one can imagine that relationships between States could be peaceful, even without federations or a world government, in circumstances in which perception and expectation of the policies of others were perfect, and in which there were tacit agreements on the conduct of foreign policy derived from experience; it takes no world order, or even any formal agreement, to restrain thermonuclear powers in their relationships with each other.

Moving the source of conflict from the State to relationships between States, is at least one step away from the pessimistic proposition that the source of conflict is in the State which, like Man, is aggressive by nature. It is also one further step toward the proposition that power might not be the only conceivable basis of relationships between States. Power politics might have its origins, not in Man or the State, or even in relations between States, but in possible misconceptions regarding the nature of Man and State.

IV. ANARCHY

Closely related to the proposition that the cause of conflict is in the relation of States is the concept of anarchy, which could cover any world system in which independent units were not wholly under the control of federations or a world government. It is not true, however, to say that if anarchy is the cause of conflict, then the remedy necessarily is government. As has already been suggested, it is possible to conceive of an international system in which separate sovereign States maintain a condition of peace with each other by reason of tacit agreements on the conduct of their foreign policies based, perhaps on experience, and perhaps on academic insights into the nature of policies which must be pursued in order to maintain a condition of peace. While it is clear that no State can itself be perfectly rational, or assume that other States will be perfectly rational in following policies designed both to pursue their own interests and to avoid conflict, it does not necessarily follow that the absence of world organization, or the existence of anarchy in this sense, will necessarily lead to conflict. The automation of foreign policy is in theory at least no more impossible than the automation of internal financial policy, which not so long ago was haphazard and conducted without insight into the operation of the financial system. It may be impossible at each point of decision to take into account all variables, and to work out a specific policy; but it is not impossible to work out a general theory as a guide to action. A limitation of the freedom of the State in its foreign policies can result from experience and insight into operation of an international system, no less than from deterrents operated by other States, and is likely by these means to be more effective.

V. THE DRIVE FOR POWER?

There is probably no greater common factor in all thinking on international relations than the assumption that States depend for their existence upon power, and achieve their objectives by power, thus making the management of power the main problem to be solved.

However one may resolve the question of the priority to be assigned to the maintenance of peace, it is clear that the problem of the management of power in international relations looms as the central issue of our time. Power exists in States. It may be used in competitive struggle, producing intolerable destruction. It may be used unilaterally, producing enslavement and degradation of its victims. In short, both survival and freedom, both existence itself and the higher values that enrich existence, are implicated in the problem of power.[1]

Schuman asserted as a general proposition that 'All politics is a struggle for power. People with power relish the joy of commanding others to do their will'.[2] He gave this general proposition a particular application: 'Foreign policy is an expression of a State's will-to-power'.[3] Hans Morgenthau made the same assumptions. 'International politics, like all politics, is a struggle for power. Whatever the ultimate aims of international politics, power is always the immediate aim.'[4]

---

[1] Claude, *Power and International Relations*, p. 5.

[2] F. L. Schuman, *International Politics*, 1941, p. 261.   [3] Schuman, p. 265.

[4] Morgenthau, *Politics among Nations* (3rd ed., 1960), p. 27.

This is an assumption based only upon evidence that power appears to have been the basic motivation in the world systems which we have known. It is an assumption that fits in well with the notion that the nature of Man as an individual is aggressive, and that the nature of the State has the same characteristics. It is an assumption that some sociologists have used to explain the institutions of society, and the degree of organization required to maintain harmony. On the basis of power it can be argued that the fundamental law of international politics is the balance-of-power, and that this law will be observed by anyone wishing to preserve his independence. By power is meant, to use Morgenthau's definition, 'man's control over the minds and actions of other men'. Interest is defined in terms of power, and whenever men and States 'strive to realize their goal by means of international politics, they do so by striving for power'.[2] Power and politics are inseparable. The justification for making power the starting point of analysis is that 'politics, like society in general, is governed by objective laws that have their roots in human nature'.

Morgenthau, who is currently widely used as the chopping block for attacks on power theory, is more explicit and more dogmatic than earlier exponents of power politics, and less inclined to examine the dilemmas, and less despairing of the conclusions reached than, for example, Rousseau; and for these reasons he has been instrumental in attracting attention to the shortcomings of orthodox theory. He stands on a pinnacle, the foundation being aggressive human nature, and it is one that has been strengthened by the political storms which have raged about it. It has been threatened only during short periods of between-war peace when idealists have attacked the foundations.

Human nature, in which the laws of politics have their roots, has not changed since the classical philosophies of China, India, and Greece endeavoured to discover these laws. Hence, novelty is not necessarily a virtue in political theory, nor is old age a defect. The fact that a theory of politics, if there be such a theory, has never been heard of before tends to create a presumption against, rather than in favour of, its soundness. Conversely, the fact that a theory of politics was developed hundreds or even thousands of years ago—as was the theory of balance-of-power—does not create a presumption that it must be outmoded and obsolete. A theory of politics must be

---

[1] *Ibid.* p. 27.

subjected to the dual test of reason and experience. To dismiss such a theory because it had its flowering in centuries past is to present not a rational argument but a modernistic prejudice that takes for granted the superiority of the present over the past.[1]

The position has been maintained for so long that those holding it can be forgiven for adopting an attitude 'whatever has been, must continue'.[2] Morgenthau claims that 'it is sufficient to state that the struggle for power is universal in time and space and is an undeniable fact of experience. It cannot be denied that throughout historic time, regardless of social, economic, and political conditions, States have met each other in contests for power'.[3] He is led to observe that 'A popular and widely held view assumed that statesmen have a choice between policies based upon the balance-of-power and more desirable policies based on morality and justice'. A second and less popular view has served as the common law of diplomats and statesmen for at least the past four centuries. It maintains that 'any given system is perpetually subject to that play of political forces which is known as the balance-of-power'.[4] 'There is a social principle underlying the relations of independent units which provides that stability can be achieved through a tendency of the separate units to establish and reestablish some kind of equilibrium'.[5]

Yet in relation to such a fundamental assumption there are a number of difficulties. The evidence supporting aggressiveness in the individual in society as an innate trait is, as we have seen, inconclusive; the evidence that States are necessarily aggressive in their relationships with each other is open to question; and there is evidence that in the nuclear age, as will later be demonstrated, the object of policy of States possessing a surplus of power is to avoid situations in which that power might be employed. In a sense, the most powerful nations have, in the nuclear era, become the least powerful.

It could be argued by those who wish to fit all forms of exercise of power into a given framework, that even political pressure is the exercise of power. It could be argued that the new nations in avoiding alliances and in escaping from power are none the less exercising it in non-military ways. But this

---

[1] S. Hoffmann, pp. 55-6.   [2] S. Hoffmann, p. 36.
[3] S. Hoffmann, pp. 68-9.   [4] *Survey of International Affairs*, 1930, p. 134.
[5] S. Hoffmann, p. 99.

liberty with the concept of power is hardly justified in the light of the way in which power politics have been described by Morgenthau and others. The concept of power politics becomes meaningless unless some definite description can be given to power. Schwarzenberger argues that power is 'the mean between influence and force' and may be defined as 'capacity to impose one's will on others by reliance on effective sanctions in case of non-compliance'. In elaboration, he says, 'the assessment of power is ability to exercise compelling pressure irrespective of its reasonableness . . . the presence, if only in the background, of the means to give effect to demands, including possible application of physical force, is the silent threat and sanctions behind power politics'.[1]

One suspects that the greater proportion of everyday human and inter-State relationships requires no exercise of power, not even the exercise of persuasion. This does not dispose of power approaches in sociology, for even a minute proportion of relationships which requires the exercise of power is sufficient to justify a theory of power politics. The assumption that politics is the pursuit of power is meaningful where a goal cannot be sought without limitation of the interest of others; there is an objective difference in interests to be resolved. It is also meaningful, though not so strikingly inevitable, where a subjective clash of interests emerges due to false perception or lack of communication.

It is relevant to observe, however, that changes in the proportions of situations involving and not involving power may be marginally significant. One could reasonably argue in the nineteenth century that the age of discovery and colonization having passed, many important sources of conflict were removed. One could argue now that objective differences in interest are lessening because of the growing independence of colonial areas, conventionalism in trade arrangements, and greater control by States of the activities of private enterprise. Even subjective differences in interest are more open to analytical consideration. However, this is marginal—one vital objective difference in interest could be sufficient to justify a theory of power politics, and the employment of war as an instrument of policy.

---

[1] Schwarzenberger, *Power Politics* (2nd ed., 1951), p. 14. In the Third Edition (1964) the passage is redrafted: 'Thus, power may be defined as capacity to impose one's will on others by reliance on effective sanctions in case of non-compliance'.

Of more importance, because they could be destructive of the theory, are the cases in which States have a common interest in avoiding international involvement in non-vital situations that could lead to nuclear confrontation. Power politics was always a game of chicken—either one side gave way or there was a head-on collision. In this eventuality all was not lost in days of conventional weapons; there was a result which usually led to benefits even to the vanquished. But in the nuclear age the game may have no results other than mutual destruction. In the nuclear age the game that has a result, in the sense of there being a winner and a loser, is the one in which there is competition in the non-exercise of power. The side which chickens out of non-exercise of power—the side which runs away from negotiation—is from the political point of view the loser. This is one feature of disarmament negotiations in which each side endeavours to put forward politically attractive proposals which it calculates the other side cannot afford to accept.

The Political Realists have no doubt overstated in order to make their point. They must be aware that power as an end in itself is but one goal of many. Peace itself may be another goal, and there are economic, religious and cultural ends to be pursued. Each of these may be sought by means of the exercise of power; but if power is an end in itself, they all compete with it.

Furthermore, the Realist is inclined to exaggerate power as a means toward an end; not all goals are sought by the exercise of power unless one so widens the definition of power as to include influences exercised merely by argument and by ordinary communication. If power is defined in such a way then the proposition that power is the prime motivating force of men and States in their relations with each other becomes nothing more than a truism. Morgenthau has something far more definite in mind when he states, 'The tendency to dominate, in particular, is an element of all human associations, from the family through fraternal and professional associations and local political organizations, to the State'.[1] His subsequent reference to the conflict between a mother-in-law and her child's spouse as fore-shadowing the conflict on the international scene between the policies of the *status quo* and the policies of imperialism, cannot be regarded in the context as being fatuous, and

[1] S. Hoffmann, p. 70.

must reflect a view which is the basis of his Political Realism. For most of us it is hard to believe that there is any continuum in power relationships starting, for example, from the exercise of influence by one on another in a quiet Quaker meeting, to influence in a school parent-and-citizen meeting, to the exercise of influence in the realm of diplomacy, to the threat of force employed in international affairs. This emphasis on power follows from pre-occupation with the goal of survival, and from the belief that most human relations are related to survival. Nor is it easy to accept Spykman's principle that whenever 'pressures become unequal, boundaries will move'[1] in the light of post-war creation of small, independent and unarmed States. To argue that these States owe their independence and their boundaries to balancing pressures of major Powers is to introduce an artificial element of unrealism merely to sustain a general theory which may be meaningful only in some aspects and at some stages of the power politics of great nations.

One curious aspect of politics in the nuclear age now needs to be taken into account. Power is employed to preserve sovereignty. Alliances with other States are one means of increasing the total pressures one State can command in its interests. In the nuclear age the tendency is to develop independent deterrents. This has been the policy, for example, of France. It represents a conflict between sovereignty and the pursuit of maximum power. It is a deliberate attempt to escape from the consequences which flow from one of the main instruments of power politics—alliances. Smaller sovereign States possessing nuclear weapons seem to prefer a bee-sting, self-destroying deterrent, rather than to strive through an alliance for an absolute deterrent which would prejudice their freedom of action, and which could cause them complete destruction even though their own vital interests were not immediately involved.

There is little doubt that moral aspects of the employment of power have some relevance to decision-making in International Relations; but despite the constant references to moral issues which appear in discussion of International Relations no sensible judgement on the importance of moral aspects can be made. Niebuhr takes the view that the moral issue is relevant because men seek to do what is right in terms of the people they represent, and because in doing so they are guided by some general

---

[1] N. Spykman, *America's Strategy in World Politics*, 1942, p. 7.

scheme of values. Others, however, take the view that the highest level of moral behaviour is the apparent reasonableness of national attitudes which ensures compatibility with the interests of other States. There is here a strong subjective element. Hoffmann is prepared to agree that in an issue such as the recognition of Communist China there is a moral issue involved as to whether a government should have dealings with the government of China.[1] The Political Realists rationalize their position by arguing that a nation is acting morally only when it is acting selfishly, and that any attempt to impose a political ideal is merely imperialism. To negotiate with a potential rival and to compromise so as to reach a solution in a particular situation is appeasement. In fact, in their view no political leader has the freedom of action which would be required to make what might be regarded as a 'moral decision' if this were incompatible with national interest. Perhaps the only satisfactory way of dealing with moral aspects of international relations is from the point of view of levels of national and international public opinion; this relates back to awareness of particular situations, opportunities of expression such as in the United Nations Assembly, and the means of communication available within and between States. In these terms moral issues become factors of information and communication. But even this view would not be accepted by Thompson who quotes Hoffmann with approval when he argues that people have acquired power which they are incapable of exercising; their attitudes are immoral if the policies which follow from them do not preserve national interests.[2]

These criticisms of the power approach to the study of International Relations are merely matters of emphasis. They have been made before from time to time, and the fortress of power politics has stood despite them, and has been rescued, sometimes at a stage approaching surrender, by the outbreaks of war which have seemed to invalidate the criticisms. The peace movements of the late nineteenth century, and the doubts being expressed regarding the approach to international politics based on power, evaporated as soon as there was a resurgence of power politics finally leading to the First World War.

More fundamental is the question whether power is a primary

---

[1] S. Hoffmann, p. 63.

[2] K. W. Thompson, *Political Realism and the Crisis of World Politics*, 1960, p. 45.

goal, or only secondary to the circumstances of relations between States which bring it into operation. It is not at all clear whether in making the assumption that power is the prime motivation of men and States, power is held to be a value in itself, or whether a means to an end. To argue that power is a value in itself, and to develop theory in International Relations on this basis, is to attribute a motivation without any scientific support, and therefore to develop a theory with widespread policy implications which could be entirely false. If it is argued that power is merely a means to an end, then at least the question is still open as to whether it is the only possible means, and whether others should be considered. Not always is this difference between power as a value and as a means made clear. Morgenthau, Niebuhr, Spykman, Thompson seem to use it in both senses; perhaps the difference is not important for their purposes. If Man or a State in their relations with other men or States employ power, then in terms of results it matters little whether power is employed as a means or whether, on the other hand, it is employed because men and States naturally seek it. For anyone, however, wishing to examine the possibilities of a system that is not power-based, the difference is important; for clearly a non-power system is not possible if men and States naturally seek power, but such a system is at least theoretically possible if men and States merely employ power, as was the case in theory in a balance-of-power system, as the only available means to the ends of peace and security.

Power as a primary goal must be associated with an otherwise static model of international relations. Even though there were no changes in the world environment, even though all participants were satisfied with the world structure, there would still be drives for power for its own sake; the desire for power itself would be the only non-static element. The structure necessary to control the exercise of power in such a model would be one in which power would be opposing power so that there would be an equilibrium position upset only by changes in relative power. The only variable or unbalancing factor would be power. If the power-politics model is not a static one in this sense, if the exercise of power is regarded as creating a dynamic system in which change can take place, then it cannot be regarded as an equilibrium model or one aimed primarily at preserving peace. As a dynamic model, one based on power as a primary motivation is a model of potential conflict and not of balance-of-power. It provides no means of change or adjustment to change except from changes in power relationships which are themselves regarded as the main changes taking place in the international relationship.

This is a distorted view of international politics. In practice power is not merely a goal but is also a means to an end, because no State is ever satisfied in respect of its non-power objectives; this dissatisfaction is another variable, and not one which can be treated as secondary to the exercise of power. Power as an end in itself may be associated with the rule of kings and dictators, though even this is doubtful; it is difficult to place power in the centre as a motivation in any international system in which centralized governments are subject to pressures which seek goals other than power. Power as a prime motivation cannot be attributed to States whose concentration is upon internal development, and in a world in which independent sovereign States do not always require national force or international guarantees for their continued independence.

The concept of power politics is far more useful in describing a dynamic world in which power is a means by which the demands for change, and resistance to change, are advanced. In this case power becomes a factor secondary to change. As such it may be no less important in practice for the end result is still power-conflict; but if power is secondary to change the analysis of power politics is completely altered, and doubt is cast upon the relevance of the devices for the regulation of power. Power becomes relevant only when the responses of a nation to change are non-passive ones. In the normal course of international relations small changes in terms of trade and relative costs of production are absorbed by other States, and give rise to no retaliatory or active response. Before, therefore, the importance of power can be assessed, it is necessary to determine what stimulates passive or non-passive responses, what types of change can be absorbed, what values can be traded, and what types of change provoke aggressive responses. Waltz has made a major contribution by drawing attention to underlying assumptions relating to Man and the State. The origin of conflict will not be found in either; and now we are forced to look elsewhere. The dynamic aspects of the system, change itself, may be a fruitful source of conflict.

5

THE FALLACY OF THE CONTINUUM

On the assumptions already outlined regarding the nature of
Man and of the State, orthodox theory suggests the need for
a balance-of-power, and when circumstances do not permit
this, a need for collective security, with the final and logical end
in sight of some form of world government in which both men
and States are subject to a universal law and order.

Claude speaks of a continuum, for he regards each of these
three devices as

differing most fundamentally in the degree of centralization of power
and authority which they imply. In this view, balance-of-power
represents the extreme of decentralization, a kind of *laissez-faire*
arrangement in the sphere of power politics. Collective security, next
in line, represents an effort to solve the power problem by super-
imposing a scheme of partially centralized management of power
upon a situation in which the possession of power remains diffused
among national units. World government, at the opposite end of the
spectrum from balance-of-power, rests upon the concept that an
institutional system involving a 'monopoly of power', comparable to
that alleged to exist in a well-ordered national State, is essential to
the successful management of the power problem in international
relations.[1]

Even though the assumptions regarding the nature of Man
and the State were unquestionably valid, no political scientist
could be satisfied with the efficiency in operation, and perhaps
not even with the relevance to current world affairs, of any of
these three devices. Each can be shown to contain certain
internal inconsistencies and impractical aspects. The conclusion
must be reached that if a solution to the problem of war is to
be found, it will not be at any point along the line of this
continuum, and that we must look therefore to quite different
approaches.

[1] Claude, *Power and International Relations*, 1962, p. 9.

I. BALANCE-OF-POWER

There is probably no concept which has been as widely held as that of the balance-of-power in international relations. 'In the fifth century BC, Thucydides explained the policy of Tissaphernes, King of the Persians, as one of holding "the balance evenly between the two contending powers", Athens and Lacedaemon. In the second century BC, Polybius, in his explanation of the policies of Hiero, makes brilliantly clear the effect of balance-of-power worries on the thinking of a states-man.'[1] While this concept has been stated and re-stated, and while it has been severely criticized as meaningless and a figment of the imagination, it still exists and explains much 'game-theory' and the attitudes of political leaders. The probability is that some kind of balance-of-power is a reality, and that policies continue to be related to it, not because it has any objective merit in modern conditions, but merely because political leaders and academic writers, both steeped in the tradition of aggres-siveness, regard some balancing as basic to foreign policy. Wolfers requests those who allege the obsolescence of the balance-of-power to ask themselves whether any alternative practical course is open to nations.[2] Haas asserts that 'The statesman who is anxious to preserve his State must have recourse to balancing principles in averting the hegemony of his rival'.[3] McLellan and his colleagues observe that 'It is possible to criticize the concept of balance-of-power, for its unreality, its imprecision, and its inherent danger. In spite of all such criticisms, the term denotes processes which actually *do* exist in international relations.'[4]

A more searching analysis reveals, however, that whatever is the content of the concept depends upon the circumstances of the time. In its pure form the balance-of-power means the main-tenance of an equilibrium so that no State or States can without good cause be an aggressor. In theory—and some historians would argue that theory and practice were not greatly separate in the nineteenth century—the balance-of-power system was one in which power was deliberately and objectively employed

---

[1] Waltz, pp. 198-9.   [2] Wolfers, p. 130.
[3] E. Haas, reprinted in McLellan, Olson and Sondermann (eds.), *The Theory and Practice of International Relations*, 1960, p. 231.   [4] *Ibid.* p. 222.

to maintain stability, and to provide in an extremity a means of change, either by force or by threatened alteration of balances. If a revisionist State wished to pursue its trading or territorial interests and these were regarded by some other States as legitimate ones, shifts in power could both give the green light to revisionism, and the red light to action by whatever States might wish to resist change. Equally, any unwarranted challenge to existing structures could be inhibited by alliances between *status quo* Powers. In theory at least, it was a system which did not exclude war as an instrument of policy, but at the same time enabled a world consensus to operate in judgements regarding legitimate national goals, and to allow change to take place.

In so far as balance-of-power did operate, it was because of favourable circumstances. It was a European system, comprising States with many common interests in existing structures, and the type of challenge which later came from States in Asia and Africa demanding independence was not the kind of challenge with which it had to deal. There are in the twentieth century features which make a balance-of-power system quite inoperative. The use of power is not, and is not likely to be, confined to balancing. Under balance-of-power, each State must, as a matter of policy, be prepared to declare in advance of changed political circumstances its willingness to switch its support from one State or group of States to another regardless of all other values. Such a condition would be possible only in a world of independent sovereign States having no cultural, political or other links with other States, and being completely indifferent on grounds other than strategic grounds with whom they had alliances; for equilibrium to be meaningful, no State could place a value on ideology, or any other interest, or even develop any close relationship with any other State, which might prejudice its easy transfer of strategic support as required to maintain equilibrium. Secondly, whatever might have been the position in the past, the idea of equilibrium in the nuclear age, in which there is tremendous reserve strike-power, seems to be irrelevant. Equilibrium, whatever the meaning, is relevant only in a world society comprising many small States, no one of which could have a determinant effect upon world politics, after the style of small firms in a condition of pure competition. Despite this the concept was most widespread at a time when there were a small number of European States with Britain in a position to hold a balance; and it must have been clear that immediately Britain lent support an imbalance was created thus placing issues of peace and war in the hands of one State.

A second meaning of balance-of-power is disequilibrium— a situation in which one or more States hold such a favourable balance-of-power that any attempt to upset the existing order can be prevented. In this sense the balance-of-power has a very close relationship with the preservation of the *status quo* by those satisfied with it. It will be seen the extent to which this particular concept of a balance-of-power reflects the good- and bad-State philosophy. Each State or group in an alliance interprets a balance-of-power in the sense of a balance favourable to it, and by which is maintained peace, be it a peace of its own choosing. There is some justification for this nationalist viewpoint in that merely an equilibrium balance-of-power, in which there was an equal chance of success or failure for a revisionist, would invite revisionism particularly by States dissatisfied with the existing order. However, one cannot imagine the situation where a balance in favour of the revolutionary against the *status quo* Powers is maintained by the revolutionary transferring its support to the *status quo*. Clearly it is a preponderance of power that is required to maintain peace, and this certainly has been the view of Western countries.

It is not clear that the purpose of the balance-of-power was to maintain peace. On the contrary, one of its purposes was to organize alliances through which war or threat of war could be used to prevent the growth in power of other alliances. Perhaps, therefore, balance-of-power can be given no more meaning than distribution of power, each State and its allies seeking to be in a position of preponderance. Certainly no claim should be made that any precise system known as a balance-of-power system now exists, still less that it is one which is automatic and predictable in its operation.

In some respects it is a system which ultimately is self-defeating. Every system must provide for continuous and smooth change, and the only means by which the balance-of-power system enables change is for a challenge to be made, and for the balance either to be upset through force or the threat of force and victory by the challenger, or to be maintained through force or threat of force and victory by those challenged. In any event it is a system which is based upon alliances, and these help to increase tensions and suspicion amongst potentially conflicting groups of States. The mechanism is capable, therefore, of creating just those conflicts its purpose is to prevent.

II. COLLECTIVE SECURITY

Collective security was not conceived by Woodrow Wilson; but by the time the League of Nations Covenant was being drafted the balance-of-power was a discredited system, and collective security the new ideal. Peace would be based not upon the chance distribution of power between alliances, but upon the overwhelming force of the vast majority of members of the League of Nations. Through it the rights and integrity of small nations would be protected, but through it also even a great Power would not be able to challenge the authority of the world organization.

In practice the two systems were soon shown to have very much in common. They were both power systems. They both assumed that good and bad States could be distinguished. Neither had any machinery by which the legitimate demands for change could effectively be met. The League of Nations was not a universal system, the United States not being a member, but even if it had been, it would have merely acted as a substitute for alliances, for it was based on a preponderance of power in favour of those States wishing to maintain the existing power distribution. In the words of Quincy Wright 'international organization to promote collective security is . . . only a planned development of the natural tendency of balance-of-power politics'.[1]

The United Nations was equally conceived as a collective security organization, but attempts were made in this case to ensure that it would act as such. For example, provision was made for the contribution by nations to an international force so that there would be a forward commitment which was lacking in the case of the League of Nations. However, the veto which was insisted upon not only by the Soviet Union, but also by the United States, ensured that if there were any collective security action, it would be directed only against smaller Powers. By accident—because the Soviet Union was not in attendance at the Security Council—so-called collective action was taken

[1] Q. Wright, *The Study of International Relations*, 1955, p. 163.

in the case of Korea. Not only was this an accident from the point of view of decision, but is was hardly collective security from the point of view of policy and strategy.

The collective security system might have been a sensible device at the time at which balance-of-power was being enunciated, at least if there had been any real desire to establish peace on this basis. The concept has no more relevance to the twentieth century than balance-of-power. Certainly it can have no application in the bipolarized thermonuclear world in which both sides to the major conflict have a strike capacity, and a second-strike deterrent capacity, which does not rest at all upon contributions from other States, and which could not be balanced even though collective security were universal.

Collective security is an acknowledgment of some of the defects of balance-of-power, and also clarifies some of its purposes. It eliminates the idea of equilibrium, and substitutes preponderance of power as the necessary requirement of peace. It seeks to eliminate alliances which divide the world into power groups. If it could achieve its objective by maintaining peace through a preponderance of power, and by avoiding alliances, it would win the widespread support even of the nonaligned nations. But to be effective it would require some machinery by which change and adjustment to change could take place, and machinery which would prevent any privileged States benefiting from the stability made possible by collective security. These are conditions impossible to fulfil, for they would require a universal collective security with each State co-operating, and in which each State was prepared to negotiate its differences when challenged by nonprivileged States. If this condition could be fulfilled then there would be an effective system of world government in which collective security was unnecessary.

In practice, as the history of collective security clearly shows, it has been balance-of-power in disguise. Collective security has been a device through which *status quo* Powers have been able to carry through the system of alliances and of favourable balance-of-power, under the respectable cloak of a League of Nations or a United Nations.

III. WORLD GOVERNMENT

It is understandable how the balance-of-power concept gave way to collective security once it was clear that a preponderance of power was the only means of maintaining stability; similarly collective security gave place to forms of world government once it was clear that to be effective collective security must be universal. Indeed, world government, being the extreme of the continuum, is the logical development from balance-of-power, and its own impracticability tends to highlight the irrelevance to the modern world of every other point along the continuum. However, the idea persists, and many voice Morgenthau's view 'that the argument of the advocates of the world State is unanswerable. There can be no permanent international peace without a State coextensive with the confines of the political world'.[1]

Most writers would be prepared to agree that 'global unity is not feasible at the present time',[2] but there is left in the minds both of politicians and the people they lead, whether they are socialist or capitalist, the idea that this is the end towards which we are working. Widespread disillusionment is likely.

IV. INTERNATIONAL LAW AND ORGANIZATION

Popular hopes and political declarations of goals have created dangerously false visions regarding what is possible. Some scientists, like Clark and Sohn, who see the possibility of peace through world law,[3] have lent support to wishful thinking by proposals which seem merely to shift the problem away from its political realities by the use of legal terms. In the popular mind legal and constitutional terms applicable in the provincial society are applicable also to the international relationship, and a world State is envisaged. There is apparently an assumption of some continuity from tribal leadership and law, to the creation of the State, and finally to the establishment of an international order. There may be uses for an analogy between a State and the world order, but there are no grounds for believing that there is a continuum. The concept of enforcement which was developed in the closed society may have no sensible application to an international society. In the national community, law enforcement is applied against a relatively few citizens who might have the desire to break a law. Almost none of these

---

[1] Claude, *Power and International Relations*, p. 209.   [2] *Ibid.*
[3] G. Clark and L. Sohn, *World Peace through World Law*, 1960.

individuals has any final social responsibilities in community decision. They must submit. They have no rights with respect to law breaking. The rights of the individual to freedom of action are regarded by law makers as relatively unimportant compared with the general interests and welfare of the millions who make up the social unit. At best, certain 'moral' rights may in some cases be recognized, the exercise of which may lead to alterations in law. In International Relations, on the other hand, there are no more than one hundred or so nations, each one of which is acting with full responsibility for its own final decisions and is prepared to defend them as being proper, justifiable, and necessary in the interests of its people. An analogy between two so totally different sets of circumstances is logically not justified.

Any enforcement of international 'law' that might take place is, therefore, enforcement by one or more States in support of their own interests and against those of others. It may be that the enforcing group claims to be acting in the interests of the world community—the claim made by democratic governments when enforcing law against the private citizen. Equally, the States against whom enforcement action is taken can claim that they represent the interests of the world community. In practice, however, neither can represent or be regarded as representing 'world interests'. There is no entirely valid analogy with national law enforcement. The closest resemblance would be found in a national society undergoing political revolution, in which one party endeavours to impose its will upon all others.

In order to overcome these difficulties, suggestions have been made to place individuals as well as States under the authority of an international organization. No clear indication has been given in such world government proposals as to the rights of the State to protect the interests of its citizens. In fact, the legal concept of world government becomes meaningful only if the world organization is comprised not of the representatives of States, but of the elected representatives of people, thus making of world government a federal system in which the central authority exercises certain defined powers, and the States residual powers. Such a federal system presupposes the transfer of all power except minor police powers to the central authority. This is tantamount to achieving disarmament and the abolition of sovereignty. Claude, who discussed world government only because others insist upon bringing it into consideration, concludes with some restraint

that the management of power in international relations cannot be achieved except by concentrating an effective monopoly of power in a central agency, which thus becomes capable of maintaining order by the threat of bringing overwhelming coercion to bear against any and all dissident elements, seems to me to misstate the position which governments occupy in national societies and to overstate both the requirements and the possibilities of the centralization of coercive capacity in the global society.[1]

Attempts to create an international structure on the basis of law do not receive support from international lawyers, and they arise more from the absence of other concrete proposals than from any conviction that a society can be created merely by the formulation of a legal structure. Law cannot create; it reflects aspects of social and cultural development, and if it is to be observed it must change with changes which take place in the social and political relations of those to whom it applies. Wherever the enforcement aspects of Law predominate through non-observance of legal restraints, order based on that law is likely to be destroyed. In the national community, while the observances of law ultimately rest upon enforcements, its practical effectiveness rests upon a general acceptance of the objectives of the law. Proposals for an international society created by legal agreements, and not related to the political and social conditions of that society, cannot reasonably be entertained.

These propositions have been well stated by Niemeyer:

Law, instead of acting as a dam, must become the helpful canal, through which functional coordination of States can be achieved, the condition under which States are able to fulfil their functional tasks. Its rules must cease to be abstract commands, they must become the articulations of the immanent laws which govern human activities in the field of political institutions. Just as the law of individuals developed in ancient times as the first *social* science, growing out of the observation and formulation of the standards according to which people actually lived and worked together, so likewise the law of international relations must be made a discipline which studies the

[1] Claude, *Power and International Relations,* pp. 270-1.

interconnectedness between States, and crystallizes the rules found in it. There is no other way that will lead to an effectual legal order of international politics.[1]

In accordance with this general proposition Niemeyer asserts that international order cannot be established merely by exercising power over the activities of separate States. 'It cannot materialize in the form of an interstate or super-State police force, but only in that of an effectual system of international law. The effectualness of international law rests fundamentally on its own merits, not on the assumption of some pressure behind it.'[2] However important law may be in relations between States, its role must be limited to recording rather than creating a level of morality or a code of behaviour.

The apparent breakdown of international law in 1919, and at other periods in history, was as much as anything due to the irrelevance of the existing law to the current political situation with which it was dealing. A system of law had been developed through the nineteenth century which reflected very much the *laissez-faire* world society '. . . in the nineteenth century, international politics and law operated largely under the assumption that the commercial activities of the nations' citizens did not concern, at least directly, the power of the States, except in the case of incidents of which these citizens were the victims in a foreign country'.[3] This system was not appropriate in an age of rapidly developing central authority in national government. The history of Japanese commercial dealings before the Second World War is one of patience, and observations of agreements and conventions in the face of severe restrictions against Japanese trade. There was no legal process by which there could be any recognition of Japanese grievances against the West. In conditions such as these, it is dodging an important issue to say that Japanese aggression signified a breakdown in law. Similarly, after the War, in cases such as the acquisition of the Suez Canal, and the forcing of the issue of West Irian, there were no means within the law, whereby these less powerful nations could obtain objective consideration of their claims.

This is not to say, however, that international law has not a positive function, and that the observance of law depends

---

[1] G. Niemeyer, *Law Without Force*, 1941, p. 24.   [2] Niemeyer, p. 21.
[3] S. Hoffmann, p. 5.

entirely upon willingness to observe it, thereby making the law itself unnecessary. On the contrary, the codification of law in a way which reflects a widespread concensus of opinion and of the prevailing concepts of justice, indirectly influences national decision-makers in the same way, if not to the same degree, as it restrains minorities in a social system. It is essential, however, that any law be subject to constant change to reflect the continuously changing cultural and political attitudes which develop in world relationships. Subject to this consideration, the invention of new legal procedures can sometimes provide solutions to otherwise intractable political difficulties.

The general position regarding the possibilities of international organization is best described by reference to the three conceptions used by Professor Schwarzenberger[1] in relation to international law. There are three aspects of international law and relations: those in which countries operate on a reciprocal basis as, for example, reciprocal aviation agreements; those in which countries agree to co-operate to their mutual advantage as, for example, in the use of rivers which pass through more than one State; and thirdly, those matters in which relations are governed by considerations of power. Clearly international agreement in the first two cases is relatively easily arrived at, and in so far as may be necessary rests upon enforcement through national procedures. Arrangements outside the reciprocal and co-operative arrangements, because they are subject to considerations of power, are not usually matters which can be dealt with by international organization or international law except to the extent that national and international public opinion, and experience in conducting political relations, can influence governments and can ensure the observance of agreements that might be entered into.

V. THE FEDERAL PATTERN

The federal pattern is a less ambitious one. Schwarzenberger claims that 'The federal pattern is the most clear-cut alternative to power politics'. But he quickly goes on to point out that a universal federation is beyond imagination, and a pattern of non-universal federation in contemporary world society would

---

[1] Schwarzenberger, *Power Politics* (3rd ed., 1964), Ch. 13.

not change the character of present-day world politics.[1] Federations within particular regions, Europe, Africa or Latin America, for example, could greatly add to regional stability, and lead to a world society comprising fewer, and perhaps more responsible, States, thus making international organization and negotiation more predictable. Once formed, federations of this type would be stable, if past experience is any guide. But the nature of the international system would remain the same.

The step from a smaller number of States to a universal federation raises problems not present in the formation of regional federations of States already possessing common cultural, economic or geographic links. There is a discontinuity in this progression no less than in the progression from the tribe to the State to world government. Schwarzenberger fully recognizes the principle of consent which a federal system requires[2] and thus in some measure avoids the objections we have noted to any system resting upon enforcement; in so doing he underlines the practical difficulties.

[1] *Ibid.* (3rd ed.), 1964, p. 527.
[2] *Ibid.* p. 533.

6

THE FAILURE OF
ORTHODOXY AS THEORY

In this criticism of orthodoxy it is useful to draw attention to two outstanding shortcomings as they appear in the context of current world politics: first, the requirement that sovereignty must be limited if power is to be managed; and second, the absence of any reliable means of fundamental change by peaceful processes within the system of power politics.

I. SOVEREIGNTY

The common characteristic of almost all schemes for international peace and security is the creation of some form of world organization which assumes responsibilities for decision-making and even enforcement. This was the nature of the United Nations created by the victorious powers after the defeat of Germany, Italy and Japan. More realistic proposals for international organization include the principle of consent by which is meant that any limitation of sovereignty is by the willing agreement of nations to give up part of their freedom of action and decision. This is, presumably, the basis of current disarmament proposals which include provision for an international organization having forces at its disposal. The scheme fails unless it can be assumed that consent once given will not be withdrawn, an assumption which is sometimes made in Law but which has no universal validity in relations between States. Proposals for world organization do not include answers to the dilemma of sovereignty in a system of collective security, and are based on the belief or hope that international organization is in itself an advance toward a world community in which sovereign powers will less and less be exercised independently. Support for the United Nations and for its progressively extending functions, and the devaluation of sovereignty, are often thought to be one and the same thing. Thompson comments, referring to the pre-war period, ' . . . an implicit if unstated assumption underlay the selection of almost every subject of inquiry: everything international was good, and everything national was bad'. He continues, 'Indeed one of the illnesses from which the study of International Relations still suffers is the cult of internationalism, with its own moral evaluations arrived at through a simple dichotomy of good internationalism and bad nationalism'.[1]

The realistic fact is that the current international scene is characterized by a universal growth of nationalism, an increased value attaching to independence and sovereignty, and in addition a very large number of newly created States. In the circumstances, it is unreasonable to look to solutions of problems of peace and security which devalue sovereignty, and which assume a progressive extension of responsibilities by an international organization. It would be more realistic to work on the assumption that international organization will not extend beyond being 'a forum within which national rivalries are adjusted through partly novel and partly historic political processes'.[2]

The cult of internationalism probably rests upon beliefs that the organization of Man will continue to progress from a tribal to a regional, to a national, to an international community. There is little to support this belief. One of very many reasons for social integration has been the threat of external enemies, and the world community is not subject to any such threat; and there are many other reasons for believing that national organization and international organization do not form part of the one continuum.[3] The faith in world organization is supported by the absence of any credible alternative in the search for solutions to the problems of peace and security. It is not yet credible that national policies can be found which would enable each independent sovereign State to live in a condition of peace with other sovereign States without resting upon the ultimate threat and use of force. The absence of an alternative, however, cannot be used as intellectual support for any proposition.

Any realistic system in current world politics must assume the continued existence of sovereign States, each exercising sovereignty by means of giving consent to international

---

[1] K. W. Thompson, pp. 18 and 19.
[2] K. W. Thompson, p. 20.
[3] See Burton, *Peace Theory*, Chapter 5.

organization, but always on the basis of the right of withdrawal. It may be that this type of organization can extend beyond obvious areas such as international health and communications, to areas which touch more importantly upon the interests of nations. But clearly, whatever extensions are possible in the future, they will remain peripheral to the central problems of peace and security. If such an assumption is destructive of long-range hopes of world government, then the sooner the validity of this assumption is acknowledged, the less likelihood there will be of widespread frustration and disillusionment in the future.

There is probably very little fundamental difference in nationalistic attitudes toward sovereignty between communist and non-communist countries. The Western nations can afford to adopt an internationalistic approach to the United Nations and world organization generally, at least while they hold a majority position, and differences in national policy statements need to be observed with this factor in mind. The Soviet view is unequivocally opposed to any restrictions on sovereignty. Any internationalism which might be in evidence in Soviet policy is based on class solidarity, and does not cut across an intense nationalism which allows of no limitations of sovereignty by reason of membership of an international organization. 'Cosmopolitism', or 'internationalism' as we would use the term, is in the communist view manifested by propaganda in favour of world government, and by attacks on the principle of national sovereignty. 'The two opposite pairs, patriotism–internationalism and nationalism–cosmopolitism, have received a permanent place in the Soviet theory of foreign policy.'[1] The Soviet view once was that effective sovereignty would require a certain degree of economic independence from imperialism. 'Since 1948, this distinction has been abandoned, and now it is stressed that the recognition of sovereignty must not be made dependent on the capabilities of a State actually to wield sovereign power over its territory.'[2] In this respect Soviet thinking is more acceptable to the new nations than Western thinking, and is, indeed, more attuned with political realism than Western thinking, which still seems to assume that national boundaries owe their existence to national forces and friendly alliances. The

---

[1] K. Törnudd, *Soviet Attitudes towards Non-Military Regional Co-operation,* 2nd edition, 1963, p. 59.
[2] Törnudd, p. 61.

enormous importance given to sovereignty both in the doctrine of Soviet international law and in Soviet practice is a political fact which must be taken into account in any discussion of the importance of sovereignty in world affairs, and of sovereignty in relation to world organization.

There are some important behavioural aspects of International Relations which support the view that sovereignty must be assumed to be a basic condition of any viable international society. These relate to the type of restraint which States are prepared to accept. For example, clearly they are prepared to accept most of the environmental limitations which are placed on their activities by their geographic position, by their population pressures on resources, by their climate, and even by the limits of their material and cultural development. Clearly, however, they are not prepared to accept limitations imposed upon them by the dominance of foreign groups. This is true within a provincial society, and is the basic cause of revolt in cases in which provincial law does not reflect the concensus of opinion of the people living under it. The refusal to accept outside domination is almost absolute in an international system. There is, therefore, a discernible difference between what might be termed objective restraints and subjective ones, and indeed between subjective restraints which are perceived as being deliberate and prejudical to the interests of those being restrained, and other restraints not so regarded.[1]

That there cannot be stability in a condition which rests upon enforcement by outside agencies is a reality we have so far failed to face. We have traditionally considered international affairs in terms of great Powers exercising their influence over smaller and undeveloped peoples. We have assumed that enforcement has been acceptable as a principle of international affairs—despite the warnings of Rousseau, Kant, Mill and others. The creation of many new and independent States which will not tolerate dominance in political, economic or strategic fields by great Powers, or by organizations controlled by them, is a revolution which might prove to be at least as important as the invention of nuclear weapons. One might be prepared to agree that if there were no sovereignty, that if there were a world order in which regional groups shared in the responsibilities of decision-making, and shared also in decisions

[1] Burton, *Peace Theory*, Chapters 4, 7.

taken in respect of enforcement, conflict would be reduced, if not eliminated. However, it cannot be argued from this proposition that sovereignty can be limited. In practice far more than limitation of sovereignty is demanded by a system of world government, for what is required is the breaking up of existing sovereign units into large numbers of smaller regional communities, each represented in the world organization.

II. CHANGE

The systems discussed above, collective security, world government and the more precise forms of world government stated in terms of law, rest upon the authority of a supra-State, or upon restraints imposed on sovereign States by other States. World government presupposes that a stage will be reached in which States will agree that the future of civilization, and the well-being of their citizens, can be preserved and advanced only by the virtual elimination of sovereignty, and in no other way. It is assumed that the world organization will be created by consent or by conquest, but however created, it will continue on the basis of consent. This in turn presupposes an assumption that whatever decisions are taken by a world organization will be accepted by States, by groups of people and by individuals, as just decisions, for without this sense of justice, there would not be consent. These assumptions seem to gloss over what could be a fundamental problem, that is, the need for change and adjustment to it, in a constant stream in order that consent would continue to be given. The amount of adjustment required is likely to be unacceptable to those nations which up to the present have been able to employ the balance-of-power and collective security to satisfy their own ends.

The chief failure of orthodoxy has been in relation to change. The outstanding feature of reality is the dynamic nature of International Relations. No general theory is appropriate which cannot take into consideration the rapidly changing technological, social and political environment in which nations are required to live in peace one with the other. But the only device for fundamental change which is possible in the context of power politics is that of war, for which reason war is recognized as a legitimate instrument of national policy. It is not surprising that International Relations has tended to be discussed in static terms, and that stability has tended to be interpreted in terms of the maintenance of the *status quo*. A dynamic approach to International Relations would immediately confront the analyst with no alternative but to acknowledge war as the only available mechanism for change.

We have argued that the source of conflict between sovereign States is neither in the nature of men nor in the nature of States. We have disputed theories which assume the existence of some basic drive for power in relations between States. Where then lies the origin of conflict? The chance relationship idea put forward by Rousseau does not take us very far, particularly when over generations there is an accumulation of experience which must offset the accidental nature of relationships. There is no reason to believe that war arises out of a relationship as such. This is made clear if one considers a static relationship between two relatively satisfied sovereign States; a condition of peace is likely to continue. It is when the relationship is a dynamic one in which States are required to make adjustments to changes which are taking place in each of them and between them, that conflict is likely to develop. In other words, the origin of conflict is more likely to be found in the dynamics of the environment in which men and States exist than in the nature of men and States themselves. Any relationship which includes change is immediately complicated by situations of objective conflict of interest.

The dynamic nature of international relations is not in doubt, and is reflected in the definitions of the study called International Relations. Hartmann, for example, says that International Relations as a field of study is focused upon 'the processes by which States adjust their national interests to those of other States'.[1] Despite the acknowledgment of change, theory does not often take it into account. Referring to the 'realist' theory of international politics, Hoffmann observes, 'reactions to shifting situations are scarcely considered by the theory'.[2] In attempting to explain the prevalence of a static approach, Hoffmann observes that the 'influence on foreign policies of factors such as geography, national resources, industrial capacity, and inherited tradition of national principles is particularly strong and relatively constant. Today, however,

---

[1] F. H. Hartmann, *The Relations of Nations* (2nd ed.), 1962, p. 5.
[2] S. Hoffmann, p. 31.

survival is almost always at stake, and technological leaps have upset the hierarchy of "stable" factors.'[1]

It is only recently in sociology that means have been found to measure and to evaluate a large number of variables simultaneously occurring. The stage in social science has not yet been reached when the variables to be considered by a student of International Relations can be dealt with as they are dealt with in some natural sciences; but at least the possibilities have been considered, and attention has therefore been drawn to the need for a dynamic approach which takes into account all relevant factors. One of the more recent attempts to do this has been that by Boulding in his treatment of 'Conflict and Defence'.[2] Perhaps the persistence of static approaches has been governed by a desire to simplify, and by the absence of more sophisticated methods.

If the origins of conflict are in the dynamics of the international system, then the nature of men and States and their understandable desire to retain what they already possess, may be regarded as the static elements around which an international system is constructed. Attention is then focused upon the dynamic aspects of the system and particularly upon processes of change and adjustment to change.

Change involves considerations other than the mere mechanics of an adjustment to an event already occurring. It cannot be assumed that all change is necessarily desirable, and that adjustments should be made automatically to it; it cannot be assumed that the demands of the revolutionary should always be met. At the same time, change has usually been considered in terms of demands by dissatisfied States which are attempting to upset an existing distribution of power or distribution of resources, and change has therefore been regarded for the most part as a threat to stability which in the interests of peace should be preserved. For this reason any nation attempting to bring about change has automatically been regarded as the aggressor, while the *status quo* powers have been regarded as those with special rights of defence. International organization has therefore been dominated by the latter, and when change has taken place, it has taken place despite them. It is the challenge of the *status quo* by the revolutionary that is the prime function of war.

[1] S. Hoffmann, p. 33.
[2] K. E. Boulding, *Conflict and Defence: A General Theory*, 1962.

Historically war has played a major part in bringing to attention, if not in satisfying, the demands of dissatisfied States. Curiously enough the demands of the dissatisfied States have in many cases thereafter been met to a large degree, even though they have been defeated in war; this was particularly the case in respect of Japan after the Second World War which won the freedom to trade in the area of South-East Asia which had been denied to it, and for which reason it had sought by force a co-prosperity sphere in that region.

Clearly, therefore, the concept of change must be related in some manner to concepts of justice, for it is only in this way that a determination can be made as to whether change and the adjustments that are required to it are justified. Whether any objective consideration can be given to concepts of justice is questionable. In Thompson's view 'Justice in concrete international situations involves "giving each man his due". We arrive through the process of endless discrimination, debate, and what philosophers call political prudence, at a tolerably acceptable concept of Man's due wherein general principles provide us with at most guides to action.'[1] Whereas it might be difficult to discuss a concept of justice in the abstract, certainly economic inequalities, discriminatory trade practices, regional discrimination, restrictions on access to raw materials and matters of this kind which provoke demands for change, are well within the understanding of peoples and governments as being matters affecting justice. When issues involving a deep sense of frustration reach a level no longer regarded as acceptable, then a challenge is likely to be made even though there is no approximation to a balance-of-power. If one were to assume that every apparently aggressive action were prompted by some awareness of injustice or some sense of frustration, and if one were to look for the cause of this, aggression would appear in a different light. When change which affects one nation adversely occurs through the acts of an identifiable State or group of States, the sense of injustice is likely to lead to responses which are retaliatory, thus forcing change on those responsible for the original change. When a deliberate intent at damage is perceived—rightly or wrongly—the responses are likely to be aggressive.

Population growth, scarcity of resources, the inventiveness of

[1] From S. Hoffmann, p. 23.

man, discovery, are all factors of change which require adjustment by the social organization and the individuals within it. There is a continuum of change from the weather and such wholly natural environmental factors, to innovation, to social change, to political change, to national policies, and wholly deliberate factors, which could, like the weather, prejudice the interests of other States. To the weather, adjustment is made, or if not made, there is no subjective element with which there could be conflict. To the national policies of other States, adjustment may or may not be made, and would less likely be made if these policies were perceived as being deliberately prejudicial, or even as being conducted without due regard to the effects upon others. On this basis a theory could be developed which would postulate power, not as a prime motivation, but as a means to an end only in those cases in which *a non-passive adjustment* was being made to a change brought about by the action of another State. Clearly, in any such theory attention would be directed primarily toward the conditions necessary to ensure the national absorption of change, and passive adjustments to it.

What is required of the social scientist is more study of change; the perception of change, the different effects upon interested parties of change introduced by objective agents, such as the weather, as compared with subjective agents, such as States or international monopolies; the means of making passive adjustments to change so that the adjustment will not lead to further aggressive responses by others; international machinery to ensure that perception of change is not distorted into the perception of a deliberate act of aggression. The inability of the West, and in particular of the United States of America, to accept and to adjust to changes in political institutions in other countries, and in particular to the People's Republic of China, the response of China and the image it has of the United States, and the further non-passive responses of the United States, have created a situation of major concern—where objectively, there appears to be little call for such tension. Research is needed into misunderstanding and failure of communication, and into a wide variety of matters not conventionally within the established discipline of International Relations. But there are limits to the usefulness of such research. Part of the data of international studies must be the inability of men to perceive accurately and all manner of irrational responses, in the same sense that geography, the weather and population growth must be taken as fixed.

The difficulty is not so much to observe the need of machinery for change, but to construct that machinery. However applicable the procedures of balance-of-power were in the past, circumstances of the nuclear age do not permit the use of violence now as the means towards change. If because of the danger of nuclear warfare, the nuclear Powers take steps to stabilize any existing situations, then situations of injustice will accumulate leading to the spread of nuclear weapons to those that wish to challenge the existing order, and finally to a challenge to the *status quo* Powers. But it is no more sensible for revisionist States to bring about change through a nuclear enforcement mechanism than it is for others to prevent such changes by these means.

The practical reality is that because the type of change which is required cannot freely be negotiated, a system of world government is not possible. To be realistic, means of change and adjustment to change have to be evolved which do not presuppose enforcement by any supra-State or organization. This would seem to limit the scope of enquiry to means by which change can be brought about through national policies, and perhaps to some degree through integrated regional and functional systems, such as are now developing and which reflect a high degree of common interest amongst participants.[1]

[1] Wolfgang Friedmann's *The Changing Structure of International Law* was available only after this book was printing. The criticisms he makes of 'traditional' approaches to International Law are in many respects the criticisms made herein of traditional approaches to the study of International Relations.

7

THE FAILURE OF
ORTHODOXY AS POLICY

If the assumption is made that States are likely to be in conflict because of universal aggressiveness, or even merely because there is an accidental relationship between them, then in the absence of a universal world system each State must anticipate aggression and order its policies accordingly. A number of policies automatically flow, each of which contains its own internal dilemmas, and each of which can be shown both in theory and in practice to be self-defeating.

I. ALLIANCES

Alliances are an integral component of power politics and balance-of-power. The balancing system clearly rests upon alliances, tacit or contracted, and upon alterations in alliances. In the classical system of balance-of-power, alliances are arranged for no purpose other than making the balancing system work, and thereby maintaining stability and preventing war. In this system power is employed only to pursue goals within the balanced system, and to prevent it becoming unbalanced. Employed in this way alliances and power are not actively directed against other States for ideological or other reasons; alliances are employed to control power, and power is employed to operate the balancing system.

Such a pure form of alliances is, however, difficult to imagine. The system pre-supposes conditions in which a balance already exists only because no State has important goals the pursuit of which would destroy the balance. The conditions of the twentieth century suggest that cultural and ideological objectives may be more important than the pursuit of power-balances, and that alliances are contracted, and power is employed, to attain these objectives. In these circumstances alliances are deliberately organized against certain States, and are disassociative in that they divide the world society into separate camps. They in turn stimulate the creation of other alliances until most leading nations are divided into camps on some ideological or other basis which appears at the time to be relevant. Far from increasing security, the military competition between the two groups, and the final bipolarization of the power structure, tends in a cumulative fashion to increase tensions and to make conflict more likely. NATO, SEATO and the Warsaw Pact may each be given credit for preventing aggression by one side or by the other; but while there is no evidence that aggression would have taken place in the absence of these alliances, there is considerable evidence that world tensions have been increased by them.

Alliances, far from relieving each member of an alliance from burdensome expenditure on armaments, create a competition between power blocs which imposes ever increasing defence expenditure upon their members. If NATO, SEATO and the Warsaw Pact commenced as measures of partial collective security, and as a means of restraining enemy expansion with the minimum expenditure by each member of the alliances, they have certainly failed in this objective.

Once national security is based on alliances other policies logically and almost inevitably follow. In many cases the consequent policies might be regarded as undesirable even by those introducing them; but one step leads to the next. George Kennan observed:

In the fabric of human events, one thing leads to another. Every mistake is in a sense the product of all the mistakes that have gone before it, from which fact it derives a sort of a cosmic forgiveness; and at the same time every mistake is in a sense the determinant of all the mistakes of the future, from which it derives a sort of cosmic unforgiveableness. Our action in the field of foreign policy is cumulative; it merges with a swelling stream of other human happenings, and we cannot trace its effects with any exactness once it has entered the fluid substance of history.[1]

Experience is that much more power is needed for successful prosecuting of a policy than anyone originally anticipates. In due course all foreign policy objectives come to be subordinate to the over-riding objectives of strategy based on alliances.

Thus since the Second World War and the formation oi

1. Hartmann (2nd ed.), p. 73.

NATO, SEATO and the Warsaw Pact, practices have developed which are logical extensions of alliances, and which, far from promoting security, tend to increase tensions and to aggravate the power struggle. Once an alliance is made with a country there is a strong interest in the continuity of the government of that country, and certainly in the prevention of any internal political change which would threaten the alliance. Thus the United States has been led to support repressive and unpopular governments rather than risk internal change. Inevitably also, economic and technical aid has developed on a discriminatory basis, determined by short-term considerations of strategy rather than long-term objectives of welfare. The formation of economic blocs, reflecting the membership of the military alliances, is something with which we are familar. Restrictions on trade and travel, non-recognition of some countries because of internal change, are amongst the stop-gap policies which in all manner of ways become self-defeating in themselves, and add to the self-defeating aspects of the original alliances.

The way in which alliances are incompatible with any notion of collective security has been made clear in the procedures of the Security Council. Clearly alliances have developed because of the failure of collective security, but equally clearly, the development of alliances has had a disassociative effect within the World Organization.

In support of the classical system of alliances and collective security it could be argued that even in the twentieth century a balancing process still operates, and even over-rides alliances contracted on an ideological basis. There has been a shift in relationships amongst the Soviet Union, China and the United States as China has progressively become politically and economically more powerful, and there has been a shift in relationships with respect to Western Germany. In both cases the defence of an ideology, and even the maintenance of formal alliances, have become of less importance, and the preservation of existing balances of more importance, in policy decisions. The formal alliances have become less disassociative by reason of other tacit alliances which over-ride them.

It may be that we are moving toward a world system over which the two thermonuclear Powers will preside in this way, allowing no State to become a dominant feature of the rest of the system, while permitting relationships amongst lesser States to alter under power and other influences, and permitting even wars between these States. Later in this study consideration will be given to such possibilities. It is to be noted, however, that this is neither a system of alliances nor of balance, in the sense that these terms have been used, and merely another device whereby those States having power can exercise it to prevent change, development, growth, alteration in relationships which would threaten their own economic, political or strategic vital interests. As such it might provide the kind of stability to be derived from effective balance-of-power or collective security; but as with all such devices it rests to an important degree upon prevention of change, and lacks sufficient means by which revisionism can operate save ultimately by the threatened or actual employment of force. In such a system Chinese revisionism could receive support from Asia, Africa and Latin America, in which case the thermonuclear States would not be perceived as balancers, but as 'haves' maintaining the *status quo*. The self-defeating features of such a system are those which have ultimately destroyed all systems which rest upon restraint of other States by imperialisms, alliances and collective security; counter-alliances, arms races, and increased conflicts amongst the States under restraint are the predictable consequence.

II. DISARMAMENT

Only one policy has emerged which has been given overt acceptance by the competing power groups, and this is the policy of disarmament. It is no new policy and has a history almost as old as the history of alliances. As increasing levels of armaments are a consequence of alliances, it is difficult to see how disarmament could be negotiated in an alliance-based system. Indeed, disarmament could be regarded not as a positive policy so much as a means toward an armament policy. As Spanier and Nogee conclude, 'disarmament and arms control plans are an integral part of the arms race, which in turn reflects the intense political conflict between the Sino-Soviet bloc and the Western democracies. The future will therefore witness the continuation of disarmament diplomacy. . . .'[1]

The fallacious assumptions on which disarmament proposals are based from time to time win acceptance in view of the

[1] J. W. Spanier and J. L. Nogee, *The Politics of Disarmament*, 1962, p. 200.

compelling need to tackle the issues presented by modern weapons. The urgency and importance of the problem tend to cloud the fallacies which could otherwise be apparent. From any cold analytical viewpoint it is clear that disarmament can be no more than a 'non-war' solution, that is, that a condition of peace would not be brought about merely by disarmament. Yet it is strenuously asserted both by East and West that the elimination of arms would be in itself a fundamental contribution to a condition of peace. If the assertion could be substantiated, then disarmament negotiations would be meaningful; but while there is even a lingering doubt it would seem impossible to achieve disarmament until all the preconditions of peaceful relationships are achieved.

However, even assuming that the removal of arms would lead to a lessening of tensions, and ultimately to a condition of peace between the major Powers, there are still fallacious assumptions underlying disarmament negotiations which make them abortive. Some of the important and less debated assumptions on which disarmament negotiations rest seem to be:

(*a*) that the problem is already one of technical and procedural negotiation;

(*b*) that an agreement arrived at between major nations can later be extended to others;

(*c*) that smaller nations will accept an international organization in place of national defence forces.

None of these assumptions should remain unquestioned; unless each is valid negotiations must fail. The conditions which would justify an assumption that disarmament was a technical and a procedural problem have to be created before a negotiation approach is appropriate. Conditions must be created in which there are no fundamental conflicts in the relations of major nuclear nations outside those arising out of competition in the development of modern weapons and means of delivery. This may be possible in respect of their own bilateral relations; but the barrier to disarmament is not confined to the immediate bilateral relations of the major Powers, and is more importantly in the relations each has with others. It is probable that it has been these third-party relationships which have always transformed the narrow bilateral relations of great States into a power rivalry. A pre-requisite to negotiation may therefore be that the two main nuclear nations at least tacitly agree, or are persuaded by circumstances over which they have no control, to employ their deterrent mechanism only to preserve their immediate territorial interests. The means toward this position is a tacit undertaking, or the emergence of circumstances, which would isolate major Powers from the regional tensions of the rest of the world in so far as these bring them into direct conflict.

A second assumption usually made is that disarmament is a problem primarily the concern of, and to be resolved by agreement between, major Powers. It is acknowledged that there are other countries with high levels of armaments and industrial capacity, and that there are reasons for their arms quite separate from those factors which are thought to promote the arms race between the major States. It is acknowledged, also, that there could not be disarmament or arms control amongst the nuclear Powers while substantial and uncontrolled levels of arms existed elsewhere. For this reason negotiations between the major Powers are regarded as an essential first step, prior to an extension to all States, of any agreements that might be reached. It is far from clear, however, that these two steps, a disarmament agreement amongst the greater nations, and its extension to others, can be negotiated separately. It might be reasonable to anticipate that the direct relationships between major Powers would be rendered so uncomplicated by withdrawal or disengagement that their disarmament would remove all tensions likely to lead to war between them; but it cannot be assumed that this would be the case in the relationships existing amongst other States. The problem of disarmament is to them one of resolving conflict-situations which are historically and currently based, which make up the day-to-day life of international politics, which are more fundamental in many respects than the current East–West conflict. Their relationships are not like those of two very great nations which are self-contained as economic and political units; and which could for the sake of avoiding nuclear war live a life apart. Their relationships rest upon interdependence, and continuously touch upon matters of vital concern. Even if there were a basis of agreement between major Powers, it does not follow that there could be amongst others.

Assumptions such as this reflect the thinking of past ages when a few great nations dominated all international relations. Now regional relationships, which comprise the bulk of international politics, cannot be put aside for settlement as though they were a side-issue of international politics. In addition to traditional fears of aggression that most sovereign States have of others, in addition to the well-known factors of prestige and personal ambition, trade competition, and other commonplace aspects of international politics, each of the countries within a region has its own special fears which lead it to maintain a high level of arms. South-East Asia, like other regions in the under-developed world, is a region in which all the internal and external problems associated with new States exist, where post-colonial disappointment in expectations causes unrest, where under-development and population pressures aggravate whatever tensions are in any event created by religious, political and other differences, where feudalism and inequalities in income and in opportunity prevail. In Malaya, Indonesia and more particularly in countries bordering upon China, there are serious internal situations which it is claimed are aggravated by the deliberate intervention of other nations, and for this reason each country has a high level of arms, and in some cases even defence agreements with countries outside the region. In addition, special tensions occur from time to time, as for example those currently existing between India and Pakistan, between Cambodia and Thailand, between Malaya and Indonesia, between India and Ceylon, between Australia and Indonesia. Most South-East Asian countries have a special problem arising out of large numbers of Chinese whose allegiances are not known, and whose diligence and capabilities are outstanding in the communities in which they have settled. All these factors combine to induce 'strong leadership', in some cases bordering upon dictatorships, and control by armies whose leaders are relatively efficient. Foreign adventure can in these circumstances be triggered off by some remnant of colonialism, or by some claim upon a territory populated by the same race but which was separated as part of earlier colonialism. No country faced with these typical regional problems can contemplate disarmament. On the contrary, the level of arms which these regional tensions independently bring about is likely to rise, to be militarily significant, and even to reach a nuclear level.

The pressures exerted upon the nuclear nations, the United States in particular, to retain their interests in the security of other countries is likely to increase the more it is realized that it is in their interests to disengage. The political implication of the creation of new States, and the military implications of nuclear strategy, are not yet fully understood by smaller States, and the United States has not yet been frank about its future policies; but the pressures are already very great. Most smaller nations have tried hard to involve the great Powers in their security by granting double-tax agreements, by encouraging capital in other ways, by following political leadership somewhat slavishly in foreign policy, and in making certain types of bases and tracking stations available. Australia, like many other countries throughout the world, has deliberately endeavoured to involve the United States in its general security problems, which are traditional ones and have only an indirect and even remote relationship to the Cold War. It, and other countries, would not automatically accept disarmament even if there were agreement between the major Powers; on the contrary, it would probably wish to increase its defence strength.

Thinking in the field of International Relations in the seventeenth century was confined almost exclusively to Christendom and to proposals which could bring universal peace in that area. The concepts of power-balances and collective security, and the proposals put forward for world organization, are merely an extension of this insular thinking to regions which in the nineteenth century could be regarded as European in the sense that they were controlled by European Powers. Universal proposals are now peculiarly irrelevant to the modern world of independent States, each of which claims sovereignty within its own territories. No proposals for world organization, and no proposals for world disarmament which rest upon agreement amongst great Powers, and which would be imposed upon smaller States, has any political relevance regardless of the preponderance of military strength which may still be held by the industrially advanced countries. The only form of world organization which could be codified is an egalitarian one in which each sovereign State, regardless of size, had the opportunity of determining its own foreign policy. Any super-structure or world organization that can operate in these circumstances can be no more than a forum for discussion at which the highest common point of agreement on general and particular matters is ascertained and later codified. This process is unlikely to be one which can take place at a universal centre in the first instance, and is one which will require preliminary regional and functional agreements. Decentralization of the United Nations in its political as well as its economic and social activities would be a departure from orthodox thinking, but one more in conformity with the requirements of the international system.[1]

III. THE END OF THE ROAD

These two examples of policy, alliances and disarmament, have been taken merely to demonstrate the dilemmas of policy and the impasse that is reached once orthodox assumptions are accepted. Neither in theory nor in practice do orthodox theories or the assumptions on which they rest measure up to the knowledge we now have of the behaviour of States, or the realities of the situation we now face.

More broadly, there appears to be an incompatibility between systems such as balance-of-power and collective security which rely upon arms, and proposals coming from within that system for disarmament as a means of removing the main threat to peace and security. Arms have been an essential part of the international system; their abolition means the abolition of the system. National arms and foreign alliances have been accepted, and the employment of force tolerated, as an inevitable part of the accepted system. Warfare has progressively become less tolerable with weapon development, and in the nuclear age wars are no longer functional, hence an even greater interest in disarmament, and a confrontation with the dilemmas inherent in the power-politics international system. It is not, however, the nuclear weapon which has created the dilemmas; it has merely made obvious some fallacies which have plagued thinking and policy on international relations throughout modern times. Failure to make balance-of-power work, or its irrelevance to altered conditions, led to intellectual escalation from balances to collective security and to world government. Balances were an emergent of the world system, and relevant at a particular time in the sense that they arose out of the policies being pursued by independent sovereign States. The deliberate escalation to collective security introduced a discontinuity in the development of the international system, attempting to transfer national decision-making to international organization

[1] See also J. W. Burton, 'Regionalism and Functionalism', *Australian Outlook*, Vol. 15, No. 1, April 1961, and *Peace Theory*, Chapter 7.

—a transfer which was complete on paper but in practice never made. The further intellectual escalation to world government is merely a logical continuation in theory of a process which has never commenced. The process which did continue after the failure of balancing, and which brought about the failure of balancing, was the pursuit of national goals regardless of the workings of the system. The real-world escalation which has continued to take place is toward greater independence of policy, corresponding with the further development of national-ism, sovereignty and the modern State.

Any theory of International Relations must rest on what is, not on what someone at some stage might like to introduce, and any national policy which reliably achieves its purposes, must be based on an analysis of what is and not what someone at some stage might think the world should be. The national goal ahead is to learn to live with arms without employing them, which is an escalation in the same continuum as power balanc-ing, for it is still within the framework of an international system of independent sovereign States. The means by which this is being done are found by analysing how the system is evolving, how it operates. Scientists in International Relations cannot afford the unscientific luxury of problem-solving or arbitrary goal-seeking, which has up to the present been their pre-occupation and caused their defeat.

There are many other assumptions employed in International Relations which require re-examination, and some are derived from other disciplines. For instance, concepts of democracy and of parliamentary government are a feature of International Relations studies often to the exclusion of a proper recognition of the wholly different circumstances which have appeared in the new nations. More recent work in the field of decision-making, of conflict resolution, and of projection has not as yet been incorporated into an integrated body of thought in the field of International Relations. The net result is that policy-makers have no objective guide, they have no recognized texts as might be available to those engaged in financial or health policy, and with all the good-will in the world they are unlikely to arrive at policies which successfully attain the aims they seek. Once we have re-checked and re-stated our assumptions, we will begin to understand the nature of international relations, and appropriate national policies will suggest themselves.

8

PEACE RESEARCH

Reference has been made to the dissatisfaction with aspects of theory of International Relations experienced by political scientists such as Waltz and Claude, and by the historian Hinsley who deplored the absence of any significant breakthrough. It is more widespread than this. In most countries where there is a high level of academic development, institutions and societies have in recent years been formed for purposes of research in a field that has most usually been called Peace or Conflict Resolution. These include the Conflict Research Society in Britain, the Canadian Peace Research Institute, Polemologisch Instituut in the Netherlands, the Section for Research on Conflict and Peace at the Norwegian Institute for Social Research, and The Center for Research on Conflict Resolution at the University of Michigan, USA. In Eastern European countries there are equivalent institutions such as the Czechoslovakian Institute of International Politics and Economics, The Group for the Scientific Study of Disarmament in the Soviet Union, the Polski Instytut Spraw Miedzynarodowych, and the Institute of International Politics and Economy in Yugoslavia.

I. A MOVEMENT OF PROTEST

The active members of some of these organizations in the West belong to natural science, and to disciplines other than International Relations. Their general view is that the established discipline has failed to adapt to the nuclear era, and in particular has been tied to a narrow national-interest approach to relations between States. The Pugwash Movement—originally almost confined to physicists and other natural scientists—is further evidence of dissatisfaction by leading scientists with the existing state of thought in International Relations.

In many instances, this dissatisfaction is no more than the reaction of intelligent and scientifically trained people who are now worried about world affairs, who for this reason have a recently-acquired interest in world affairs, but who have not had the opportunity to find out what political scientists have been and are thinking. Furthermore, they have not had the opportunity to consider the implications of some terms and concepts they accept; for instance, many physicists concerned with disarmament seem, judging from their own documents, not to see any special problems in 'collective security'. Nevertheless, those concerned with Peace and Conflict Research have contributed an altered emphasis. They have protested against orthodox approaches to International Relations which presuppose that little can be done in the way of preventing or diverting conflict even in the long term. While orthodox approaches seem to assume the inevitability of power conflicts unless restrained by some form of deterrence, Peace Research, on the other hand, makes no such assumptions, and endeavours to examine the sources of conflict. It tends to base its researches upon conflict resolution within the provincial society. The difference between the two approaches is the difference between conditions of 'non-war' and of 'peace'.

The peace movement is nothing new, and from the middle of the nineteenth century it was perhaps as highly organized on a non-official international basis as it is at the present time. The first universal peace conference was organized by the British and American peace societies in London in 1843, and there was a mushroom growth of peace organizations of one kind or another which had a remarkable effect on policy right through the latter half of the nineteenth century. It reflected the different viewpoint which had developed throughout the past centuries, and the new approaches of the political scientists of the day. In peace congresses in the nineties there were represented, and in conflict, the views of the British and American religious societies, those of the secular pacifist organizations, those of the federalists, and those who favoured an approach to international organization through international law. Finally the pacifist and non-institutional viewpoint gave ground, and at the end of the century peace congresses were freely discussing organization and enforcement proposals. Governments were influenced by the peace movement and met at The Hague conferences of 1899 and 1907 where they demonstrated both their anxiety to arrive at an agreement, and their inability to accept any proposal which would in any way limit their freedom of action; this suggested the impossibility of effective arbitration or enforcement systems. Political scientists and the peace movement were forced to fall back upon federalist schemes, and this not through conviction, but merely in the absence of any other workable possibility.[1]

World War I ended discussion of narrow European federations, and yet brought to attention the impossibility of any federal State for all the world. The League of Nations, with ambitious objectives, but with a weak enforcement structure, was the consequence. The peace movement and peace research as it then existed were diverted away from the basic philosophy of Kant, Bentham and Mill, to an institutional approach which seemed to be the only realistic one in a world of power-politics.

It could be argued that the peace research of the present era will suffer the same fate if and when the relations between major Powers allow of nothing but national approaches to problems of peace and war. There is, however, an important difference between the peace movement of the last century, and the thinking of the fifties and sixties of this century. Peace research is a challenge to the concept of power-politics; but it is not the challenge of Bentham and Mill who shunned both international organization and the power of sovereign States. Nor is it the approach of the federalists who preceded and followed them; it draws from both institutionalists and non-institutionalists. It is concerned to promote international organization, specially that which is supported by the desire of governments for reciprocity in some matters, and for coordination in other of their independent activities. In relation to the most vital field of International Relations, that is the field dominated by power politics, the peace movement is not necessarily institutional, non-institutional, federalist or non-federalist. It is far more concerned with underlying factors, aspects of decision-making both by governments and by people, the nature of conflict itself, and the question whether power is a primary motivation or merely means to an end, and with the elemental nature of aggression.

The issue which was perhaps uppermost in the minds of those concerned with these matters at the end of the last century, the issue of enforcement in an international society, is one in which

[1] Hinsley in *Power and the Pursuit of Peace* deals at some length with the peace movement of the nineteenth century.

there is no clear consensus of opinion in the peace movement of this century. The question is open, as it was in the days of Bentham and Mill, as to whether an international system can be based upon independent sovereign States restrained only by consideration of public opinion and morality, or whether some system which includes enforcement is required and is practicable. Those within the traditional study of International Relations, such as Morgenthau and Herz, are, as we have already seen, giving thought to a system based neither upon enforcement nor upon public opinion, but upon a nationalistic universalism forced upon governments by the circumstances of the nuclear age.

The interest in background circumstances—the nature and origin of conflict—is the distinctive feature of Peace Research. At no time in the consideration of issues of peace and war has so much attention been given to what Kelman terms 'societal' and 'attitudinal' aspects,[1] and perhaps the reason is that at no time have these been as important as they are in the twentieth century. Technology in weaponry and in communications are amongst societal factors which have radically changed power relationships, and the further development of the State and international institutions has both imposed restraints upon governments and given them greater opportunities in policy decision. Attitudinal factors which affect the individual have become more important because of the greater opportunities of the individual and the spread of education. It is not surprising, therefore, that those concerned with Peace Research include both natural and social scientists. In terms of discussions and conferences, Peace Research is an 'interdisciplinary' one, and there are few disciplines which are not a qualification for participation. The relevance of the speciality of those concerned is not always apparent, but there is a common attempt to be scientific, to be objective, to learn all viewpoints, and finally to arrive at some common judgements on what is relevant.

The reason for this deeper search is because what is required in the nuclear age is the prevention of war and not merely steps which might reduce its probability. In these circumstances the study of International Relations cannot sensibly be primarily the study of maintaining a non-war position, but must be the study of a condition of peace; it cannot be concerned with

[1] H. C. Kelman, *Journal of Social Issues*, Vol. XI, No. 1 (1955).

power-balances, and other devices aimed at controlling States, as much as with finding those national policies which if pursued by independent States would enable each to live in a condition of peace with others; it cannot be concerned with means by which a *status quo* can be maintained as much as with the legitimate claims of nations, and how change can be brought about peacefully. The Peace Research groups have paid less attention to the immediate problems of disarmament, deterrence and strategic stability, and more to conflict resolution, public attitudes, decision-making, and other fundamental aspects of conflict resolution and management.

II. PEACE RESEARCH AND INTERNATIONAL RELATIONS

Most new studies commence as an inter-disciplinary study; and it is only when they cease to be this that they develop a body of thought which can be recognized as a discipline. The inter-disciplinary nature of a study becomes a function of the individual rather than a function of inter-disciplinary organization. It is now possible to train students in International Relations, and they approach the subject not as lawyers, economists, or students of politics, but as students of International Relations. As such they see less and less value in an approach from any one discipline, and find that clarity, precise thinking, and avoidance of false analogies are achieved by casting aside terminology and concepts which may be meaningful in the discipline in which they originated, but which are misleading if applied to International Relations. Any study of a subject on an inter-disciplinary basis is likely to degenerate in a particular institution into a branch of one discipline, depending on who fathers the study, and the relative strength of the disciplines and the persons represented. If 'inter-disciplinary' can be given any practical meaning in this context it must mean that there will be a number of persons scattered around various disciplines who have been thinking about Peace Research or International Relations from one point of view or another as a full time occupation, who have come to similar viewpoints, and who can communicate with each other in a terminology which is meaningful. In doing this such persons gradually lose touch with many aspects of the discipline in which they are trained, and absorb areas on the periphery of other disciplines, in due course working in a common field of agreed boundaries, and creating an independent discipline. The distinction between an inter-disciplinary attitude, and inter-disciplinary procedures, is an important one to make in the development of a new field of study.

Peace Research, being an inter-disciplinary approach to problems of peace and war, is in danger of falling into method-ological errors. Those engaged in a particular discipline are inclined to transfer their terminology and concepts from their discipline to the field of International Relations without realising that they are merely employing models and analogy. For example, the pathogenesis of war seems to be based on an assumption that there is some direct relationship between individual abnormal behaviour and warfare. The fact is that warfare is a legitimate, reasonable and time-honoured instru-ment of national policy in conditions in which there are no peaceful means of change. Again, theories of aggression in animals may or may not be valid; but even if valid they cannot be used to prove the existence of aggression between States. The use of analogy, and of models which do not stand up to reality-testing, is a particular danger in an inter-disciplinary approach.

In due course, as International Relations as a research and teaching subject advances into this area, and as Peace Research delves more deeply into International Relations, the distinctions between the two will seem less real. At the moment they certainly appear real to those interested in Peace Research, and who are not always aware of new emphases being introduced into International Relations. Perhaps the position is that popular interest in Peace Research is giving a jolt to International Relations which those working in this backward discipline will ultimately welcome.

Peace Research in the twentieth century is a recognition that there is an academic problem to be solved; it is in sharp contradiction to the thesis implicit in the activist Peace Move-ment that all that is required is to persuade or force policy-makers to act in certain ways in relation to certain issues. Peace Research is more directed to the question, what advice can be given to policy-makers?

International studies can conveniently be departmentalized. Within the broad group of natural and political scientists seeking to avoid war, there have developed two schools, the 'armers' and the 'disarmers', that is, those who seek stability through improved military balances and deterrence, and those who seek to remove or to control conflicts. The 'armers' may be broken down into those concerned with maintaining stability by improved deterrents, and those most interested in arms control and disarmament. The stability-deterrence studies are of two kinds: firstly the orthodox approaches of balance-of-power, and secondly, the more technical and specific studies of nuclear deterrence.

The peace studies are differentiated by reason of the fact that they make no assumptions regarding the nature of men or States. They are of two kinds, the one examining the elements of conflict, decision-making techniques, conflict-resolution, the role of education, difficulties in communication and other matters of this order. The other branch is the study of the policies which independent States would be required to follow if each were to maintain a peaceful relationship with the other. This does not exclude the study of international organization, but in so far as it includes it, there is no importance attached to enforcement powers.

Those concerned with Peace Research are inclined to argue that they are looking at international society as a whole, and endeavouring to examine conflict from an international viewpoint, whereas orthodox studies have tended to approach International Relations from the point of view of the interests of separate States whose responsibility it is to maintain their own security. There is undoubtedly a different emphasis of this nature, and it is probably because of its international approach that the Peace Research studies have failed to persist once nations are involved in crisis situations.

The Peace Research institutes, to which reference has been made, have already promoted a greater interest in the study of issues of war and peace, and directly or indirectly have led to increased University teaching and research in International Relations. Not unexpectedly, this movement of protest is orthodox bound: there is an acute awareness of the dilemmas of orthodox approaches, but no alternative theories of International Relations seem to have emerged. The trends within International Relations away from the study of structures, and toward processes of decision-making, were well established before Peace Research became widespread. Furthermore, the pamphlets and publications for which Peace Research is responsible suggest that the study of conflict is adding to knowledge in special fields related to International Relations, but is not providing a break-through, or any significant new approach, or alternative general theory. Peace and Conflict Research centres are providing useful and stimulating perspectives, they are goading International Relations to develop improved techniques and more realistic models.

PART III

THE ALTERED
WORLD ENVIRONMENT

9

IMPLICATIONS OF
NUCLEAR STRATEGY

'Aggression' is war by another name, and war has been accepted as a proper instrument of national policy at least in conditions in which there is no adequate mechanism for peaceful change and adjustment to change; nationalism and sovereign independence have progressively been placed higher in the scale of values of States; responsibility for foreign-policy decision-making has become more widespread and has been more and more influenced by national and international processes of democratization; considerations of 'justice' associated with claims for independence and non-discriminatory treatment have restrained Great Powers in the pursuit or preservation of privileged positions; communications, education, travel, further developments in the modern State, new philosophies, have all exercised influences on relations between States, especially since the Second World War.

Ever-present, in the forefront of attention, are the implications of nuclear strategy; but the political and nuclear influences affect each other. Nuclear strategy could conceivably have taken quite different forms, in the absence of this altering political background, for instance, some form of world imperialism dominated by the thermonuclear States; and the influence of these background circumstances may have been unimportant, or at least greatly lessened, if it were not for the dilemmas of nuclear strategy.

I. THE DEFECTS OF THE NUCLEAR DETERRENT

The possession by each of the two Great Powers of a nuclear capacity, sufficient to achieve unacceptable destruction of the other, constitutes a deterrent to the use by either side of nuclear weapons, and to aggression generally when this might lead to the use of nuclear weapons. This balance of terror is, in the current world situation, a saefguard against war between the

Great Powers, and as such enters into strategic calculations whenever serious conflict is likely. Because the Cold War struggle is between two blocs of nations which include most of the major Powers, important world disputes are finally controlled by the deterrent threat of nuclear war.

However, the nuclear deterrent is a haphazard contrivance; it did not develop out of any deliberate planning of international relations, and has major defects as a workable international institution. It has obvious technical defects; the risks of irresponsible or accidental use of nuclear weapons may diminish with the invention of safeguards, but they will nevertheless increase with the spread of the weapon to more countries. It is also unstable, for the balance of terror can be upset by technological break-throughs, or even by an accumulation of stocks of weapons by one side sufficient to destroy the capabilities of retaliation by the other after a preventive strike.

The technical defects, though frighteningly serious, are in the long term the least dangerous; because they are technical they can probably be overcome, and an awareness of the risks of accidental warfare is in itself a stimulus to scientists and politicians to overcome at least these known causes. There are other defects which are inherent in the device: for example, the operation of the nuclear deterrent is uncertain. It cannot be stated with any certainty that nations will heed the threat of nuclear warfare any more than they heeded past threats of widespread destruction. There are nuclear scientists who are so impressed with the break in continuum of weapon development created by the discovery of thermonuclear energy, that they argue that the nuclear deterrent is different from previous deterrents in kind, and not merely in a matter of degree. This is an optimistic viewpoint. In the pre-nuclear age risks were taken of massive retaliations, yet they were taken; there were situations which, in the view of the political and the military leaders of Germany, Italy and Japan, justified taking these risks. It is not difficult to imagine in the nuclear age a situation in which a power struggle is being lost by one side, and a decision is taken to risk even greater massive retaliation rather than to suffer certain defeat. China with its large and dispersed population presents a case in which the use of nuclear weapons, even with the risks of retaliation, could be regarded by its leaders as rational; running the risks of nuclear warfare might seem the only means of changing a world structure which denied China equitable opportunities for economic progress. Indeed, China is in this respect in a position similar to that of Japan before it sought, at the risk of almost certain failure, to acquire by force a co-prosperity sphere under its own political control. Nor can it be stated with certainty that the nuclear Powers would use nuclear weapons even after threatening to do so. Far from promoting stability, the threatening of nuclear destruction without implementing the threat, could lead in time to behaviour which ignored the existence of nuclear weapons, thus destroying their deterrent effect. Brinkmanship, piecemeal aggression, and extensive use of subversive tactics and of conventional weapons, could ultimately create a condition of international instability that could bring the nuclear weapon into play unexpectedly, and in relation to a relatively unimportant dispute.

The deterrent effect of possession of nuclear weapons by both Russia and the United States is at best no more than to prevent open warfare; it clearly can make no positive contribution to the resolution of conflict, and cannot of itself lead to a reduction of weapons of mass destruction. Moreover, the weapons on which the deterrent rests cannot be removed because of the kind of difficulties which have been experienced in disarmament negotiations, and because also of the fear of rearmament. The position could be reached in which outstanding political issues between the Great Powers had been settled by negotiation, and yet the danger of war still remained merely because of the existence of the weapons of mass destruction. The nuclear deterrent is, therefore, not merely negative in the sense of making no contribution to the resolution of conflict, but is also self-perpetuating.

One of the effects of the deterrent is to keep in existence situations which in the interests of stability and peace should undergo change; over a period there tends to accumulate a number of potential conflict-situations which in other circumstances would be resolved. The nuclear deterrent is a Great Power device, and as such is as likely to be employed to maintain inherently local positions, such as unpopular regimes, as to maintain ones which are inherently stable and made unstable merely by some temporary or accidental circumstances.

One of the most serious defects of the system of nuclear deterrence is that the foreign policies which flow from it include a high degree of local activity and interference in domestic affairs, and do not achieve stability, but tend on the contrary to create additional conflict situations. The threat of overwhelming force, which the United States used during the last days of 1953 as its answer to communist influence in countries in Asia, was no longer appropriate once Russia possessed nuclear weapons and their means of delivery. There had then to be a build-up of conventional weapons and forces at strategic points, and an increase throughout the whole range of weaponry. Accompanying this, support had to be given to whichever governments were anti-communist, both by direct military assistance and through defence pacts. The United States in this way became committed to supporting administrations which in the normal course would have been defeated by popular movements, and would not have attracted United States support. The conflict in the minds of American policy-makers between the defence of politically backward States against Communism, and dislike for corrupt and inefficient administration, led to acts which achieved neither regional security nor social progress in these States. Assuming that Communism was aggressive and a threat to the United States, the nuclear deterrent gave the United States little option but to defend its interests in this way. It would be reasonable to assume that these failures of Western policy, which are now widely acknowledged,[1] could be matched with similar failures of the policies of the opposing bloc, though we know little of the debates which took place within it.

II. THE 'NEW-ISOLATIONISM'

As the Great Powers reassess their interests in the light of their own failure to find a solution to the problem of disarmament, in the light of the growing complexities of the nuclear deterrent, in the light of technological developments, and in the light of the rapid extension of nonalignment, they tend to see their strategic interests in an altered perspective. Their attention is drawn toward evolving means by which they can live with nuclear weapons without using them, to the avoidance of situations in which they might become involved, to the stabilization of

[1] J. H. Herz, *International Politics in the Atomic Age*, 1959. In Chapter 8, 'Impact of the New Weapons', Herz deals at some length with the difficulties inherent in nuclear deterrence.

political relations throughout the world, and to the peaceful settlement of disputes between other countries as they occur.

More recent technical developments of the nuclear weapon and its means of delivery have made even more desperate the need for Great Powers to avoid situations in which there could be risk of nuclear warfare; but these technical developments have at the same time provided the Great Powers with means of avoiding conflict situations. Now that both possess long-range missiles, long-range submarines, and other means of delivery of nuclear weapons from their own installations, their systems of deterrence do not rely upon foreign bases and alliances. In these circumstances there are good reasons for not complicating their own dangerous deterrent systems, and their own dangerous power-relations, by commitments which add nothing to the protection of their vital interests.

On any assessment of interests, the nuclear Powers cannot afford the risks of employing the nuclear deterrent system in all conflict situations which might occur between middle Powers, or even in all cases in which they have an alliance with one of them. A border dispute, a dispute between States over the future status of a territory such as Laos or Cuba, or a conflict of interests in a country in the Middle East, would not seem to justify a threat of nuclear warfare—though this obvious fact had to be learned by reality-testing in the Cuban crisis. The Soviet refusal to underwrite Chinese policies of eliminating colonialism in Asia, and the refusal of the United States to share with its allies its responsibilities for the use of the deterrent, are both indications of a realized need not to be involved in situations which unnecessarily bring the two thermonuclear Powers into direct opposition on matters not of vital concern to them, while leaving them free to decide which are of vital concern. The thermonuclear deterrent is promoting a new isolationism on the part of thermonuclear States.

The increasing support of the Great Powers for the neutralization of countries by nonalignment is understandable in this context. So also would be policies adopted by both Powers to contract out of many of their obligations which they have assumed as a result of alliances with other countries. This applies particularly to the United States which, because of a now outmoded strategy, has become involved in every corner of the globe, and continues to be involved in many cases merely because some of its allied governments have taken advantage of the Cold War situation and the United States need for bases, to preserve themselves against some internal threat, or against some traditional threat of aggression. Withdrawal of bases, withdrawal of military support, and reliance upon a nuclear deterrent wholly under the control of the Great Powers, is a trend already perceptible.

However, no simple plan of disengagement is possible, for the centrally-based nuclear deterrent is not an appropriate means of dealing with the typical conflict situation which is of importance to a Great Power, but which by itself would not justify risking nuclear warfare. Conventional weapons and local defences continue to be required to ensure stability. This is a serious weakness of the nuclear deterrent; technically the deterrent system can deal with any threat of aggression, but because the weapons on which it is based are so powerful and would lead to devastation of many nations if used, the deterrent cannot be employed in the many typical local situations which occur. On the other hand the use of conventional forces on a large scale could lead to the use of nuclear weapons, and therefore in the nuclear age even they are not an appropriate means of dealing with these typical conflict situations unless there is some guarantee in advance—which there cannot be—that a relatively minor dispute and small-scale fighting will not build up into major warfare. The only resolution of this dilemma is for each Great Power to avoid involvement in any dispute unless its rival becomes a party to it, even at the risk of losing some strategic or political interest.

III. NEUTRALIZATION BY NONALIGNMENT

Withdrawal of extensive regions of the world from the area of Great Power conflict has helped the nuclear Powers to avoid some conflict situations. In these regions the Great Powers cannot establish military bases, obtain privileged rights in trade or resource exploitation, indulge in uncontrolled propaganda, or conduct aggressive activities in other ways. Their economic aid and technical assistance must be given competitively, and to an increasing degree without obligation. As nonaligned or neutralized areas increase, the opportunities for waging the Cold War and for preparing for military activities, will progressively be limited. The establishment of an extensive nonaligned area also removes a danger inherent in the winning of the Cold War by one side: the danger that there will be a desperate nuclear response from the loser. Greatly extending nonalignment means that neither side can win or lose, and the nuclear stalemate is, therefore, being provided with a useful political reinforcement.

However, it is particularly in relation to the efficiency of the nuclear deterrent that the withdrawal of regions from the areas of conflict is important. The struggle between the Soviet bloc and the Western Alliance is not one in isolation from the rest of the world; it is not one in which each Power seeks to occupy or to destroy the territories of the other. It is a power-struggle primarily between two great nations but taking place in a world environment; it is a struggle directed toward areas of the world outside the territories of the main contestants. Each party seeks to extend its spheres of influence; the areas of conflict include areas of Europe, Africa, Asia, and even Latin America. If the deterrent mechanism were required only to ensure that nuclear weapons would not be employed as a result of conflict of interests arising directly in United States–Soviet territorial relations, it would rarely be alerted; but when it is required to prevent open warfare between nuclear Powers in every conflict of interests occurring in Europe, the Middle East, Africa, Asia and Latin America, it overshadows world politics. The weapons and the risks involved have no sensible relationship to the relatively minor local interests which are in conflict. If the nuclear deterrent were absolutely efficient, no dangers would arise from the wide responsibility thrust upon it. But because the efficiency of the nuclear deterrent is not absolute, and because there is a risk of failure, every increase in the area of conflict and in the number of conflict-situations to be controlled by it, increases the chances of nuclear warfare. The neutralization of nonaligned nations helps to reduce the responsibilities of the nuclear deterrent to the limits of its efficiency.

Even though required to deal with a number of situations limited by reason of neutralization of regions, the deterrent system still remains an instrument suitable only for enforcing the peace at the thermonuclear level between thermonuclear Powers, and not relevant to the task of establishing a system of peaceful relations.

IV. THE PERMANENCE OF THE SYSTEM OF DETERRENCE

The power conflict, and the possession of nuclear weapons by
the parties to it, are enduring features of international relationships. This is a realistic view-point now accepted by many
observers, some of whom believe that disarmament negotiations
have become little more than a continuing diplomatic exercise
carried on for Cold War political purposes. Professor Rabinowitch went so far as to suggest that 'further negotiations
on disarmament may be fraught with the danger of enhancing
the existing distrust rather than reducing it',[1] Lord Russell
held out little hope for disarmament without the solution of
underlying problems,[2] and George Kennan adopted a similar
view.[3] The disarmament negotiations have led to a growing
opinion that the problem of disarmament is not a technical one;
that even though a fool-proof scheme could be devised whereby
weapons could be abolished without endangering either power
group in the process, there would still not be agreement at a
political level.

The nuclear deterrent is a continuing institution, just as the
deterrence of conventional forces was in the past, and the
international system will continue to be based on it. The
problem of disarmament in the nuclear world appears to be no
more tractable than it was in the pre-war period, despite the
difference in the magnitude of the weapons to be abolished; the
problem awaiting solution is not the problem of disarmament
and supervision to ensure that arms will not be produced again,
but the problem of establishing conditions in which they will
not be used. The greatly increased destructive power which
nuclear weapons provide cannot be regarded as making disarmament any more practical from a political point of view than
it was previously; it may be regarded as making the abolition
of war, as an institution of national policy, a practical possibility
through the acceptance of a world system of relationships which
makes major weapons and war irrelevant.

The nuclear deterrent neutralizes the military power of both
thermonuclear States; it makes these States less free to pursue

---

[1] E. Rabinowitch, *Bulletin of the Atomic Scientists*, Vol. XVI, No. 2, p. 37.
[2] B. Russell, *Common Sense and Nuclear Warfare*, 1959.
[3] G. F. Kennan, *Russia, the Atom and the West*, 1958.

policies of power politics than other States that possess only conventional weapons. In a sense each is powerless, and both must conduct their foreign policies as if they possessed no military power. Other restraints of a political character, to which reference is made in the next Chapter, similarly reduce the political and economic influence of these two Great Powers. It would be a mistake, however, to draw the conclusion that, having been forced to conduct relations as though power did not exist, the power possessed has no function and could be removed. Some analogy with gold reserves in a bank seems to be required to describe this situation in which power is both useless and indispensable, or some reference to the difference between potential and kinetic energy to describe the existence of a deterrent force which may not be set in motion. In due course the gold reserve can be reduced once confidence grows in the operation of a system which no longer requires it; but a national and apparently sensible elimination of the reserve would destroy confidence in the alternative, and developing system. The international system is no longer one based on relative power any more than the financial one is a gold standard; but the dependence of power, like gold, persists.

As the two thermonuclear States progress from one system to the other under pressure of deterrence, they are confronted with runs on their reserves initiated by third parties. The future stability of relations between other countries, especially the middle Powers—those nations with a developed industry and with an actual or possible nuclear capability—is important in their own relationships. In the future there are likely to occur many serious conflicts in developing regions, but assuming that the nonaligned nations of Africa and Asia can evolve regional systems of defence and conflict-resolution, and can maintain the system of nonalignment, and assuming that the Great Powers are not in danger of direct conflict by reason of their own bi-lateral relations, attention then becomes focused in particular upon problems of the Middle Powers. The Middle Powers are not within the system of nonalignment, nor are they principal participants within the system of deterrence. Two of them possess nuclear weapons, and some others have an industrial potential which would support production of them.

The nuclear capability of a Middle Power is technically relevant to its own strategic relations with other Middle Powers, and not to those with either of the two Great Powers. But the capability is sought in relations to a Great Power because there is no confidence that it will not be left undefended, not only in a conflict with other Middle Powers, but more particularly with a Great Power. Middle Powers seek their own nuclear deterrent, despite warnings such as those of the United States Secretary of Defence who said: 'limited nuclear capabilities, operating independently, are dangerous, expensive, prone to adolescence, and lacking in credibility.'[1]

However, from the point of view of the Middle Power the policy of acquiring an independent deterrent is self-defeating, for the Great Power can then argue that its responsibilities are taken over, and that it can withdraw from the local scene. Equally, the policy of withdrawal from the local scene could be self-defeating from the point of view of the Great Power. The reluctance of the Great Power to risk nuclear warfare could leave the Middle Powers unprotected; but equally it leaves them (and all other Powers including African and Asian nations which are strongly armed) free to carry on the type of power politics which prevailed before the nuclear age, and through which major changes in strategic balances could take place. Thus, situations in Europe, Africa, and the Middle East, involving smaller Powers, could lead to conflict; in each case the conflict could be confined to these nations, but in each case the interests of the main nuclear Powers are likely ultimately to be involved.

China is a special and an even more difficult case. It is a Middle Power not so fearful of nuclear reprisals, and suffering an enforced isolation by reason of Western policies, of its Chinese minority problems in Asia, and of its strained relations with Russia. No nation the size of China, no nation in which nationalism has reached such a high level, is likely to accept isolation of this kind, and counter-responses may be anticipated. Short of nonaligned countries working out a relationship with China, and short of full recognition of China in world councils,

[1] Those succeeding him have accepted Mr Churchill's views stated in the Commons on 1 March 1955 (*New York Times*, 2 March 1955): 'Unless we make a contribution of our own . . . we cannot be sure that in an emergency the resources of other Powers would be planned exactly as we would wish or that targets which would threaten us would be given the necessary priority . . . I cannot feel that we should have much influence over their policy or actions while we are largely dependent, as we are today, upon their protection.'

China cannot be regarded as being effectively restrained by any of the forces operating upon other Powers.

Disarmament is no more possible for the Middle Powers than it is for the Great Powers, especially those with the traditions of the leading European nations. The assumption must be made in respect of them also, that they will remain armed, and endeavour to have their own deterrent under their own sovereign control. The incentives for this will increase as the interests of the thermonuclear Powers in what has been called 'new isolationism' become more evident. Sufficient has been said of the self-defeating policies relating to nuclear deterrence to indicate the high degree of uncertainty that nuclear policies will add to the security of Middle Powers. The uncertainties can be used to justify increased nuclear capabilities, and independent deterrents; one possible development in Europe is the creation of super-States out of groups of nations, each with a deterrent capability approaching that of the Great Powers, and another is the possession of nuclear weapons by all the main industrial countries. The Middle Powers would then face the problem, as do the Great Powers, of living with nuclear weapons without using them, and they would face all the same dilemmas about conventional and nuclear weapons, and the same problems relating to the avoidance of conflict situations.

10

THE ALTERED POLITICAL ENVIRONMENT

Hinsley argues that in the first half of the twentieth century there has been 'an increased moral aversion from violence in most men's minds' which he suggests is not due solely to the greater efficiency of destructive power, but also due to 'a news service of unparalleled efficiency in bringing violence to men's attention'.[1] He believes that 'men with power were being subjected to quite unprecedented restraints'.[2] He emphasizes the emergence of a better informed public opinion, and the growth of technical deterrents.[3] Furthermore, he demonstrates that since the failure of the League there has been a far greater understanding of problems of change, of responsibilities of *status quo* Powers, and of the subjective nature of judgements regarding 'just and unjust wars'.[4] Influences such as these are strengthened by the dangers of the nuclear deterrent, and the logical consequences of nuclear strategy.

There are many alterations in the political environment which together are significant in world affairs; amongst these are the national and international democratization of foreign-policy decision-making, the seeming incompatible re-introduction of an international aristocracy of decision-makers, the political-strategic relationship between nuclear powers and the body of new States, the closely related respect for independence and territorial integrity which seems to have increased under pressure of nuclear and political circumstances, the role of subversion, and the increasingly important inter-play of economic relations between developed and developing economies. There are many others to which importance might be attached, but some discussion even of these will demonstrate the extent of political change which has occurred in the twenty-year period since 1945.

---

[1] Hinsley, p. 276.   [2] Hinsley, p. 284.   [3] Hinsley, p. 284.
[4] Hinsley, p. 319.

I. THE DEMOCRATIZATION OF FOREIGN POLICY

Nuclear strategy is not the only factor which, in the nuclear age, limits the freedom of action of great Powers. The change which has taken place in the international community, of which the creation of new States and the use of the international forum of the United Nations by them are only symptoms, has not yet been fully appreciated. Professor Partridge has drawn attention to this change by using a useful analogy:

The revolution that has occurred in international society in the last three or four decades is crucial here. The elements of that revolution are familiar. A large number of communities, which previously existed below the threshold of articulate international politics, have emerged to statehood. Coinciding with that, international political society has become, as it never was before, an 'open' society: I refer to the emergence of a condition of open, continuous, international debate in which the majority of the independent nations expect to participate, within the United Nations Assembly and outside. This, I think, is something new in the world; and it makes the discussions of the World War I period about the advantages and disadvantages of 'open' and 'secret' diplomacy seem archaic to us. The intense excitation of world wide political agitation and controversy has been hastened and intensified by the rivalry between the two super-Powers; and there is another analogy with internal politics here. Just as Marx and Lenin have argued that the political awakening and strengthening of politically submerged or 'oppressed' classes have often been fostered by struggles within the ruling class, so the struggle between the USSR and the USA is a very important factor in the political emancipation and maturing of the smaller, newer States. It has been assisted, of course, also by many other developments: the 'shrinking of the world', the revolution in techniques of communication, and so on: in fact, the very same technological and social changes which, in internal politics, have brought the age of pressure-group democracy to full flower have had very similar effects upon international society.

Now, this revolution in the structure of the international 'system', the emergence of a politically highly active, open, pressure-group democracy type of international order seems to me to be important for the following reason. Political scientists and international lawyers have much debated whether there is anything that can be called an international community, one capable of supporting a legal order. Whether or not this is a profitable question to raise or discuss, we may at least say this, that the appearance of the 'open' international society is perceptibly creating one important quality of that integrated political community which we call the state, *viz* a structure of claims, expectations, of imputed rights and duties which the members of the system (and especially its more privileged and powerful members) are expected to acknowledge and comply with. It is a process not dissimilar to the process by which, in the histories of the great States of Europe, the slow passage was made from a state of privileged autocracy plus the political anonymity of the bulk of the population to one in which every man and group has its 'rights' and is very vocal about them: the condition in short in which citizenship and the privileges and opportunities of citizenship have been established. Students of contemporary international affairs have not paid enough attention to this change in the character of the moral, ideological and political dimension of the international system; but we have a familiar example of it in the beliefs that now circulate about the duty to give and the right to receive economic aid. Citizens of the affluent Western societies now commonly display towards Asian and African peoples something reminiscent of the 'bad conscience' that Western middle class intellectuals have often displayed in the past in their attitudes towards the working classes of their own country. This is a change in the nature of international society which is important because it changes quite radically the moral and political context in which great States now pursue their national policies.[1]

II. INTERNATIONAL ARISTOCRACY

In the view of Morgenthau, a deterioration of international morality occurred as a result of the substitution of democratic for aristocratic responsibility in foreign affairs, and the substitution of nationalistic standards of action for universal ones.[2] However, changes in the world environment now lead one to suggest the development of a 'nationalist universalism', as though the pressures of world and national public opinion, which first destroyed morality and internationalism, were turning full circle, and helping to promote them. A similar view has been taken by Herz.[3] The logical development of nuclear strategy is forcing States to take a longer-term view of their shorter-term strategic interest. A nationalist universal-

---

[1] P. H. Partridge, 'Images of the International Order', *The Australian Journal of Politics and History*, Vol. IX, No. 1, May 1963, pp. 10-11.

[2] Morgenthau, *Politics among Nations*, 1960, p. 254.

[3] Herz, 1959, Chapter 12.

ism—that is, a long-term view of national interest—is an inevitable consequence of thermonuclear strategy, and the fact that it is incompatible with supra-nationalism and international organization with enforcement powers does not necessarily mean it cannot promote a condition of peace and security.

Morgenthau would agree with his colleague Thompson, who believes that 'The people have acquired power which they are incapable of exercising, and the governments they elect have lost powers which they must recover if they are to govern'.[1] The difference between the two viewpoints, first that there is an internationalism developing, and second that democratic processes have led to dangerous nationalism, is not so great as might at first appear. The atomic age, as Herz points out, is placing greater responsibility for decision upon national leaders, and despite the democratization of decision-making at a national and an international level, the international aristocracy of the days of princes and emperors has been restored in an altered form. The international aristocracy, which through intermarriage and direct communication tended to control or guide excessive nationalism into channels compatible with an international system and a developing international community, has a modern equivalent created by technical developments in the fields of weaponry and communication. In the nuclear age, as was clearly demonstrated during the Cuban crisis, hour-by-hour decisions were required in circumstances in which allies could not be consulted, and it is doubtful if there was even consultation within the national groups directly concerned of all the decision-makers who would believe that they had a role to play. In so far as other governments endeavoured to influence the course of events, the initiative had to be with the active head of State rather than with a cabinet or parliament. Since the Cuban crisis the installation of the 'hot line' has provided the emergency communication between heads of States. Undoubtedly the decisions taken by heads of States without consultation with their colleagues in a particular crisis must reflect political pressures which have over a period been the experience of the political leaders concerned; equally undoubtedly, some of the personal responsibility to which Morgenthau attached such importance has been re-introduced.

[1] K. W. Thompson, p. 45.

The two processes, the democratization of foreign policy and the development of an international aristocracy which is active at crisis periods, are by no means incompatible. On the contrary, from many points of view both systems tend to operate against powerfully organized interest groups, because these are less effective in achieving their purposes in the very long term (where public opinion is effective), and in the very short term (where decision-making is left with political leaders), than in the medium term where their lobbying is most efficient. It could be argued that the international system is now gaining the best of both worlds, first pressure on governments by reason of informed national and international discussion of foreign affairs, and second responsibility placed finally upon leaders who must, whether they like it or not, form an aristocracy and communicate with each other as members of it.

III. NONALIGNMENT AND NUCLEAR POLITICS

The Great Powers are restrained in their decision-making, not only by nuclear deterrence, but by reason of the existence of nations which remain outside their alliances. The institution of alliances has for centuries dominated world affairs: membership of alliances and counter-alliances has been the experience of most nations. Neutrality has never been widespread, however much it might have been desired by each sovereign State. When it has occurred it has been possible owing to the power interests of the greater States, which sometimes found 'buffer States' useful in peace time, and neutrals useful in war; there were occasions on which each rival Power preferred to respect the independence of a small State rather than to risk the extinction of that independence at the hands of the other Power. Neutrality, when it did exist, was made possible by the fear each Power, or each alliance, had of the opposing one. In terms of past experience, the nonalignment of the 'fifties and 'sixties could be regarded as another outcrop of neutralism, existing only through the mutual fears of the two opposing power blocs, and therefore stable only in so far as the neutralism suited the strategic interests of the major Powers. One view frequently expressed, especially in the United States, is that, in addition, nonalignment owes its existence to the tolerance if not the protection of the West in whose traditional spheres of influence nonaligned countries are located.

The mutual fears of the main rivals are greater in the nuclear age than ever before, and the nuclear deterrent is at least a restraint upon the use even of conventional weapons. It can be assumed that the caution of major Powers which enabled smaller nations to be neutral before the Second World War still exists now on an even greater scale. The fear each of the Great Powers has of the other is in the nuclear age so much greater than before, that any nation which chooses to be neutral should be able to enjoy an independent status for as long as the deterrent operates.

However, the nuclear deterrent is far from perfect in its operation. It cannot be regarded as proof against non-military means of aggression, against the use of conventional weapons in many border disputes, or against situations which could threaten the independence of smaller nations. Indeed, in some respects the nuclear deterrent system invites brinkmanship on the grounds that no Great Power would finally employ nuclear weapons except in the defence of an interest directly vital to it. As a consequence, if the nonaligned nations owe their status to the mutual fears of the Great Powers, they may be even less secure than pre-war neutrals.

There are, however, certain features inherent in nonalignment which increase its stability. Nonalignment developed as the national foreign policy of a number of countries despite the opposition of colonial Powers. The origin of nonalignment was in the nationalist movement of independence of colonial territories. The strength and success of these movements, assisted by the circumstances of war, took the colonial Powers by surprise. The expectation, or at least the hope of the colonial powers to which they formerly owed allegiance, was that the new nations would maintain their old trading, cultural and other ties. It was anticipated that in matters of defence and military alignments, as in trade, a continuing relationship would persist; but this did not often happen.

There were pressures on the nonaligned countries from both sides in the Cold War to declare themselves, as both sides found this extensive neutralism an embarrassment to them; but these pressures were strongly resisted. The nonaligned countries were then regarded as a liability; they could not be relied upon for military bases or as instruments in the Cold War, and they were capable of active opposition in relation to issues disputed between the Great Powers. At the United Nations they became an embarrassment to both sides, tolerated only because of their combined voting strength.

On these grounds it is difficult to sustain the view that nonalignment is a function merely of the power-conflict as was neutrality. The nonaligned nations had a special status as a group, even though each was acting as an independent nation. As a group they were capable of limiting the freedom of political action of the Great Powers in a way which a passive neutral could not do.

This effect was at least in part due to the adoption within a few years of nonalignment by a large number of countries in widely separated regions of the world. Most cases of neutrality have been isolated ones: a particular nation being neutral in a particular power conflict, and if there were several neutrals they were usually in the one region. The current nonalignment spreads from Southern Europe, through Africa and Asia to Latin America; it is a political movement as well as a foreign policy for a number of nations.

As a widespread political movement, nonalignment is an institution to which Great Powers must pay attention in determining their policies. No major Power can afford to ignore it, and the policies of the Great Powers are conditioned by it. One form the power conflict has taken is economic competition in the underdeveloped areas of the world, in which the allegiance of small nations is sought. Economic aid is one weapon used by the Great Powers, and its use provides an increased and not a decreased motivation for nonalignment, as there is competition between the Powers in giving the aid. The nonaligned nations, therefore, do not respond to aid as was intended: they are more, and not less, confirmed in their nonalignment. The response of the two Great Powers to failure to achieve their political objectives could reasonably be to decrease or eliminate their aid. But if one were to do this, the immediate effect would be to present a political advantage to the Power which continued the aid. Short of an agreement between these Powers not to grant aid, nonalignment traps them into competing, not for any benefit each might derive, but merely to prevent the other obtaining a benefit. Whereas rival States virtually isolate neutrals, and mutually agree to preserve the neutral status, they attempt to win over nonaligned countries and in doing so confirm them in their nonalignment.

Nonalignment rests, however, on a surer foundation than the competition between States for spheres of influence. There is an important difference between the status of a neutral nation or a buffer State arising out of political or military strategy amongst Powers each seeking to win a final political or military advantage, and the status of a nonaligned nation arising out of a nuclear stale-mate position in which it is in the interests of the Great Powers to avoid all warfare, and therefore all forms of competition leading or likely to lead to war. In both cases the status is in some respects a function of the power-conflict; but in the first case it is part of the strategy of conflict, and in the second it is part of the strategy of avoiding conflict.

Admittedly, this latter status is a recent development. The Great Powers were opposed to nonalignment originally, and tried to break it down. Only in the 'sixties did they begin to see its advantages in conditions in which there is a continuous threat of nuclear war, a failure to reach agreement of disarmament, and a need therefore to learn to live with nuclear weapons. Nonalignment is making a positive contribution to the solution of the power struggle in the nuclear age, and its stability is increasing the more the Great Powers appreciate this and take advantage of the opportunities nonalignment offers.

The usefulness of the nonaligned nations in this respect arises out of the fact that they withdraw large areas and populations from the power conflict, and in addition work actively to restrict the area of conflict. Never before has a group of nations stood outside a power-conflict, and actively worked to maintain non-bloc status of each of its members, while deliberately attempting to influence the behaviour and policies of the major Powers. Never before has a group of nations not involved in the power dispute been in a position to intervene as the nonaligned nations do at the United Nations, as some of them did in relation to Laos. Their contribution may not have been of great significance, but the fact that they have this function, that they have a positive role in world affairs, that they are a relevant part of a developing international system in the nuclear age, gives them a status and a stability wholly unlike any previous form of noninvolvement in conflict.

IV. RESPECT FOR SOVEREIGN INTEGRITY

Since the Second World War there have been changes in the political environment which have given increased opportunities to nations to pursue independent policies. The creation of many new States, the widespread recognition of their independence, and their equal status in a world organization, have helped to support sovereign independence and equality in international relations. Thus nonalignment is more practical than it would have been previously, and a system of nonalignment is relevant to the political and strategic circumstances of the post-war world.

The respect for sovereign integrity, which is basic to a system of nonalignment, is a post-war change in international relations second in importance only to the possession of nuclear weapons by Great Powers. In describing the pre-nuclear system, Herz shows how the inequality of power destroyed the independence of small nations:

The units of this system, the 'independent' and 'sovereign' nation-states, precariously survived, but they were forever threatened in their interests and in their very existence by superior power. They were legally protected to some extent by mutual recognition of 'rights' (such as 'fundamental rights' to existence) and 'duties' (for instance, duty of non-intervention), and politically, through the functioning of the balance-of-power system. In fact, however, insecurity ('international anarchy') ruled supreme, because of the actual inequality in power and the permissibility (even in a legal sense, namely, through the process known as war) to use superior power to destroy the inferior.[1]

The acceptance and support of sovereignty, and the need therefore to evolve an international system based on equal sovereign rights, is an important consequence of the emergence of new nations. As this equality of sovereignty is acknowledged by all Powers, regardless of the size of the internal system, or of the strategic value of the countries concerned, many sources of conflict are eliminated.[2]

By 'sovereignty' in this context is meant what has been termed

[1] Herz, 1959, p. 39.
[2] J. W. Burton, *Peace Theory,* Chapter 5, 'The Self-defeating Nature of Traditional Policies and Institutions'.

'territoriality', and this is in some respects a better term.[1] The creation of new States out of former colonial territories has helped to make effective what was previously only a theoretical principle, that is respect for the territorial integrity of nations, and respect for the right of each State to control the activities of other nations within its own boundaries.

One suspects that the open discussion of problems of small nations, of their struggles for independence, of their poverty,and of the past exploitation of their resources, has led to the creation of a sympathetic public opinion in the more advanced communities. This sympathy seems to extend beyond economic aid to a respect for their independence, as was demonstrated in the Suez crisis of 1956 when the British Government was strongly criticized, not only in Britain, but also in other Commonwealth countries and the United States. One could imagine that in a past age this small military exercise would have been carried out quickly by Britain and France, perhaps being met by mild opposition, being stoutly defended by the governing élite, and then quickly forgotten. Certainly the British and French Governments had no previous experience that would have warned them of the consequences of their actions in this case. The rights of independence, the right of nations to nationalize foreign industries in the interests of their underprivileged peoples, seem now to have more than mere legal justification, for they can be preserved even when attacked by major Powers. Morgenthau has argued[2] that 'wherever one probes beneath the surface of popular phraseology, one finds that a world public opinion restraining the international policies of national governments does not exist'. He was writing in the early 'fifties, before Suez, and since then the 'open' society has begun to operate, well over one hundred nations taking part. One suspects that the failure of the United States in the early 'sixties to control political developments in Cuba, despite clear support within the United States for strong action, was due to an appreciation within the administration of a world public opinion.

Closely associated with this sympathy for underprivileged peoples is a greatly increased awareness of and interest in their problems. The end of colonialism, and the creation of many

[1] Herz, 1959, Chapter headed 'The Nature of Territoriality'.
[2] Morgenthau, *Politics among Nations*, 1960, p. 269.

small independent States each struggling with pressing economic and administrative problems, has created an international political environment in which interference with independence would receive little support even within the aggressor country. Indeed, one is led to speculate that the so-called inherent aggressive behaviour of nations, and of the aggressive nature of international competition, may now be less in evidence. The post-war world has features quite different from those of the period of exploration, colonialization and exploitation in which these expansionist features were observed. What has been assumed to be an inherent characteristic of the behaviour of nations may have merely reflected the national interests of the time. In the modern world (whatever were the circumstances of the past), a small State seems to be able to exercise its rights to independence with a high degree of success without having to protect its borders; sovereignty or territoriality no longer rests upon ability to protect it. These are conditions conducive to the development not only of independence, but of independent policies.

This change in attitudes toward small States may not be credible to those who treat power as the prime, and finally the decisive factor in world affairs. It becomes understandable and credible, however, if a communications model is employed to explain decision-making.[1] The status of the new and small nations does not rest on power: their influence at the United Nations is not one based on power—except voting power. Their emergence as nations, their role in world society, their influence on world public opinion, and attitudes adopted to them by governments of powerful nations, was and is a function of communications more than of power, or balances-of-power. Their future stability and international status likewise cannot reliably be estimated in terms only of power.

V. SUBVERSION

In such a world environment, and especially in the nuclear age, means of pursuing national interests are likely to emerge which are more subtle than those traditional ones employed in the attempt to retain control of the Suez Canal; and subversion in various forms has been developed since the Second World War as a major instrument of defence and of revisionism. The stabil-

---

[1] The communications model is discussed in Part IV below.

ity of independence and of nonalignment depends at least in part on the ability of new nations to withstand this particular technique.

This is a difficult matter to discuss without reference to the particular situation; all countries are subject to foreign influences, and to an increasing extent as means of communication improve. There is a wide range of influence from the normal acquisition of knowledge to actual interference in the political life of a nation, and in between there are many border-line cases over which there is argument as to whether subversion exists. Furthermore, it cannot always be determined to what extent internal changes are indigenous, and to what extent they are inspired by a foreign source.

In a system of nonalignment, foreign contacts are likely to be greater and not less than in a system in which there is a deliberate attempt to isolate a community from those against whom it is aligned. Everyday foreign influences are likely to be most significant in the development of a nonaligned State which is at an early stage of political and economic growth, and receptive to new approaches to its pressing problems.

The decision as to what constitutes subversion can be made only by the functioning government as an exercise of its national sovereignty, or 'territoriality'. In doing this it is not bound to observe any principles except those which it may be obliged to observe by reason of its own and world public opinion. So also in respect of the action to be taken to prevent foreign or internal activities associated with subversion; the exercise of national powers is limited only by internal legal restrictions and conventions. When governments are able to exercise power effectively, then subversion as defined by them can be controlled. It is when subversion is associated with strong internal political movements which governments find difficult to control that determination by them of subversion leads to disputes and even unrest; any uncontrollable domestic movement is likely to be dubbed subversive if associated with a foreign creed even if influenced only insignificantly by it.

The nonaligned government of India did not hesitate to legislate in order to deal with internal pressure groups which it believed to be associated with foreign Powers, on the grounds that their activities were disruptive. If a sufficient number of Indians had regarded this repressive legislation as unwarranted, or discriminatory in its application against views which they supported, then this would have led to political conflicts. If in such an internal dispute a government were not able to maintain itself, then political change could take place, which would in turn alter international relationships. In other words, it is for the government to determine what is undue pressure or influence from outside, and what is the normal and acceptable level of influence through intellectual, cultural and commercial contacts. Its failure to enforce its decisions may in due course induce political change, and altered international relationships.

Controversy over what is and what is not undue foreign influence has occurred most frequently in relation to situations in aligned countries where attempts have been made by local authorities, and by Powers supporting them, to prevent changes taking place which would alter international relationship. In many cases the subversion is encouraged if not inspired by a foreign Power; the real problem of subversion, however, arises out of support for the movements of revolt so inspired, and out of the lack of strong support for the government of the day. In a nonaligned country, subversion is less controversial: an internal movement would either be suppressed or lead to a change in government, for by definition no foreign protection of the government could be sought.

Subversion is a weapon which any nation may use, and its use is not confined to the Great Powers. However, in respect to the stability of nonaligned nations, it is Great Power subversion which is significant. Diplomatic activities, economic aid, the influence of foreign capital enterprises, and of foreign-inspired political parties, all have a place in the wide range of subversive activities. The stability of any independent nation may ultimately depend upon the extent to which the Great Powers are prepared to accept nonalignment as useful, and to respect it as they have frequently respected neutrality.

From an international point of view, nonalignment is both a foreign policy and an international movement, and its stability in each aspect rests mainly upon its relevance to the world situation, which is in the present case a nuclear environment in which the main interests of the Great Powers are in finding means of avoiding nuclear conflict. As such it is in fact a function of the Great Power struggle, but unlike neutrality, a function of that aspect of the struggle concerned with the avoidance of open conflict. It is relevant, too, in the sense that it is a development in a changing world political environment in which many small States have emerged, each taking a part in an 'open' society. Because it is relevant, its zone of acceptance is wide, and every expansion of the area of nonalignment helps to entrench it as a useful system, and helps therefore to promote its stability. Whatever may have been the initial world reaction to nonalignment, international influences are likely to increase, and not to decrease its stability.

VI. ECONOMIC CONSEQUENCES OF NONALIGNMENT

The new States will in forty years have a population of some 2500 million. The present communist States together will have a similar population, while the Western World will contain some 1200 million.[1] The new States are underdeveloped; but their natural resources and the markets they provide are of importance to the further development and stability of the developed economies. In any event, the inescapable connection between politics, strategy and economics renders their economic and commercial arrangements important to the Great Powers.

In accordance with the general opposition to blocs as such, the nonaligned nations at first actively discouraged economic associations which were suggested from time to time. The formation of the Asian and South Asian States (Malaya, Thailand and the Philippines) was consistently resisted by Indonesia and other countries whose co-operation was required for such an association to be practical. The fear was that any economic organization, especially such as this which included aligned nations, would develop a political flavour, and be inconsistent with nonalignment. Suggestions for Asian economic co-operation were advanced at the Bandung Conference in 1955 by Ceylon, but there was little enthusiasm even for these. Mr Nehru seemed to have changed his view to some extent by December 1961 when he addressed the Third Conference of the Afro-Asian Organization for Economic Co-operation; at this conference serious consideration seems to have been given to problems of economic co-operation almost for the first time. Even at this conference, however, it was noticeable that India in particular was aware of the political implications of any

[1] F. Baade, *The Race to the Year 2000*, 1962, p. 15.

economic organization, and cautious therefore with respect to any proposals for the creation of an Afro-Asian bloc.

The proposal of a European Common Market appears to have greatly affected the thinking of Asian-African countries, and of the nonaligned countries in particular. As far as the smaller nations were concerned, the Common Market was but one more example of neo-colonialism, just another attempt by the privileged communities to preserve their position at the expense of the underdeveloped economies. They were once again to be thrown back on their own resources, and no amount of aid could offset the long-term trade disadvantages. The Common Market was an extension of military and political alignments into economic arrangements. At the September 1961 Conference of nonaligned nations at Belgrade, Nkrumah asked the rhetorical question: 'What is this Common Market if it is not a new design for reimposing Europe's domination and exploitation of Africa?'

One of the recommendations of the Belgrade conference was that:

The participating countries invite all the countries in the course of development to co-operate effectively in the economic and commercial fields so as to face the policies of pressure in the economic sphere, as well as the harmful results which may be created by the economic blocs of the industrial countries. They invite all the countries concerned to consider to convene, as soon as possible, an international conference to discuss their common problems and to reach an agreement on the ways and means of repelling all damage which may hinder their development; and to discuss and agree upon the most effective measures to ensure the realization of their economic and social development.

This did not state clearly whether members favoured the formation of a separate bloc, or alternatively steps to break down the Common Market. The latter seemed to be in mind, for in June 1962 at a conference at Accra the principles of non-alignment were reaffirmed in relation to economic organization:

We believe that the world's trade should know no ideological frontiers and that discriminatory economic practices should be opposed and abolished. Restrictions on trade between all nations can only aggravate the world's economic problems and intensify international strains. We therefore deprecate the extension of the Cold War by way of economic boycotts and bans on trade. We also oppose the setting up of high tariff areas and cartels which affect under-developed nations. We welcome economic integration but we deplore all areas of economic discrimination which tend to crystallize the alignments of the Cold War in the field of trade, and to be a further obstacle to disengagement. We are in favour of the international stabilization of commodity prices in view of the great reliance of many of the less developed nations on the sale of primary products.

Those African nations which had an opportunity to be associated with the Common Market faced the same problem as the neutrals of Europe. They saw the Common Market as a political, and not merely a trading alliance. In this they agreed with the neutral Switzerland, whose government made it clear to the EEC Council of Ministers that limits were required to safeguard 'her neutrality—guarantee of her independence—her federalist structure and her system of direct democracy'. While a policy of neutrality was not, in the Swiss view, opposed to economic co-operation, the following three reservations were required: first the maintenence of neutrality, second, the maintenance of a sufficient basis of supply for a wartime economy, and third, the freedom to terminate the agreement in any political situation which a neutral must take into account.[1]

The situation presented by the Common Market proposal called for some rethinking of their position by nonaligned nations. On the one hand they were likely to suffer economically if they were excluded from trading blocs, on the other they were in principle against joining such blocs if invited, or themselves creating such blocs.

It seems that it was Yugoslavs who were first to face up to the conflict of interests. Janez Stanovnik observed in 1962:

As a result of political antagonism between blocs we are witnessing regional 'integration' and 'specialization'. Both sides speak of a rational division of labour amongst nations with the aim of reducing costs of production and achieving greater welfare. Both economic blocs take the 'international division of labour' to mean division within their own geo-political spheres. They prevent a genuine division of labour on a world-wide scale either by means of pre-ferential tariffs or by state monopoly of foreign trade. Only those countries which join the blocs can expect to benefit from such

[1] Statement by the Swiss Government to the EEC Council of Ministers, 24 September 1962.

international division of labour. Countries which do not join the blocs due to political or other considerations must automatically suffer from economic discrimination.[1]

Another Yugoslav, Bogdan Crnobrnja, was more forthright and argued that economic organization is not inconsistent with nonalignment and could, incidentally, help to promote it. 'The policy of nonalignment cannot be considered only as a by-product of policies pure and simple, since the question primarily concerns the co-operation between the nonaligned nations themselves. Economic co-operation for these countries already is, and will be even more so in future, a potent instrument in bringing them closer together and of consolidating their independence.'[2] These were amongst the first hints that economic nonalignment might take on the appearance of economic alignment between nonaligned countries.

In June 1962 the Casablanca Summit Conference, comprising the nonaligned countries of Africa, concentrated on economic co-operation and considered the admission of other African countries into the Casablanca group for this purpose. In July in Cairo the Conference on the Problems of Economic Development was held. Though this conference was sponsored in the main by the nonaligned nations there was a wider representation of African countries. In addition, there were some other countries including Malaya and Singapore, while Chile, Ecuador, Uruguay and Venezuela were represented by observers. As a result of decisions taken at this conference it was subsequently possible to have common views brought before GATT, and other international economic conferences.

The Cairo Conference seems to be the point at which 'economic nonalignment', or active co-operation amongst nonaligned countries in economic affairs, was launched. While no firm decisions were taken as to the direction of future co-operation, it was clear that this economic group intended to co-operate to bring pressure in economic discussions as they had done at the United Nations in political discussion. It was clear

[1] Article entitled 'The Economics of Nonalignment' translated from Serbo-Croatian by C. Kiriloff of the Australian National University. See also articles in *International Problems,* The Institute for International Politics and Economy, Belgrade, 1963.

[2] This statement is taken from a Yugoslav publication *Krsto Bulajic* and the translation was made from the Serbo-Croatian by C. Kiriloff, of the Australian National University.

also that there were no longer strong inhibitions against economic organization amongst themselves as a group, if this proved possible and desirable. A bloc of economically under-developed countries may be technically and economically an impractical one; but free of nonalignment principles, after Cairo the nonaligned nations could engage in negotiations amongst themselves aiming at limited bilateral or multilateral agreements.

One effect of the Common Market proposals was that nonalignment reached out to all underdeveloped countries, or more precisely, to all countries which regarded themselves as being prejudiced in their development by reason of continuing political and economic control over them by major Powers. As has been noted, Malaya and certain Latin American countries were represented at Cairo. Latin America was regarded by most of the leaders of nonaligned countries as comprising a group of nations which should be included in any future Afro-Asian consultations. When in 1962 Indonesia suggested a second Afro-Asian conference, the response of other nonaligned nations was that no such limited conference was appropriate in the new circumstances created by the Common Market.

The emerging concept of economic nonalignment led to subtle changes in attitudes toward the West. A review of Western intentions took place, the Common Market provided a sharp jolt to the new nations which had been prepared to accept aid as evidence of a new and more liberal approach by the West. Quite suddenly, the Afro-Asian-Latin American countries reappraised aid, and became aware, as was in evidence at Cairo, that pressures exercised by them to ensure a shift in their favour in the terms of trade, were likely to bring results of greater benefit than any likely economic aid. It took some years for the new nations to realize that the responsibility was on them to prevent internal political pressures being exercised by great Powers: they slowly realized that the dangers of 'neo-colonialism' could be met, not by pleas and by complaints, but only by their own actions. Similarly, in respect to economic relations, the Cairo Conference, in great measure stimulated by the Common Market, marked the point at which the new nations realized that their economic development could not rest upon the accidental acquisition of economic assistance which resulted from the Cold War. In the long term it would be their own economic organization, and their own combined activities in international discussions, which produced for them the conditions in which their economic development could take place. Stanovnik concludes his article referred to above by saying: 'The Cairo Conference has warned the economic theoreticians that solutions of economic problems connected with developing countries should not involve any mechanical transplantation of experiences drawn from history, nor should they consist in an uncritical application of econometric formulae from developed countries. Any further progress of economic theory requires generalization of concrete experience gathered by the developing countries themselves.'

Thus there is being forced upon the Great Powers a shift in their competition from the field of economic and technical aid, to the field of international organization, that is, from the field of aid to the field of trade. A shift of this nature will direct critical attention to the domestic economic policies of the major industrial nations in the same way as their military policies have been criticized. Once the total value of economic aid (that is, aid which has no military significance) is seen to be small in comparison with the value of losses sustained through shifts in the terms of trade against the underdeveloped countries, a concerted attack can be expected on Western economic policies. If there is no constructive response to this attack then aid will be regarded as a payment made by the West for the privilege of continuing policies which are detrimental to the economically underdeveloped countries. For instance, subsidized production of agricultural commodities both for local consumption and for export, the production of synthetic products such as rubber, tariffs and the invisible protection of light manufactures such as textiles, regional arrangements such as the Common Market which discriminate against the new countries, high duties on products such as coffee which come only from the under-developed areas, are amongst the circumstances which the West defends but which effectively prevent a type of economic development which it claims to sponsor. Equally, obligations to raise levels of employment and to bring about better distribution of real income in the main consuming areas such as the United States and Europe, which directly affect markets for the products of the underdeveloped countries, will in due course be a matter of international consideration. In the past the demand that domestic economic conditions be regarded as a matter of international concern has come only from countries such as Australia, New Zealand and Canada whose high standard of living has not evoked sympathy in the United States and elsewhere; the same demand from the very many small underdeveloped nations is likely to be harder to resist.

The shift in competition from aid to trade is likely to favour the communist bloc and, therefore, to increase tensions between the new nations and the West. Whereas the Common Market must be a somewhat rigid structure based on tariffs and various protective devices, the communist system could be far more arbitrary and flexible. It is based on a State monopoly of trade, and special arrangements can be made relatively easily for imports from underdeveloped countries and for trading relations advantageous to them. The position has developed, therefore, in which a European organization which was contrived as a protection against the competition of the Communist Bloc, and as a means of welding together the smaller countries of Europe, is likely to be self-defeating. As at this time of writing no binding decisions have been taken by the United Kingdom for entry into the Common Market. If entry were not finally sought or not finally agreed upon, Britain, in association with other major Commonwealth countries, would then become the natural leader of the excluded nations, probably to its own advantage, thus constituting the third economic area which the nonaligned countries seek to develop as a first step in breaking down the two existing economic-military power blocs.

Economic co-operation amongst nonaligned nations is at an early stage. There are no circumstances more likely to weld them together, along with other Afro-Asian countries, than exclusive economic arrangements such as the Common Market. Their reactions against forms of 'neo-colonialism' add to their unity and effectiveness as a group of independent nations. At the same time, their co-operation in economic affairs is leading progressively to formal arrangements which are tending to constitute the nonaligned nations as a bloc. Even though the intention is to confine their joint activities to economic matters of common concern, there are obvious political implications, for their pursuit of economic objectives can only be by political means; gradually they are acting as a bloc in more and more matters. This is a dilemma that has yet to be faced.

11

HISTORIC PERSPECTIVES

The relevance of nonalignment, as a response to the conditions of the nuclear age, will be no surprise to a historian. The long-term trends in the development of modern States, and in relations between them, suggest that nationalism and sovereignty would have increased, and international structures with enforcement capabilities would have decreased, even in the absence of nuclear strategy. The progressive development of the power-model 'continuum' from national defence, to alliances, to collective security, to a world government with centralized police or enforcement powers on the model of a municipal society, is quite contrary to basic and persistent trends over centuries. Furthermore, it would be quite contrary to behaviourist analysis of relations between States to expect enforcement to be acceptable by sovereign States, or for value attached to nationalism and sovereign independence universally to diminish. Just as realistic power politics as a theory and as a policy has survival by default, so has the unreal solution of world government. World organization is and will continue to develop; but its basis is the voluntary association of independence units, each exercising and preserving its sovereignty in the association, with no possibility of acceptance of enforcement against it by the association or by any supra-State or alliance of States.

I. TRENDS

Throughout a period of some seven centuries there has been a change in thinking on International Relations from almost complete acceptance of enforcement to an almost complete rejection of it. In the thirteenth century most thinking was directed toward the re-establishment of a European empire which would maintain the peace and security of each of its constituent parts. This was the approach of Dante in Monarchia at the beginning of the fourteenth century; but almost at the same time Dubois was taking a different view realizing that for reasons of distance and diversity no one individual or one authority could rule the world. Marsilius, a few years later, seemed to take a similar view. Then came the gradual growth of the sovereign State and some weakening of the viewpoint that peace and security could best be achieved by a universal organization. The Jesuits in the sixteenth century and Grotius early in the seventeenth century were prepared to admit a need for conflict amongst independent units, and to make a distinction between just and unjust wars; and Crucé favoured association of independent States to maintain peace. Various schemes followed which from this time on retained an enforcement element, but which also reflected serious doubt as to the degree of enforcement which was possible in a system of sovereign States. William Penn, the Quaker pacifist, in 1693 was prepared to contemplate enforcement as part of a plan, but only because he believed that if in fact provision were made for it there would be no need to use it: he believed in deterrence. The outstanding feature in thinking concerning relations between States in the period between the fifteenth and nineteenth centuries is the dispute between those who took an institutional approach to peace with an emphasis on enforcement and those who valued sovereignty. In the eighteenth century Kant, who strongly held the view that the problem of war and peace could not be solved by the suppression of States, and Bentham and Mill seemed to try to overcome the dilemma by devaluing not only enforcement but sovereignty as well, and by devaluing all forms of international organization which in their view merely increased the powers of sovereign States. They, and Mazzini later, had far more confidence in a system basically of anarchy but controlled by public opinion, than in any system of international authority. They were opposed both to absolute independence of the State, and to centralization of international power.

The intellectual dispute was in due course resolved by circumstances. States showed clearly at the Hague Conferences of 1899 and 1907 that there was little likelihood of agreement on a governmental basis to any international organization which would limit their independence and freedom of action. Illogically but realistically this led to even greater support for systems of international enforcement. Then World War I seemed to demonstrate the need for an international organization with enforcement powers to prevent a repetition of such a catastrophe, and the intellectual debate was resolved in favour of those who supported enforcement. In so far as the debate continued after World War I, it was again resolved by World War II in favour of an enforcement organization despite the failures of the League. Since the drafting of the Charter of the United Nations, and because of many factors including the logical consequences of nuclear strategy, and a greater understanding of the nature of conflict, and in particular conflict between those seeking change and those who have an interest in the existing order, opinion has swung sharply away from the possibilities of enforcement through an international organization such as was contemplated when the Security Council was established.

There has been throughout the same period a mirror development; there was a virtual absence of any interest in sovereignty until about the tenth century, but the further growth of the modern State finally led to the high value attached to sovereignty at the present time. This is a value held not merely by newly created States, but also, because of the implications of nuclear strategy, by nuclear States themselves, and by middle Powers that hope to be nuclear nations. There has been a resurgence of nationalism, for example, in France, Japan and elsewhere, and even in the United States there is discussion about 'the new isolationism'.

These clear trends in thinking suggest that we are living in an era in which we are thinking in ways dramatically different from any that has preceded. The period from the fifteenth century on, in which there was dispute between those who supported enforcement and those who supported sovereignty, could be regarded theoretically as a period of great instability, and indeed it was so. Now we are living in an era in which the high value attached to sovereignty has almost eliminated any possibility of a universal world government system with police powers. The interesting question is whether peace and security in such conditions are possible.

II. THE NEW CONTINUUM

Internationalism and sovereignty have been generally regarded as incompatible, at least by those who would hope to see the development of world organization to a level of world government. The popular view, the view of many scientists—and indeed the view of those who have drafted current disarmament proposals—is that States must accept some limitation on the sovereign independence in favour of a supra-State. But the realistic fact, whether it is welcome or not, is that there has been a progressive growth in nationalism and in values attaching to sovereignty, and no limitations of sovereignty are in prospect.

World organization cannot provide enforcement as a means toward peace and security for sovereignty and enforcement are ultimately incompatible. Realistically world organization is based on the principle of consent—consent being widely interpreted to include a right of withdrawal, or unanimity of decision. Sovereignty and *non-enforcement* functions of a world organization are clearly not incompatible; they are an extension of the normal relations between nations carried on through diplomacy, trade and other means. World organization of this kind is a more efficient means of communication, in which a multilateral mechanism is substituted for a series of bilateral relationships: this is the limit of the capabilities of world organization.

The world organization today embraces all matters of international concern, at least in relation to the powers of discussion at the General Assembly. Let us imagine a column to represent all matters of international concern. Employing Schwarzenberger's classifications,[1] at the top of this column could be placed those matters on which governments are in agreement on a basis of *reciprocity,* for instance civil aviation agreements, and a little lower those matters on which governments enter agreement on the basis of *co-ordination,* health and trade agreements for example. In neither case is enforcement important, and in both cases in so far as enforcement is necessary, it is carried out nationally by member States within their own jurisdiction. For instance, agreements on health are administered and policed on a national basis. There are other matters outside those of reciprocity and co-operation, and which rest upon *power politics.* They include banning of nuclear tests, and could in the future include matters concerning disarmament. In so far as these are likely to be subject to international agreement they must rest upon national and not international enforcement.

[1] Schwarzenberger (3rd ed.), Chapter 13.

It will be seen that there are two continui in respect of International Organization, the first is an imaginary or idealistic one which progresses from alliances and balance-of-power to wishful-thinking collective security and world organization on an enforcement basis. The solution to problems of peace and war will not be found at any point along it. The second is the historic one, and rests on sovereign independence; successive points are degrees of independence in policy, reflected in agreements based on reciprocity, agreements based on co-operation, and tacit and other agreements forced upon nations, not by any supra-State, by the operation of the modern international system.

III. A NON-ENFORCEMENT SYSTEM

An international system of this latter type was foreseen by Bentham and Mill; but it was not regarded as either realistic or credible on the circumstances of the day. Today consideration of such a system is being negatively encouraged by the type of thoughtful analyses of Waltz[1] and Claude[2] who, without reference to current developments, and on the basis of analysis of thought and system, have effectively destroyed the assumptions and devices of orthodox theories of power politics; no longer can we assume that the aggressive nature of Man or State is the origin of war, and no longer can we assume that alliances and collective security provide the answer to the problems of conflict. We must now turn to the dynamic nature of the system, to the problem of change and adjustment to it, to find the origins of conflict. A nationally-based non-enforcement system is being encouraged positively by circumstances to which States have no option but to make adjustments. This is the system, it seems, which Herz and others have been describing if one interprets correctly their conception of 'nationalistic universalism'—that is, a system of policies based on short-term nation interest which are in the long-term national interest, and in the universal interest. It is one which circumstances have dictated, and which has become credible through the national and international democratization of foreign policy, and through greater insight and experience in determining national interest—both powerfully promoted

---

[1] Waltz, *Man, the State and War.*
[2] Claude, *Power and International Relations.*

by the realities of modern weapons. Governments will adjust policies at the pace demanded by the circumstances, and there is already evidence that States, large and small, nuclear and non-nuclear, are attempting to escape from power, and from the limitations on their freedom of action imposed by their power and their alliances; nonaligned countries have been in the vanguard of this movement, with the middle Powers capable of independent deterrents not far behind, followed by the nuclear nations which are most eager to be relieved of responsibilities outside their vital interests.

Collective security schemes and alliances provide, as has already been argued, no effective means of radical change, short of war or threat of war, and radical change is a requirement of any international system, such as the one in which we live, in which sharp inequalities of resources and opportunities prevail. Acceptance of change, of principles of domestic jurisdiction in respect of internal political change, the studied pursuit of national policies designed to avoid non-passive responses by others, reference to principles of non-interference, and public debate of alleged infringements, are no longer strange features of the international system. The position is no longer that there is no alternative to power politics; the position is that the essence of power politics is now the endeavour to escape from power into a system beyond power politics resting on a calculated avoidance of the employment of power as an instrument of foreign policy in cases where demands for change are being made and supported within the composite framework of 'nationalist universalism' and of non-enforceable world government.

Grotius, in the seventeenth century, postulated two basic principles which would overcome the conflicts inherent in a world structure comprising nations of unequal military and economic power. According to an interpretation by Otto Butz, the principles of Grotius were as follows: 'The first was that the political and legal reality of the sovereign State had to be accepted as a permanent fact. All States had to be considered as completely independent, not only of one another but also of any supranational authority. Within the territory under his control, therefore, each sovereign must be acknowledged as supreme in all matters.' Grotius' second and related initial assumption was that 'all sovereign States, by the fact of their being such, must

be considered as legally and diplomatically equal. In terms of
rights and prerogatives there can be no distinction between
them. They are all on a par, whether large or small, old or new,
militarily powerful or weak, and regardless of their type of
government.'[1] Nonalignment policies are compatible with these
general principles of Grotius, frequently restated since. They
postulate a system in which each nation claims certain national
rights, and in observing the same rights of others, adopts policies
which avoid retaliatory and aggressive responses by others. In
the nonaligned system of international relations, foreign policies
fully recognize territoriality, and therefore do not seek to take
advantage of the possession of power to influence or to control
other nations in their domestic or foreign policies. A system of
nonalignment presupposes an acceptance of the *status quo*, an
acceptance of different forms of government, different economic
standards, varying military might, and the existence of unrest
within nations. There are certain corollaries. Each government
has a right to resist any interference from others in domestic
matters, and in so far as it succeeds it remains the legitimate
government. The legitimate government ceases to exist and
another legitimate government takes its place if conflict in the
closed society results in changes of internal power. These
internal political changes, even those employing force, must be
allowed to take place within each nation without interference
from outside. In particular, in the struggle between factions
trying to preserve what is, and those attempting to make fundamental changes even by revolution, no outside Power is entitled
to interfere; systems of privilege receive no protection when they
are under challenge internally, and no government is regarded
as the 'legitimate' government which has not the popular support
or means to maintain itself without outside assistance.[2] Thus,
while a system of nonalignment is a system which preserves the
status quo, it also includes provision for domestic change through
which ultimately there is alteration in international relationships.

Grotius and others after him were faced with the problem of
how such independent States could be persuaded or compelled
to accept and to abide by these rules of international conduct.
His answer rested upon enlightened self-interest for there was no
way to enforce conformity to international law. Nations would

---

[1] O. Butz, *Of Man and Politics*, 1961, p. 96.
[2] See Friedmann, pp. 264 ff.

observe laws, he argued, because they were the expression of the universal self-evident rationality, morality, and common sense of Natural Law. However, experience soon indicated that Natural Law was either not recognized or not observed. Conflicts still occurred because in a world system in which there were great and small Powers, there could be no independence of the smaller States while rights to press national interests upon others were claimed and acted upon; there was an incompatibility in such a system between the ability to press national policies upon others, and the right of smaller States to have an independent status.

The principles of Grotius are now more relevant to international circumstances than they were in his day; the nuclear discovery, and the creation and the acceptance within one international system of the sovereign independence of many small States, have forced upon all nations an appreciation of the practical value of principles which were previously only of theoretical interest. It is now possible realistically to consider a system in which national rights to interfere are no longer claimed, in which it is policy, even the policy of major Powers, not to intervene, to influence, to discriminate, to form alliances, nor to assert policies, in ways which might limit the sovereign powers and independence of others. The existence of large and small nations does not now necessarily lead to the strengthening of the already strong, for each nation has an equal status, and no special rights need arise out of the possession of superior economic or political power.

Kant, at the end of the eighteenth century, was even more explicit, and much of what he said could be said today by leaders of nonaligned States:

For States in their relation to each other there cannot according to reason be any other way to avoid the lawless condition which contains nothing but war than to give up (just like individual men) their wild and lawless freedom, to accept public and enforceable laws, and thus to form a world State of all nations . . . . But States do not want this, as not in keeping with their idea of a law of nations, and thus they reject in fact what is true in theory. Therefore, unless all is lost, the positive idea of a *world republic* must be replaced by the negative substitute of a union of nations which maintains itself, prevents wars and steadily expands.[1]

[1] *Perpetual Peace,* quoted from Hinsley, p. 63.

In his view, to quote Hinsley,[1] 'It was no more logical to hope to solve the international problem by the supersession of the States than it would have been logical to try to end the civil state of nature by the abolition of individuals'.

Bentham and James Mill not only agreed that the continuing independence of States was inescapable, but argued in addition that peace would be maintained if only governments did not intervene. This is an almost self-evident observation, if not a circular argument. This *laissez-faire* attitude is not shared by the nonaligned States; but the intent is the same. In a system of nonalignment, by definition, any policy-decision affecting relations between States must be non-discriminatory, and this is close to the reasoning of Bentham and Mill. Bentham's argument, that Mill restated in *Law of Nations*, was that 'war could be avoided by independent civilized States with the aid of nothing but public opinion and a rational body of international law.'[2] Mill went further, and came nearer the nonaligned concept by the behaviourist observation that 'an independent nation would resent . . . a command . . . by another'.[3]

The self-defeating nature of peace through preparation for war, which Mr Nehru has so often pointed out, had already been observed by Rousseau. 'War is born of peace, or at least of the precautions which men have taken for the purposes of achieving durable peace.'[4] All the dilemmas involved in basing peace on the ultimate sanction of force had been observed by Penn, Bellers and Saint-Pierre, and Penn was able to avoid them and his conscience by believing that once a deterrent were organized, it would not have to be used. Bentham and Mill were prepared to reject this optimism—which has persisted to the present day, merely by default.

The rejection of the power politics assumption that Man and State are inherently aggressive, changes the character of thought on the subject; the continuity of development in the modern State, and the way in which philosophers have observed relations between States, point to a non-power model as being historically relevant. Professor Röling has recently observed:

[1] Hinsley, p. 62. [2] Hinsley, p. 88.
[3] James Mill, *Essays on Government*, quoted from Hinsley, p. 88.
[4] Hinsley, p. 51.

The Theory of International Relations is still in the phase of its vital errors. The theory of power and interest—generally adhered to by the present leading scholars—has served its main function: to put an end to the unrealistic 'idealism' of the inter-war period. In many theories of this 'twenty years' crisis', it seemed as if in international relations, morality and law formed the last word. The disappointment about the hypocracy of that time brought to the fore the almost cynical theory of power and interest, presented as the naked truth.[1]

The power model was one which lent itself to what was claimed to be 'Political Realism', and it helped and still helps to explain important features of the international system, especially in circumstances in which war is acceptable as a means of achieving national goals. However, the claim to be politically 'realistic' is one which is based upon circular thinking; the realism of the assumptions is not proved by the allegedly realistic conclusions. 'Political Realism' has led to many unrealistic observations. As has previously been suggested, power is not the only, and may not be even the main, influence in social organization.

The strongest challenge to the orthodox study of International Relations has come from within it. The fundamental criticisms regarding both the nature of men and States, and the institution of alliances and collective security, have been essentially negative. Neither of the main critics to which reference has been made, Waltz and Claude, have put forward any clear alternative to the concept of power politics. More recently, Deutsch has argued that 'it might be more profitable to look upon government somewhat less as a problem of power and somewhat more as a problem of steering'.[2] This is the conclusion to be drawn from the above criticism of orthodoxy and evaluation of alterations in world politics.

[1] B. A. V. Röling, from a foreword to C. H. Boasson, *Approaches to the Study of International Relations*, 1963.

[2] Deutsch, *The Nerves of Government*, 1963.

PART IV
NEW MODELS

12

FROM POWER TO STEERING

Fresh concepts and terminology help to overcome what could reasonably be described as habits of thought, if not traditional prejudice. New terms—the jargon of a discipline—are not generally welcome, and clearly must be justified. Nevertheless, they should not lightly be rejected in favour of customary language, for it is by a slight shift in emphasis, or the slightly altered perspective of new terms, that thought has developed. Furthermore, we need to remind ourselves that all common language was once 'jargon'. 'Power', 'equilibrium', 'balance-of-power', are terms derived from mechanics. If altered conditions, or different perspectives attract attention to features not specifically included in a former concept, then new terminology is justified. We will be referring to 'steering' and to 'communication' processes within a system. Power and steering refer to different aspects of a mechanical system; both are analogous and derived from the sciences, and the one is no more jargon than the other.

The manner in which the political environment has been altering, and the effects of political change and of nuclear strategy upon policies of States, are not readily comprehended or immediately credible to any of us accustomed to power-concepts and terminology. This includes most of us: relations between States have been thought of as being predominantly power-relations. The question we now face is whether power is the dominant feature of relations between States, and whether the power-model—including balances, equilibrium bipolarization—adequately describes and explains these relations.

I. FROM POWER TO INFLUENCE

Let us take a spectrum on which at one end is force, and at the other influence exercised without power. In between, there are graduations of power short of force, exercised by all manner of political and economic means.

The extreme point at the left of the spectrum represents the condition in which a State has adequate force at its disposal, and is not restrained by any political consideration, and uses this force in the pursuit of its objectives. The decision-making process is simple; once the goal is perceived, the decision is taken to achieve it, and it can be achieved by force with certainty.

This is now not often a typical condition, though it might one day have been. It is, however, the theoretical condition of a balance-of-power; a State perceives that the balance of forces has altered, and regardless of any political, cultural, ideological or other considerations, shifts its military power as required to maintain the military balance. In the modern world, force is in the background, and political and economic power is employed supported by the threat of force. This is the meaning of 'power'. The exercise of power is tempered by law, morality and institutions, but it is nevertheless the ability to impose the policy of one State upon another that is less powerful.

When power is dominant, that is, when States operate in ways associated with the force end of the spectrum, the power-model and terminology are adequate. The assumption is that if there are any non-power influences present, they are of no practical significance. A dispute over a territory, or over an oil concession, will have an outcome wholly determined by relative power exercised by a number of interested parties—and this can readily be represented by a simple mechanical model.

We have noted that such models are static ones; they describe the end-result of power-bargaining, the new balance. In this sense the power-model is very similar to the historic approach by which events are described at successive points of time. The processes by which the new equilibrium is established are not explained by the mechanical model. The assumption is made that the processes are power processes—a simple matter of power-bargaining. The continuing social mechanism is a power one, and the dynamics of the system are no more than repetitive patterns of power relations. Thus, the inductive thinker who employs the power-model will approach any historic or current situation on the assumption that it is predominantly a power situation, and by using the power-model will have no opportunity to ascertain whether there are other influences. Thus it is that the power approach contains a theory as well as a model; the inductive approach, together with the situation analysis with

which the power approach in International Relations is associated, is based on a theory of power.

The assumption or theory that power is dominant in relations
between States may or may not be valid; what is clear is that
the approach provides no means of ascertaining whether it is
valid, whether there are influences present other than power.
This is one explanation of why the trends described in the three
preceding Chapters may not seem credible to those accustomed
to power-concepts.

Once there is any movement along the spectrum away from
Force toward Influence, once it is assumed that factors other
than power play a significant role, the power-model is not only
inadequate, but seriously misleading from the point of view both
of analysis and policy.

Nuclear deterrence and world political consensus have, we
have argued, imposed restraints on States in addition to those of
law, morality and institutions. These restraints not merely temper,
they prevent the employment of force wherever the force is
likely to be nuclear. They therefore also prevent the exercise
of economic or political power which rests upon force in the
background. The nuclear deterrent and world political pressures
have thus inserted a break in the spectrum—political and
economic power is no longer connected with force and the threat
of force. This means that the political and economic bargaining
power of dominant States is weakened; there can be no certainty
of outcome. Power no longer exists in terms of the definition that
it is the ability ultimately to force the policy of one State upon
others, except in circumstances of vital security. Power exists
only in the sense that it is power to bargain within the limits
imposed by the political and economic environment, and
without ultimate reference to force. Political and economic
power have come adrift from force; the point of the spectrum at
which States operate in the nuclear era is significantly further
toward the Influence extreme than it was previously. Decision-
making processes are in these circumstances far more complicated; the responses of other States, political consensus, long-
term effects, must all be weighed.

What is now required is some model or terminology which
exposes the processes by which decisions are taken. The possible
exercise of power in extreme circumstances will be one factor to
be taken into account. Any adequate model, clearly, should be

useful in explaining situations based on force, or power or influence. Only in this way can the circular features of the power approach be avoided; power may still be dominant in relations between States, a theory of power politics may finally be shown to be valid, and in any event force is still in the background even if in the nuclear age it cannot be used; but the model has to be such that if other influences exist, they can be observed and estimated.

II. FROM POWER TO DECISION-MAKING

The traditional power-model is an international one—it has been concerned with a balance or an imbalance created between States by their changing policies and capabilities. A decision-making model is necessarily a national one. Whereas the traditional model demonstrates the resultant of all national pressures which operate and lead to changes in balances, a decision-making model focuses attention on the nature of each national pressure.

There is no reason why there should not be a decision-making model concerned only with power, and the way in which balance-of-power operates from a national and decision-making point of view. Modelski once observed that while there could be little disagreement with the view that power was of prime importance in relations between States, and while it 'bulks large in the literature of international relations', power has not been examined in terms of foreign policy analysis. 'At present, the study of power has become associated with the proposition that "Power is the generalized end of all politics", but the detailed treatment of the subject has been strongly descriptive and lacking in analytical penetration.' In his view, power has scarcely been regarded as relevant to foreign-policy analysis.[1]

Modelski has no quarrel with the power approach and the assumptions on which it is based; his complaint is that in the treatment of power in international politics, the decision-making processes have been neglected. He introduced a 'power-inputs' and 'power outputs' model, and was able to attract attention to the elements of decision-making and foreign-policy analysis.

[1] G. Modelski, *A Theory of Foreign Policy*, 1962, pp. 21 ff.

This is a useful starting-point in the introduction of new models because it serves to introduce decision-making without necessarily challenging the assumptions of the power approach. A relatively simple input–output model is sufficient for decision-making based on these assumptions. However, in the nuclear age, the decision-making process is more complicated than a power-model suggests. Modelski took into account the fact that the output of one State is the input of another; no decision can be taken without considering the responses of other States. But alternatives, such as between making internal adjustments to changed conditions and forcing adjustment on to others, must be considered, and alterations in decisions and in goals are an important part of decision-making. Consequently, a model is required which enables insight into decision-making in these circumstances, and into the possibilities of avoiding conflict by decision-making processes, such as the employment of alternative adjustments and the changing of goals. Power-input is concerned merely with means toward ends; world consensus, non-power influences and objectives, morality and law, convention, values and justice, universal objectives in addition to national ones, all need to be exposed within the decision-making process.

The important process from the point of view of relations between States seems to be that which takes place between the point of input and the point of output—the process of accumulating facts and information, classifying, sifting, the process of goal determination and the use of information in relation to it, the selection of alternatives in the pursuit of goals, and so on. If we have a model which can cope with these inner processes, then we are less limited in consideration of input and output, and can take into account factors other than power, including limitations of power and restraints on the exercise of power.

The great number of variables introduced in any realistic decision-making is particularly challenging in an age in which quantitative analysis is so widely held to be the only useful analysis. The theory of games was one attempt to overcome some of these difficulties. By reducing the variables, however, it eliminated just those aspects of decision-making which are important.[1]

[1] See Deutsch for a critical appreciation of the use of games theory.

III. STEERING AND DECISION-MAKING

The model which seems most appropriate is one related to 'guiding the ship of State'—but guiding it in the electronic age. Wiener in 1941 introduced the term 'cybernetics' which he derived from a Greek word meaning 'steersman'.[1] 'Cybernetics' refers especially to the idea that the human brain and a high-speed electronic computer have many characteristics in common. Both send and receive messages, store and reproduce data, and remember facts and formulas.[2] The ship of State is not, however, the traditional one with captain or Prime Minister at the wheel, but one which, thanks to electronic processes, determines its position, adjusts automatically its course on the perception of drift, avoids obstacles in the way once they appear on the radar screen, and generally is capable of all the complex processes of decision-making in the modern world. The part of the ship which is of interest is that part in which the communication takes place within the steering mechanism. The model in which we are interested is a communications model. We are interested in communications outside and into the steering mechanism; but we are far more concerned with the communications system within the steering mechanism itself. It is the processes of national data collection, sifting, screening, and course determination prior to action which is of most interest in international relations.

Deutsch has made a major contribution in this respect.[3] International Relations can be described in terms of the history of relations between States, of the history of thought on the subject, or of the development of theory. But Deutsch has described International Relations by reference to the history of model-making or processes of thought in sciences generally. Maps and curves were early examples of models, simple balances later ones, and when science had progressed sufficiently far it was possible for political scientists to think in terms of mechanical and organizational concepts. Deutsch argues that it was only after the 'forties that it was possible to think in terms of communication for it was only then that communication

---

[1] N. Wiener, *The Human Use of Human Beings,* 1950.
[2] E. McNall Burns, *Ideas in Conflict,* 1963, p. 553.
[3] Deutsch, *The Nerves of Government.*

engineering had developed sufficiently far to demonstrate self-monitoring, self-controlling, self-steering automatic processes.

The inadequacies of earlier mechanical models are clear. They were confined to balances and static concepts. The whole was taken to be equivalent to the sum of the parts, and the parts did not appear to modify each other. Such models gave no insight into growth or change and led to static social theory. The organism models, relating to an age in which there was an interest in anatomy, gave some insight into processes of growth. However, there was no insight into structure or processes of learning with the result that 'natural' laws had to be regarded as a sufficient explanation of many phenomena. The history models paid some attention to development and growth, and enabled political scientists to comprehend innovation and invention, but provided no understanding of the inner structure of these processes. There was observation relative to successive points of change, but not of the progressive processes of change.

One incidental advantage of the cybernetic or steering model is that it gives a better perspective on power. In terms of communication needs, power is unimportant. When a system is fully integrated, receiving information, classifying it, and reacting, and is subject to feed-back controls, and when through this process it can change its goals and adapt itself to changing situations, power is seen as of incidental importance, no matter how important it might happen to appear at any point of history. Power is seen as the means to achieve unaltered goals in a system committed to some particular view, or policy or goal. A model of this order helps to explain how it is that a State, the size of the United States, can misjudge a situation, such as South Vietnam, and find it is powerless to achieve the result sought. It can equally explain how a smaller country such as Ceylon can be effective in reducing tensions between China and India. It helps to explain why it is that the new States can adjust themselves to the Great Power conflict without losing their own integrity; because they are new, because they are not committed, they have a learning and adjustment capacity beyond the comprehension of established States committed to certain types of institutions, ideologies and policies.

From a policy point of view a communication model is instructive. While power can compensate for a low degree of achievement of goals, its use, like the institution of war, is in practice limited to that of a last-resort device. When the Western Powers sought to promote stability in South-East Asia, they adopted the procedure of supporting feudal regimes. In fact, this policy had the effect of provoking communist reaction. The communications model, which provides for corrective steps, and warns against over-compensation in goal-seeking and in adjustment, is a good deal more instructive from a policy point of view than the model of power politics.

Any model which focuses attention upon national decision-making is an improvement on a static conception of balances. Power is employed as a last resort, when goals cannot be sought in any other way—and be it emphasized, when States are not prepared to alter goals. The use of force is a measure of ability not to have to learn, to adjust, to accept change by peaceful means. Power is a *status quo* concept, it is the means by which an existing situation is maintained by those who believe they possess superior power. Those who attempt to upset the existing structure are aggressors. Aggression thus can be defined as the response of a State upon which has been forced an intolerable option: either it must accept intolerable conditions which limit its development, or it must become an aggressor against those with superior or at least equal capacity, despite all the risks involved. One suspects many histories of 'aggression' would lend themsleves to such an interpretation. The Western Powers over a period gave Japan one such intolerable option—the choice between aggression, and continuing to live in world conditions which heavily discriminated against Japan. From a point of view of power politics, it was not relevant to consider the decision-making processes which would be forced upon Japan; the only relevant consideration was the power and the interests of the Western States. If, however, the decision processes were understood in sufficient detail to enable each nation to anticipate the responses of others, then some of these intolerable options would be avoided.

Models concerning decision-making are more applicable to the nuclear age than any models based on power and the transference of power. For example, there must be in the nuclear age a high degree of goal-changing, which is not a concept compatible with power politics. The type of goal-changing which is likely to take place is the switch from the immediate objective of national security, to the ultimate objective of preservation of civilization, which includes national security. Herz has put forward 'Universalism as Alternative to the Power Dilemma'.[1] He was taking up the concept of 'nationalist universalism' put forward earlier by Hans Morgenthau. Neither of these scientists had at their disposal a model which would make explicit their theories, but both are turning away from a power concept towards one related to communication.

IV. THE ALTERED NATURE OF INTERNATIONAL RELATIONS

Modelski's contribution to decision-making, and his criticisms of traditional power approaches to the study of International Relations, is evidence that scientists became aware firstly of the importance of decision-making and consequentially of the need to provide for some means of its analysis. At the same time, the invention of new models and terminology, by which decision-making can be examined, has itself done much to attract attention to its importance. The nature and significance of International Relations has altered as a consequence. The study traditionally was concerned with the history of power-balances, the history of policies of the leading States, the history of International Institutions, and the Collective Security structures which have been advocated. It was concerned with speculation about World Government, or Federations which could be one step toward World Government. The main issues in relations between States were not clearly discerned; it was thought they were the means of control on an international plane; whereas it now appears that they are those aspects of national policy that lead to conflict, and those that enable States to live in a condition of peace one with another. There has now been a switch in interest from international forms and structures to national processes. Attention of theorists, and of policy-makers, is thus focused upon the national scene. The inter-play of politics at the national and international level is not merely an interesting side-issue; it is now the central problem of International Relations. The options are to pursue national interest by action to prevent change and to promote change by force, or on the other hand to carry out adjustments internally and share the burden of adjustment by negotiation, as is the case in any community.

[1] Herz, 1959, Chapter 12.

The internal flexibility of an economy, the education systems, degrees of ideological commitment and social and political rigidities, are all matters of the utmost concern to International Relations.

According to Professor Sprout, International Relations is the term used 'to designate all human behaviour that originates on one side of a national political boundary, and affects human behaviour on the other side of that boundary'.[1] Relations between States are the sum total of all activities that take place in each State that affect other States. The model relevant to such a definition is the national one which depicts the national unit, and the decision-making processes within that unit which take into account the policies and activities of each other unit. If International Relations in these terms becomes far more complex, covering many areas previously regarded as being within the field of politics, psychology or anthropology, then this is only a step toward reality, even though a challenge to the scientist to find means to deal with the greater complexity and the greater number of variables.

The challenge could be rewarding. The power-model suggests there is no logical outcome of international conflict but disaster for the human race. A world imperialism, acquired by world conquest after an atomic war, is the most positive suggestion that can be made on the power approach to international politics. There is no natural law on which it can be argued that there must be another solution to problems of peace and security; but the communications model gives insight into the ways in which international relations are in practice being conducted, and suggests that there are alternatives to the fatalistic one which is the conclusion of power politics. The goal-changing, the options confronting decision-makers, are not those which were apparent when States had unrestrained force at their disposal; but they are those which States are in fact facing in the nuclear age. The Political Scientist, in revealing the behaviour forced upon the decision-maker, can make him even more aware of his options.

[1] See C. A. W. Manning, *The University Teaching of Social Sciences: International Relations,* 1954.

13

FROM SOCIETY TO COMMUNITY

We are aware of factors within the world system which in recent years have exercised an influence on the policies of States, even the thermonuclear States, which cannot be defined precisely in terms of their power relationships, or of morality, law, political pressures or other factors which feed into decision-making processes. There has not yet been an explanation of the events of the Suez crisis of 1956 that satisfied all aspects of it; they cannot be described only in terms of United Kingdom and United States relations or the position of the Soviet Union, or in terms of public opinion in the United Kingdom. There are aspects of the 1962 Cuban crisis, and of the earlier stages of conflict when the United States, it would seem, could have made a greater success of invasion attempts, and even of a boycott, not easily explained without consideration of a world consensus of opinion. The fading out of border conflicts, such as the one between Algiers and Morocco in 1964, and between India and China in 1963, are not wholly explicable in terms of the power relations of these States, or the intervention of third parties.

We have spoken of a world 'society' to distinguish it from a world 'community'; a society is an organized whole but loosely bound, while a community is more integrated, reciprocity and co-ordination playing an important role. Orthodox International Relations has been concerned with world Society, and customary terminology is in relation to such a world. Are there aspects of world politics which do not fit into this framework? Unless our methods and concepts enable us to discern features not yet apparent, not only will an explanation of International Relations be inadequate and misleading, but opportunities to encourage or to discourage developments and trends are likely to be missed. The power-model does not enable us to observe decision-making processes which include influences other than power; by concentration upon a decision-making model are we not in danger of missing some other incipient aspects of the world community? Once the balance-of-power failed, the world

had super-imposed on its institutions a scheme for collective
security as one step toward government, which we now see as
a plan based upon a false interpretation of historic trends; does
a communications or decision-making model lead to policies
which likewise fail to take into account as yet unobserved
features of the world society?

The communications model is nationally orientated; it
concentrates upon the decision-making process of a particular
State in order to find out what influences, including power-
influences, affect relations between States. This may be justified
on the grounds that International Relations are an abstract;
there are no relations between States that do not trace back
to the policies and acts of independent States. International
Relations and foreign policies are concerned with all those acts
taking place on one side of a border which affect States on the
other side, and these acts include almost every national
activity. A decision to subsidize an industry or to reserve places
at schools for foreign citizens is no less a matter of international
concern than a decision to impose a tariff wall or to have a
discriminatory immigration policy. Alliances, political pressures
at the General Assembly, have no relevance unless fed through
the national decision-making process. In these terms, international relations do not exist separately from the activities of
States. The question arises, however, as to whether there is any
cosmopolitan, as distinct from international, relationship. Is
there a plane of thought and activity which directly affects
relations between States, without being channelled through the
national decision-making process? Can even the cybernetic
model adequately explain the subtle something of which we are
aware, and which leads sometimes to an outcome of a situation
which was not expected and not sought?

I. MAKING THE SYSTEM WORK

In so far as the collective security system did operate in the
nineteenth century, it was due to balancing taking priority over
other immediate national interests—or put in another form, it
was due to the fact that no other national interests were so
important as to justify acts which would destroy the system.
States were prepared to observe the rules of balance-of-power.
No game can be played unless certain rules are observed;

either side in any contest can break rules, and if penalties are not sufficient to deter and to compensate, and thereby to make the game playable, order and system vanish and there is no game. It only required one player at the close of the nineteenth century to place other national interests before the obligations of balancing, and the game ceased. Equally, if collective security was ever to be played, a basic rule was to commit forces in advance to deter an aggressor, regardless of economic, ideological, cultural or other considerations. This game was never played; since the Second World War there have been certain States committed to maintain certain political attitudes and to oppose others, and the only order that has occurred derived from the fact that both parties acquired weapons which themselves created another game. In relation to the nuclear deterrence system there are certain rules, and the system will continue to operate with some element of order only in so far as certain rules are perceived as being part of the game, understood as to their function, and in practice obeyed. That nuclear deterrence is not in itself a deterrent restraining the Great Powers in their policies, but depends upon their observance of certain rules, is not always understood. The deterrent system is not necessarily any more stable than was balance-of-power; the stability rests upon a judgement of advantage to be derived from maintaining the system or challenging it. From a national viewpoint the challenge could succeed in a particular instance; nuclear war would not necessarily follow the calling of nuclear bluff. Once successfully challenged, however, the system would be destroyed, the ordered game would be finished.

This becomes apparent when it is realized that nuclear deterrence is based upon the assumptions of irrationality in decision-making. The mutual terror associated with nuclear deterrence exists only if each State assumes the other is irrational. The State which appears in its decision-making the most irrational is most to be feared. Take first of all the case of accidental strike. Game-theory and general consideration of nuclear strategy reveal that the response of State X to an accidental and limited attack by State Y would not be all-out retaliation, for such retaliation would lead to an all-out second strike. This is a rational response on the part of State X to a limited attack by accident. If the attack were not accidental, but nevertheless limited, it would be rational to retaliate by limited response. The attack and the response could even be on a third and allied party as a warning to the opposing nuclear State.

The same reasoning applies to deterrence in respect of all-out attack; it is fear of the irrational behaviour of the party attacked which deters the attacker. All-out retaliation cannot prevent a second strike; but it could ensure complete destruction to all parties and to others.

Irrationality is not a rational assumption for an analyst to make. Consideration of accidental strike has forced him to assume rationality in all nuclear strategy. Once this is done, the mutual deterrent is no longer credible. The only rational support for the deterrent is the possibility of escalation; but experience is that a pragmatic approach to this is likely to be taken, probing, brinkmanship, and military testing being some of the means.

What then makes the deterrent system operate? When President Kennedy and Chairman Khrushchev made their vital decisions during the Cuban crisis, was it fear of irrational retaliation that guided them or was it a realization that if either assumed rationality and successfully called the bluff, the consequences would have been the destruction of the deterrent system, allowing both to operate in other spheres without heed to nuclear deterrence? President Kennedy knew that he could have called the Soviet bluff—why would Chairman Khrushchev risk universal destruction just for Cuba?—and equally he realized he would subsequently have had his bluff called over strategic areas in Europe. In political terms far more critical decision-making would have been shifted to situations such as Berlin.

The nuclear deterrent system is little different from balance-of-power in this respect; it is a game to be played, and so long as it appears to be in the interests of all parties to play it according to the rules, it can continue to be played, and even improved by introducing new rules. Once either side is persuaded by circumstances to call the bluff and to act heedless of possible consequences, nuclear warfare does not immediately follow, but a system break-down occurs. Neither side can then predict the consequences, for there are no pre-determined rules. There is usually in international politics no new game or new set of rules to which the players can immediately and smoothly transfer.

Circumstances in which the game can be terminated are not hard to imagine. There could be a stage of competition at which one side might consider the game has to end. But even assuming that the two thermonuclear States continue to perceive their own interests in maintaining the game, there are other States concerned. If, for example, China or the States of Africa were in the future to act despite threats from one or both thermonuclear Powers, and if the threats were not implemented, nuclear deterrence would no longer be credible as a control of other States. With the proliferation of nuclear weapons, more and more threats will be made, increasing the likelihood of bluff being called, and if this does occur, credibility in the system will no longer exist. Once the bluff has been called by a nonnuclear Power, it is a short step toward calling bluff by a nuclear State.

It is only the game-playing aspect of the deterrence system which endows it with rationality. Game-playing is no new feature in International Relations and history is a record of surprises when a player has decided no longer to observe the rules. In the balance-of-power there were some inherent difficulties because war was part of the recognized game. In the nuclear age escalation rules out war as a reasonable institution, and the consequences of ending the game are greater; but it is not always clear at what point a breach of rules destroys the game. Cuba was a case in which a breach would have had this effect; but what of Suez and Hungary? Understanding of the game and of the consequences of not playing may have increased at least within the thermonuclear States, but there is evidence that this understanding is not universal.

The nonaligned States also have certain rules to observe, to which reference will be made; from these rules develop principles of policy such as non-discrimination in the treatment of all other States. In the Sino-Indian border dispute Mr Nehru was careful to place nonalignment before what some of his advisers regarded as immediate strategic interests. He had to consider not only the immediate military situation, but also the position of India if he had opted out of the nonalignment game.

The genesis of the world community is probably to be found in an awareness of a common interest in continuity in gameplaying; if rules have to be broken or altered, this needs to be accomplished in such a way as not to stop the game. It will be observed how relevant is the new international aristocracy, and the reaons why Morgenthau, Thompson, Lippmann and others have deplored the democratization of foreign policy, and the elimination of the old international aristocracy. Most States are power oriented, and a State such as the United States includes institutions developed and employed by pressure groups that support the use of national power for particularized purposes. 'Irrationality' could easily be introduced into decision-making in these circumstances. In the nuclear age, however, there is necessarily one point of final decision in each State, thus establishing an effective international aristocracy in a position to adopt the approach which Morgenthau described as 'international morality'.

II. INTERNATIONAL ADMINISTRATION

A second continuing feature of world society, relevant to the emergence of a world community, is the influence of the growing international administration. Langrod observed, after referring to the diplomat and the soldier as symbolizing the main relations between States, diplomacy and war:

Nevertheless in this 'theatre of nations' on the stage where in theory there is room only for these 'representatives' of States, a third person has appeared who by definition is neither a protagonist nor a referee, who, by virtue of constitutional provisions in force, 'represents' no one, who thus occupies a special place without precedent in history. He must work in the common interest, rising above all particularism, but respecting the values which each people contributes to humanity. Neither a diplomat nor a soldier, but the personification of world solidarity, the international civil servant, if he is indeed impartial, occupies a strategic position of the highest importance in a pluralist world whose mentality is governed by, and tends toward force. He symbolizes the breach with the methods of the past, and by his very existence opposes anarchy between nations, since his function is to introduce elements of order and stability among them.[1]

The international administration is essentially a new phenomenon. There were over two hundred 'unions' already in existence before the First World War. Communication unions such as the Universal Postal Union were early examples. The first administration to receive diplomatic status, on the grounds that its members were not instructed by governments, was the International Institute of Agriculture at Rome in 1905, and the

[1] G. Langrod, *The International Civil Service*, 1963, p. 25.

international civil service could be regarded as being established at this time.[1]

The growth since the Second World War has been tremendous, the evidence being the increased number of specialized agencies, and regional organizations related to the United Nations. What, if any, influence does this international civil service have in the development of a world community? If some influence, what is the means of discerning it? On what model do we rely in describing the effects upon a State of consultation between UNESCO and the Children's Fund? Both are ultimately under the control of members of the United Nations and of the Economic and Social Council; but is there not a plane of operations here which cannot be described in terms of decision-making processes at the national level?

Students of politics are familar with the role of the public service in a developed political system; the role of the public service is thought to be of great significance, supplying a continuity to policy, and bringing opposing policies together so that, in office, parties are hardly distinguishable. Whether this is due to the public service as much as to the effects on decision-makers of a sense of responsibility, is not known; but the resistances of the public service to discontinuity in policies, and the continuity of influence supplied is known to be important. There are occasions on which political leaders do not wish to take responsibility for some necessary but unpopular decision, some alteration in the bank rate or restriction on imports. On such occasions, they rely upon the recommendation of 'experts'. The decision-making process is then reduced to reference to experts, or their text-books, or some generally accepted theory. The politician merely states the goals; the experts determine the means to them. Sectional interests which are affected must submit to the general interest, unless their pressures are such that the politician is prepared to intervene, to alter the theory, or to control its implementation. To what extent are these community and society elements existing in the world organization of States? Can we be satisfied with the formal argument that all actions of all administrations are always under United Nations control, and therefore under State control? Or in practice, should we take into account the experience of any decentralization of authority, and the operations of a vast

[1] Langrod, p. 42.

public service, some departments of which negotiate with others in relation to the world community?

One knows from conversation that the ECAFE official, who moves about the relevant region freely, who makes high-level contact with the governments concerned, who has acquired a deep personal interest in the political affairs and relations of the States within the region, who sees a direct relationship between his economic work and the political stability of the area, is aware of the opportunities he has to promote understanding and to influence policies so that there is a community result. One is aware, too, that the international public servant finds greater opportunities or a more receptive audience in Asian and African areas than elsewhere, perhaps explained simply by the greater urgency of the situations being faced. But we are still far from quantifying this aspect of world organization.

One of the effects of an international public service is to introduce some absolutes into an international system otherwise dominated by compromises. The impartiality of the international public official, which is the impartiality also claimed by many of the new States in their assessments of the activities of the Great Powers, establishes some standards, and a relevance for facts and objective judgement not previously a feature of relations between States.

The influence of the civil service is not easily discerned in a communications, and nationally-oriented model. This is not as yet necessarily a serious defect, provided one is aware of the possibilities of influences emerging which are essentially cosmopolitan.

III. ASIAN-AFRICAN INFLUENCE

A third influence toward a world community is the introduction as actors of a large number of independent States in Asia and Africa, most of which cannot base their policies on power, and rely upon co-operation amongst themselves and with developed States. Their own disputes have a communal aspect which, in terms of European society, is not readily understood. For example, the Prime Minister of India convened a conference at Delhi in 1949 to discuss the Dutch-Indonesian dispute, and the future of the territories which formerly were the Netherlands

East Indies. There were at this conference representatives of Asian and Middle East countries, who could readily have used the occasion for their own purposes, to make a bargain for support to Indonesia in return for Indian assistance in their own Middle East problems. From the opening session, through the committee discussions, to the stage of final agreement, the outstanding feature was the relevance of discussion, and the outcome was a balanced judgement that was persuasive at the United Nations when it was reported. There was an absence of the bargaining and negotiating approach which is characteristic of most Western conferences of this nature.

Perhaps in no areas will there be more disputes in the future than in the Asian and African regions; but one suspects that they will be settled in due course within the regions, by processes which make little sense to Westerners, and even less sense in terms of power bargaining. There appears to be an approach to politics and to community relations in Africa and Asia which is not easily pictured by Western terminology, especially power terminology.

One other way in which we might move nearer an understanding of this phenomenon is to examine gatherings such as the Bandung Conference of 1955, and the Belgrade Conference of nonaligned States of 1961. Both of these were played down in Western circles, at least before they took place. Both had a profound effect, which was belatedly recognized. Both demonstrated that there was little Western understanding of what was transpiring, and one reason seems to be that the power or bargaining approach is not a sufficient explanation to such Asian and African exchanges.

IV. REGIONAL INTEGRATION

Perhaps one factor in the growth of a world community of sovereign States is technological development generally, and in particular post-war transport and communications, press and radio. Increased national educational opportunities and international scholarships, many official and unofficial international gatherings, the forum of the Assembly, the spread of scientific and technological knowledge, may all have contributed to a community outlook in world affairs.

Whether it is a cause or a consequence of greater integration and co-operation, there has since the Second World War been an impressive growth both in regional and functional organization. Some of this is disassociative, that is, it divides rather than integrates, consolidates world society rather than helps to create a world community—the NATO, SEATO, Warsaw pacts are of this kind. The significant growth has been in associative, non-discriminatory regional and functional organizations, which rest upon mutual interest, and which are either universal in character or are not directed against non-members. Bandung, Belgrade, the Alliance for Progress, Pan-African regional arrangements, the regional and functional agencies of the United Nations, are of this character. Claude concludes his survey of functionalism with the comment that 'it may be that the economic and social work of international organization will prove to be one of the means of developing a system whereby Man can control his political climate'.[1]

At this stage of our knowledge, we can go no further than postulate a factor which could be termed 'world consensus'; it seems to be not only a real one but an influential one. New States, developing world organization, an international and responsible decision-making elite conscious of the need to balance national and universal goals, along with communications and education, might explain 'world consensus' in broad terms; what it is in more detail and how it operates are matters for further thought and analysis. At this stage one can only observe that these intangibles must be taken into account in any description or theory of international relations, and analogies or models which cannot reflect them are likely to be misleading.

[1] Claude, *Swords into Plowshares* (2nd ed., 1959), p. 402.

PART V
NONALIGNMENT

14

THE RELEVANCE OF
NONALIGNMENT

I. THE RELEVANCE FOR THEORY

No theory of international relations is complete without an explanation of the development of, and a theory of, nonalignment. It is particularly relevant to this study, not merely because it is important in world affairs, but because, first, nonalignment is a special feature of the current world system to which the communications, rather than the power, model is suited; second, because it reflects some of the features of a developing world community described in the previous chapter, and in this sense is itself a useful corrective to the communications model; third, nonalignment has inherent within it certain features which are developing amongst aligned States, and throws some light upon the relations between aligned States; and fourth, nonalignment offers an alternative game and set of rules which is likely to be important once nuclear deterrence is no longer credible.

Some confusion may appear as to whether nonalignment is referred to in the following chapters of this study as a model in the academic or comparative sense, or a model in the exemplary sense. As already indicated, we must be interested in nonalignment in itself as an important feature of and influence upon world affairs. There are, however, certain aspects of nonalignment which throw light upon the behaviour of other States. Nonalignment is consequentially of interest as an academic model, which is 'an analytical tool—fashioned by the observer for his own purposes or chosen from existing stocks. It is an artificial device for comparing, measuring, experimenting, and guiding observation—all with respect to empirical phenomena. One of the most important functions of models is to generate hypotheses which otherwise might not occur to the observer and which can be tested by reference to factual data.'[1]

[1] Snyder, Bruck and Sapin, p. 30.

It is not suggested that nonalignment as a system is a model which other States should or could follow; on the contrary, the features which are in common arise out of opposing forces. Nonaligned States are powerless in terms of force compared with thermonuclear States, whose isolationism is due to the consequences of their power, and their need to avoid its employment. Nonaligned States can afford to be objective in assessing the merits of some great Power conflicts, but only because they are not involved, whereas the great Powers are much concerned with almost every event in world affairs. It is however suggested that the two systems have features in common and are complementary to each other to the extent that nonalignment does appear to offer an alternative game and some rules which would enable the thermonuclear States to re-establish order if their own rules were not observed. In this limited respect nonalignment does offer a model which is exemplary.

II. NONALIGNMENT AS AN INTERNATIONAL INSTITUTION

The term 'nonalignment' is commonly used to describe the foreign policies of nations which are not in an alliance with either the Communist or the Western bloc, despite the feeling of the political leaders of the nonaligned nations that it does not convey satisfactorily a description of their policies. 'Nonalignment' has no positive value or connotation; yet it is precisely this positive value which they wish most to express. In Belgrade, Cairo, Delhi, and at other centres of nonalignment, other and even less satisfactory terms are frequently used: 'non-bloc', 'uncommitted', 'actively neutral', are some of those. Long phrases and even speeches are sometimes the only means of overcoming frustrations experienced as a result of the absence of any term which is as yet sufficiently meaningful. For want of a better term 'nonalignment' has now been adopted very generally, and it is the term used in this Study.

When nonalignment was adopted as a foreign policy first by India, Burma, Ceylon and Indonesia on obtaining their independence shortly after the Second World War, the majority of other States were formally or tacitly aligned with one of the two contestants, the Soviet Union and the United States of America. Nonalignment had, therefore, the appearance of being the exception, to be explained by special national circumstances.

Even though the number of nonaligned nations has since rapidly increased,[1] it is still commonly regarded in this way. Unlike neutrality,[2] which too was the exception, nonalignment is in relation to a power rivalry which is taking place in the absence of war; and furthermore, the nonaligned nations claim a right to be non-neutral, to participate actively in world affairs including certain aspects of the main rivalry. In this sense nonalignment appears to be a new phenomenon.

Appearing to be both the exception and novel, nonalignment has been under judgement. Ultimately it might prove to be in-appropriate to a world structure that is based on alliances, and in which powerful nations continue to exercise their economic, political and military strength in competition with each other with only incidental regard for the independence and interests of smaller nations. Furthermore, even though it were in theory appropriate, nonalignment could reasonably be regarded as potentially unstable because of the obvious weaknesses of the particular nations which are at present nonaligned. On the other hand, it could prove most relevant to the circumstances of the post-war world, and if this were so it could be a viable policy despite the instability of those adhering to it. As such it would be of interest to all other nations, including the major nations and the two Great Powers, which all still seek relevant adjustments to the circumstances of the nuclear age.

So far nonalignment has been studied primarily in a national context; nonalignment in Burma, Ceylon, Egypt, India, Indonesia, Yugoslavia, and countries of Africa, has been described as an emergent of the historic and current national circumstances of each of these nations.[3] Alone these national studies are not satisfactory, for they do not distinguish those national influences which are unique to nonalignment, from

---

[1] See page 214 for a list of countries which have now declared themselves to be 'nonaligned'.

[2] See Chapter 18 below for the differences between neutrality and nonalignment.

[3] Besides the numerous texts on Indian foreign policy, and the general works on the foreign policies of many of these nations, there are some others of particular relevance to nonalignment. The series of Papers presented to the Fourth International Conference on World Politics contains studies on Afghanistan, Ethiopia, India, and some general studies about African and Middle East countries. Other case studies of interest are: M. Leifer, *Cambodia and Neutrality*, 1962; G. Hoffman and F. Neal, *Yugoslavia and the New Communism*, 1962; Erskine Childers, *Common Sense about the Arab World*, 1960; Dr U. Maung Maung, *Burma in the Family of Nations*, 1957; P. Lyon, *Neutralism*, 1963, is a recent systematized study.

others which are common to aligned and to nonaligned alike. In the case study of Cambodia, Leifer observed that nationalism and anti-colonialism were of significance as a cause of non-alignment.[1] It was undoubtedly relevant to draw attention to these features; but their significance as a cause of nonalignment is not clear once it is observed that they are not confined to the nonaligned countries. By themselves national case histories also tend to attribute more importance to local and current influences than a broader perspective would justify. For instance, to use again Leifer's study of Cambodia, the development of non-alignment appeared to be the consequence of local circumstances and even chance events: relations with neighbours which were traditionally tense, two meetings between Mr Nehru and Prince Sihanouk, the failure of the United States to provide security through SEATO, the friendly approach of the Chinese at the Bandung Conference, the character and personality of Prince Sihanouk, and many other Cambodian experiences and circumstances clearly relevant to a national history. Similarly, the nonalignment of Yugoslavia has been attributed to certain unique geographical and political circumstances, that of Egypt predominantly to the fear of attack in the event of war between other Powers, and that of African States to their desire to play one Great Power against another for a material benefit. In several cases the surveys have been made by nationals who are themselves absorbed in local politics, and impressed with the spontaneous and separate development of nonalignment within their own territories. Talking to political and academic leaders in nonaligned countries one is struck by their obviously sincere belief that nonalignment was first conceived as a policy in their own country in response to special local circumstances.

That there are most important local causations, and therefore characteristic national differences in policies of nonalignment, is clear; but there is also strong evidence of common features, and common causation. There is a remarkable similarity of thought and expression to be found in all parts of Africa and Asia, and the same approach to problems of international relations is shared by Africans and Asians to a degree that is impressive to anyone moving from country to country, or who is attending conferences at which Africans and Asians are present. The similarity of ideas also emerges from the statements

[1] Leifer, p. 1.

of leaders of nonaligned countries, despite the tremendous regional differences in history and in circumstances. On the practical side, the fact that nonaligned nations have met together as such, and work together at the United Nations, suggests that their policies may have some common origins and objectives not explained merely by the local circumstances which come to light in a national case study. Furthermore, a relationship has been established amongst nonaligned States, and between them and other nations. Nonalignment has become an institution, and moreover one which does not necessarily rest upon the continued existence of rivalry between two power groupings; the termination of the Cold War, the elimination of tensions between States, could make 'nonalignment' as a policy more and not less relevant to political circumstances. These, which are the most interesting aspects of nonalignment, do not emerge from national case studies.

For these reasons a study which is complementary to national case studies is required, one that is more concerned with the background and relevance of nonalignment to African and Asian States, and the influences which have been operating in the critical period since the Second World War; one that can explain the occurrence of nonalignment in a similar form in a number of nations almost simultaneously, despite local circumstances which appear from national studies to be unique.

Despite the many speeches of Prime Minister Nehru, President Nasser, President Sukarno, President Tito, President Nkrumah, and other political leaders of the nonaligned States, there has been no full treatment of the concept, no analysis and precise description, no exposition through which others might estimate the significance and future prospects of policies of nonalignment. What analysis there is has been made by Western political scientists. The result is that while the term is now in common usage as a means of categorizing the countries which are uncommitted in the Cold War, the growing body of thought it represents to those who are nonaligned is still unclear to others. Certainly, there is not in the West any popular comprehension of the full meaning of 'nonalignment', and Western political leaders who must deal daily with the attitudes, policies and hopes it represents are still thoroughly confused. Misunderstanding is mutual: on the one hand it sometimes appears that the exponents of nonalignment are claiming for their policies some lasting and positive significance, a model of international behaviour which all countries should follow in the interests of peaceful relations, an inspired response to the problems of the nuclear age, and a solution—for everyone—to the central problems of international relations which currently appear to be intractable; on the other hand the *aligned* nations, small and large, East and West, appear to have an image of *nonalignment* from which they deduce that it is a shifting policy of unrealistic expediency, of blackmail, and of irresponsibility, likely not to be permanent, and to be even a danger to world peace.

Nonalignment may or may not be a policy of expedience, an immoral attempt to obtain the best of both ideological worlds. There can be no complaint, even by the nonaligned nations, against a Western assertion that nonalignment is a policy of national interest—for this is a characteristic of all foreign policies. (The surprising thing is that so much space and feeling is devoted in Western comment to this self-evident observation.) A serious intellectual complaint may be made, however, if nonalignment as an international political institution is not subjected to further study, merely because it might appear to be associated with short-term expediency, instability, irresponsibility and behaviour destructive of peaceful international relations. The institution of *laissez-faire*, of multilateral balance-of-power, of party-parliamentary government, of marriage, and all other institutions known to civilization, have been developed out of expediency, and a degree of self-interest; it is time which has honoured and conventionalized them, and it is the rationalizations of theorists which have given them an explanation within the context of a history of civilization, and finally a legitimacy which sometimes has outlived their period of usefulness. Even though nonalignment were merely a self-seeking policy of national self-interest, and a current threat to international stability as conceived by the two main opposing Powers, it still requires to be studied as a system; one which has developed in, and may therefore be a relevant response to, the nuclear age; one which may be given a sound theoretical basis; one which could become a lasting and universal institution in international relations.

15

THE DEVELOPMENT OF
ALIGNMENTS

In the broadest terms, *nonalignment* is promoted by whatever factors contribute to the widespread, if not universal desire of nations for independence, and by whatever current advantages there happen to be in non-involvement in the conflicts of others; and *alignment* occurs when defence and related national interests that require foreign assistance are sufficient to more than offset these nonalignment influences. Alliances and non-alignment are resultants of these two sets of forces simultaneously operating upon nations with varying intensities. Both sets of forces require analysis and assessment before either alignment or nonalignment can be explained in any particular case, or as a general phenomenon. There is, in reality, a totality of forces that persuades some governments, despite the value that they attach to their independence, to enter into alliances which restrict their freedom of action; and there is a totality of forces which induces other governments, despite the value they attach to their security, to avoid alliances and to assert their freedom of action in world affairs. Nonalignment as an aim or as a doctrine may be described and explained as though the desire for independence were the only relevant factor, and indeed in political speeches this is done; but nonalignment as an accomplished fact can be explained only by taking into account also the strength and causes of alignment pressures.

The policies of nonalignment are the policies every government would follow in an ideal world of sovereign States in which there were no power conflicts or threats to independence that called for special defence arrangements or alliances. In the 'thirties, Dr G. Cohn, then Chief of the International Law Section of the Danish Foreign Office, made use of the term '*neo-neutrality*' to describe non-participation in war by a country which was endeavouring to make a contribution to war prevention. Cohn observed that traditional thinking regarded war as a normal and legal institution, and neutrality as an important by-product of it, whereas in his view, neutrality should be regarded as a 'normal and positive condition of the law-abiding States, and war as an abnormal disturbance of public order'.[1] He was demonstrating that what is usual has become confused with what is 'normal'. Tradition has similarly given a status of normality to alignment, because of its prevalence, whereas it is nonalignment which is the 'norm' of foreign policy, the independent equilibrium position as it were, from which nations are moved by pressures and circumstances. In an address to the Heads of State at a Conference of Non-Aligned Countries in Belgrade in September 1961, President Sukarno took this view:

Every nation, without exception, basically desires such a policy, knows that it could help preserve world peace by the adoption of such a policy. But the possibility of conducting a policy of nonalignment depends not upon desire alone. It may be because of historical background, because of the immediate national interest, because of the geographical position, many countries do not have the opportunity, or even the capacity, to conduct a policy of nonalignment.'[2]

President Sukarno went on to assert that where nonalignment did not exist, this was due to persisting forms of 'colonialism and imperialism', which could be interpreted more broadly as meaning pressures exerted upon weaker countries by far more powerful ones. In some of the African and Asian cases of most interest to him, this view could be supported; but more generally alliances have been and continue to be due to a variety of other influences, and the explanation of them is far more elusive than he suggested. Pakistan and Burma after independence were two countries in the same geographical area, with a similar background, similar living standards, and similar strategic value to the more powerful nations, yet one chose to be aligned with a Power-bloc, and the other felt free to be nonaligned. Malaya provided a base for foreign forces while Indonesia claimed a status of nonalignment. Yugoslavia was a nonaligned nation, while neighbouring Greece was a member of NATO. What, more precisely, are the pressures that persuade or force a nation to accept the limitations on freedom of action implied in alignment?

On the assumption that the desire of all governments is to be

---

[1] G. Cohn, *Neo-Neutrality*, 1939, p. 4.

[2] The Official Report of *The Conference of Heads of State or Government of Non-Aligned Countries*, published in Belgrade, 1961, p. 26.

independent and at peace, alignment is in some degree involuntary—each aligned State presumably considers that it has no option in the existing circumstances but to belong to an alliance. Certainly, stronger Powers can impose alignment on weaker ones by the forced installation of a particular government, or by the protection of some particular governing elite. There have been some cases of this kind: the people of Germany, Korea and Vietnam were divided, and it was more than a mere coincidence that the Governments of the Western sectors happened to support Western policies, that those in the Eastern sectors happened to be in support of Communism, and, moreover, that both wished to be militarily aligned with the corresponding Great Power. However, clear cases of continuing imposed alignment are unusual; they occur when some strategic position must be held at all costs. It is not generally expedient for a major Power to continue indefinitely to occupy or to control any nation; to ensure alignment it tries to create institutions and governments designed to maintain a favourably aligned policy. Western intervention in the latter stages of the Second World War in Greece, Italy and areas of the Middle East and South East Asia, and Soviet intervention in countries of Eastern Europe, resulted in governments prepared to maintain alliances with the respective power bloc. As a result of popular indifference, the elimination of organized oppositions, the persuasive means of propaganda, and the institutions which were established, there were reasonable prospects that the kinds of governments created would remain, and that the alliances would be maintained.

In the majority of cases, however, alignment is neither imposed nor is it a consequence of imposition; it is a deliberate response by a nation to a set of circumstances which, in the view of its leaders, compel it to seek the protection of another Power. Usually the initiative for an alliance is taken by smaller Powers, and indeed the anxiety regarding the continuation of the alliance and the fulfilment of mutual undertakings is experienced as much by the smaller nation as by the major Power with which the alliance is made.

I. TRADITIONAL EXPECTATIONS OF AGGRESSION

Traditional thinking on relations between sovereign States is in itself an influence upon foreign and strategic policy decisions leading to alignment. It is a traditional and widely held view that international politics stem from a power struggle amongst a number of small and large units each of which is aggressively inclined, and each prepared to exercise superior power in the pursuit of an important interest. This view, as we have already seen, underlies most theories and journalistic observations on international affairs.

The validity or realism of traditional expectations of aggression cannot easily be tested by experience, for an expectation itself may induce the results expected. When aggression is expected, policies introduced to prevent it are likely to provoke it; if peaceful conditions were expected, the policies adopted could tend to induce them. Furthermore, the final outcome of a situation depends upon an interplay of expectations, fulfilment of expectations seeming to validate and to support the policies associated with them and disappointment in expectations seeming to justify changed policies. In an actual situation there are so many inter-twined influences that the final outcome cannot reliably be held either to validate or to invalidate any expectations. Nevertheless, the traditional expectations of aggression, re-enforced by the traditional attitudes of psychology and political science, remain a reality, and therefore a cause of alliances.

Where there is a major power conflict already existing, such as the current rivalry between the Western and the Communist nations, traditional expectations of aggression—valid or not—are supported by the political outlook of the contestants, by propaganda, by racial prejudice, and by other subjective factors which enter into conflict situations. Because of this subjectivity there is rarely agreement on expectations of aggression even within any one military bloc. There were, for instance, those within the Western Bloc who argued that the former colonies of French Indo-China were likely to be stable and independent once the indigenous revolutionary movements were complete; there were others who took the view that the nationalist movements were communist inspired and that they would therefore pave the way for communist aggression. This tug-of-war in viewpoints characterized debate on Western policies when nationalism in South-East Asia was first apparent in the post-war period; and the policies pursued guaranteed the appearance of aggressiveness. There is little doubt that in the communist bloc the same kind of debate took place; there would have been those who expected stability as a result of nationalist revolutions, and those who expected the absence of Chinese intervention to invite further encirclement of China. Indeed, this disagreement in expectations was an important feature of differences between Russia and China. The Chinese had an image of the West as aggressive by reason of past colonialism and of attempts in the Cold War period to secure bases in Asia; while the Russians believed the West was on the retreat, and if not provoked, would be content not to expand its domain or to threaten either Russia or China. Whenever differences in expectations of aggression occur within an alliance, the alliance seems to be weakened; but military caution and the pressures of traditional thinking are usually decisive in leading nations to maintain alliances or to seek new ones.

Expectations of aggression are, understandably, greater once nations are directly involved in a political struggle. In the late 'fifties the expectations of Thailand, South Vietnam, and the Western Governments directly concerned, were that there would be continuous Chinese aggression in the absence of containment. On the Chinese side, the expectation was that any colonial administration or government which appeared to have little local support because of its economic or political institutions, would call in foreign help, and that such foreign help would be forthcoming, thus providing yet another threat to China. Once there is confrontation, expectations of aggression become self-supporting, and in due course no dissenting view is tolerated. Whether valid or not, traditional expectations of aggression are an important background factor in the establishment of alliances, and they are part of the explanation as to why nations join alliances even in circumstances in which no specific or discernible threat can objectively be established.

II. COLD WAR ALLIANCES

In the Cold War many countries are aligned with one or other Great Power as though they were directly involved with it in a common ideological struggle. However, their alliances have in many cases very little to do with the central conflict. They are entered into in the hope (a diminishing hope in the nuclear age) that there will be military assistance accorded to them even though the threat to be met does not come directly and undeniably from the opposing Great Power or one of its allies. Australia, Canada and New Zealand, for example, are aligned nations; they aligned with the United States against Communism. None has had, or is likely to have, any significant internal communist problem. None could demonstrate any internal or external communist threat which would justify extensive alignments (though for domestic political purposes Communism has frequently been made to appear in these countries as a serious threat). The Australian alignment is through SEATO and ANZUS, two military pacts covering the South-East Asian and the Pacific areas. They are not primarily anticommunist pacts as far as Australia is concerned. Communist China, and the new States of Asia whose political philosophies are not yet determined, are regarded with apprehension; but not primarily because they may be communist. They have merely taken the place of Japan, once the threat, and now thought to be under American control. China and the new States of Asia are to the Australian merely a continuation of the threat from Asia which has so much dominated Australian foreign policies since Australians were first conscious of their isolated position in the Pacific. Opposition by Australia in 1961-2 to Indonesian claims to West Irian was not based primarily on belief in self-determination. It arose spontaneously in the community (and before the extent of Soviet military assistance to Indonesia was known) out of fears of non-Europeans being close to Australian shores. The alliances with the United States of America were entered into as a substitute for pre-war British protection based on Singapore, and pre-war Dutch and French interest in the stability of the region.

Pakistan is another interesting case of a Cold War alliance which has little to do with the Cold War. The forces operating in the direction of nonalignment have been as strong upon Pakistan as anywhere. Pakistan is regarded by observers as intensely anti-colonial, nationalistic, and unconvinced regarding the merits of the conflict between the Great Powers.[1]

[1] Statements by political leaders in Pakistan during the late 'fifties made it clear that Pakistan had no conviction about the balance of righteousness between the West and the Communist powers, that they were confident that Islamic socialism would prevail in a struggle with Communism, that the dangers of hostile action from the Soviet Union were much smaller than the risks of Indian aggression, and

History, traditions, religious ties with countries of the Middle East, and relations with Russia and China on the one hand and with Western countries on the other, would seem to make Pakistan a classical case for nonalignment. But in 1954 and 1955 Pakistan went to the limit in alignments by concluding a mutual defence agreement with the United States, and by joining both the South-East Asia Treaty Organization and the Baghdad Pact. The Government did this despite strong opposition in the Assembly, and the reason is to be found in Pakistan's general defence problems. Pakistan has land frontiers with India, Iran, Afghanistan, China and Burma, and partition had left it with virtually no defence industries, for these had passed to India. Of all its potential enemies India was regarded as the most likely aggressor, and the dispute over Kashmir appeared to be evidence of this. However, no nation showed any desire to support Pakistan at the risk of offending India; British Commonwealth support was lacking, and Russia and the United States showed no interest. Pakistan felt rebuffed and isolated. The change in the situation came in 1953 when 'Mr Dulles wished to sign up players for his team and Pakistan was willing to come to terms'.[1] Dulles felt that 'the strong spiritual faith and martial spirit of the peoples make them a dependable bulwark against communism'[2] and for its part 'Pakistan had expected that after joining SEATO and the Baghdad Pact, the United States would give her, besides economic and military aid, full moral and political support in finding an amicable settlement of the Kashmir dispute, which is a constant threat to her peace'.[3] Since that time Pakistan has frequently been disappointed by absence of support, and by the support given to India, and from time to time suggestions have been made that membership of SEATO is a liability. The alignment of Pakistan, therefore, had little to do with the Cold War; Pakistan was a member of Cold War alliances to interest other countries in its defence against a nonaligned nation, as a means of obtaining military equipment and economic aid, and as a remedy to the isolation from which its government was suffering. The

that 'Western Imperialism' was a greater threat to independence than Communism. See K. Callard, *Pakistan: A Political Study*, 1957, and by the same author a paper on Pakistan's Foreign Policy presented to the Thirteenth Conference of the Institute of Pacific Relations.

[1] Callard, 'Pakistan's Foreign Policy'.   [2] *Ibid.*
[3] Mohammed Ahsen Chaudhri, quoted from ibid.

alignment of Pakistan could prove to be unstable, especially if nonaligned nations can obtain similar benefits without in any way having to sacrifice freedom to be objective and critical in relation to the issues of the Cold War.

European alliances, which are more directly concerned with the major power conflict, also have some of these features. Alliances have been traditional in Europe, and would occur even in the absence of the world conflict between the Western and the Communist systems. The existence of this particular conflict has helped merely to determine the nature of the defences and the alliances. But while the Western European alliances are designed to counter a possible communist aggression, this does not necessarily mean that all attention has been diverted from the types of aggression which have led to European wars in the past. The result is that major nations in Western Europe are not prepared to follow nuclear strategy and technology to its logical limit, and to hand over to the United States all responsibility for determining when and what situations call for deterrent action. They are prepared to enter into an alliance through which total Western European military strength is increased; but the hope also exists that the NATO alliance will provide some protection against potential aggressors in Western Europe itself.

It is by these deliberate extensions of traditional and current national fears of aggression into the East–West confrontation that the ideological conflict has become widespread, alignments have become consolidated, and a power-rivalry between two major countries has taken on the complexion of a bi-polarized conflict.

III. INTERNAL UNREST AND ALIGNMENTS

In the Cold War conflict in which ideology appears to be significant, in which the allegiance of small nations to the two military blocs is of strategic significance, internal political conditions of many strategically placed nations are relevant to the overall conflict. There are cases of alliance, or of military arrangements which can be regarded as alliances, where there is no active threat from another country, and where internal political conditions are almost solely responsible for a government seeking an alliance with a party to the Cold War conflict. The immediate post-war situations in the Philippines and Malaya were of this kind. In both cases the 'guerrillas', who had fought the Japanese during occupation of these territories in the Second World War, established local administrations. In Malaya in particular the guerrillas assumed that after the Japanese defeat they would be given special consideration, if not an effective part in the future administration of the country. They were no different in this respect from the guerrilla forces in Yugoslavia whose administration finally took over the country. In the Philippines they were concerned primarily with land reform and with the break-up of the feudal system of agriculture which prevailed before the war. In both cases Western occupation forces re-established their pre-war administrations, and later defended nominated governments against the opposition of the 'rebel' groups, that is, those which had fought the Japanese, which had established local administrations, but which were rejected by the returning colonial Power in favour of factions many of whose members had collaborated with the Japanese.[1]

The reason for this Western action was that, as was the case in Yugoslavia, the guerrillas in Asia were groups which were organized primarily by anti-colonial, nationalistic, if not avowedly communist parties, and post-war administration by them would have been communist. In Yugoslavia the pre-war government, which had formed a government in exile, and whose supporters in Yugoslavia failed in their leadership against the Germans, had forfeited its claim to govern, and could not easily have been reinstated even with Western military support.[2] In Asia, however, the returning colonial Powers were in almost complete military control of the liberated territories, and could push aside the nationalist or guerrilla administrations, as was done in Indonesia, Indo-China, the Philippines and Malaya. In Indonesia and Indo-China nationalist movements could not be suppressed once allied forces were withdrawn; but in the Philippines and Malaya the Western-supported governments were stabilized by the suppression of the rebel factions.

In the cases of Indonesia and even parts of Indo-China, nationalism not only led to freedom from colonial control, but

[1] See V. Purcell, *Malaya: Communist or Free?*, 1954 (under auspices of Institute of Pacific Relations); L. A. Mill, *British Malaya 1824-1867*, 1925; W. O. Douglas, *North of Malaya*, 1954.

[2] See Hoffman and Neal, and the Sixth Volume (*Triumph and Tragedy*) of Churchill's account of *The Second World War*, 1954.

finally proved, as it did in Yugoslavia, greater than any foreign influence, and nonalignment emerged. In the case of Malaya, the suppression of the revolutionary movement led to an anomalous position, reflected in foreign policies which were neither alignment nor nonalignment. The Western-supported Government of Malaya was a government primarily of Malays, and it tried to keep a balance between two Chinese communities. There were Chinese in Malaya who supported the guerrillas, and who continued to support the social and political reforms they contemplated, and whose sympathies were with the Communist Government at Peking because it was sympathetic to the guerrillas during the long period of 'emergency'. There were also Chinese in Malaya many of whom collaborated with the Japanese, whose sympathies were with the Government at Formosa. The Government of Malaya could not recognize the Government of the People's Republic of China for fear of offending one group, and its failure to recognize this government antagonized the other group even though care had been taken not to recognize the government at Formosa either. For the same reasons, and also because of Malaya's relations with other Asian and African countries, the government could not afford to accept United States military assistance, and in the view of some Ministers of the Government the presence of Australian forces in Malaya was an embarrassment. Grave misgivings were held about SEATO, membership of which was avoided, for this alliance had the effect of sharpening differences between communities of overseas Chinese without affording any guarantee against communist aggression. Internal repression continued to be necessary, and the incorporation of Singapore in Malaysia was a means by which greater control could be exercised over potentially subversive elements. Nonalignment had an attraction for many of Malaya's leaders, as such a policy would help to remove a situation in which Chinese communities must choose between one side or the other in the Cold War, and would help to establish a domestic environment in which the Cold War would no longer have repercussions. A final decision on foreign policy in Malaysia rests upon expectations of internal developments more than upon expectations of foreign influences.[1]

[1] These statements on Malay attitudes cannot be documented; they are impressions gained during 1962 as the result of conversations with Ministers and officials, and subsequently checked with other observers at Kuala Lumpur.

A contribution by Vernon Aspaturian to *Neutralism and Non-alignment* is evidence of a growing realization in the United States of America that there are sensible alternatives to the support of unpopular regimes. He points out that the United States could defend 'existing feudal regimes', support 'revolution from above' carried out by elements within the existing ruling classes, or thirdly 'abandon feudal classes to their historical fate and support the rising middle-class nationalist movements'. This last strategy he regards as the most radical of any; but observes that it requires less positive action by the United States than any other. 'It is not required that the United States stimulate these revolutions: they are developing spontaneously in response to existing conditions.'[1] This is tantamount to breaking up alliances the United States has with some countries, and allowing the nationalist forces to fight their own battles, and to preserve their integrity against all comers, internal and external, in the same way as the nonaligned nations have done. The fear that withdrawal of support would now lead to a vacuum and not to the early establishment of a viable nationalist government, inviting control by elements hostile to the West, and reluctance actively to intervene in the political affairs of a country in order to help in middle-class movements, have left United States policy where it was fifteen years ago, despite a greater insight into the requirements of stability. The fifteen-year-old image of American thought which the Communist and the Asian, African and Latin American countries have, is false; but their image of American policy is still a real one. Similar comments could undoubtedly be made in respect of Communist alliances, Communist thinking, and Communist policies. In both East and West, alliances and defence of indefensible governments go hand in hand.

IV. SUBVERSION AND ALIGNMENTS

There are cases in which internal unrest is inspired or assisted by foreign agents for purposes of obtaining a strategic or political advantage in the Cold War. This was probably the case in the states of French Indo-China immediately after the war, in the Philippines, in Malaya, in Thailand and adjacent regions, and in many countries of Africa, the Middle East and

[1] Martin (ed.), *Neutralism and Nonalignment*, pp. 188-93.

Latin America. Any doubt that foreign subversion exists has now passed in almost all areas of active dispute in the Cold War; instances of communist subversion can be substantiated in South-East Asia, and with little doubt the Russians and the Chinese have evidence of similar activities. Subversion is for all parties involved in military situations now one of the most important non-military means of achieving victory. Alliances can now be justified in the face of clear evidence of attacks being made on the independent status of countries in the region.

However, as has already been observed, once there are expectations of aggression and defence policies based on these expectations, aggressive actions are likely to follow; the fact that subversion can now be substantiated, and that alliances are now justified, does not necessarily demonstrate that the original expectations were justified. In order to ascertain how the alliances came into existence it is necessary to enquire into the situation as it appeared at an earlier stage, the stage of alleged aggression and subversion.

The evidence is that it was governments which faced internal demands for social and political change which sought foreign military assistance. Their expectation was not of foreign aggression in the military sense; but one of foreign assistance to indigenous revolutionary elements. The nationalist movements which came into prominence during and immediately after the Second World War were revolts against foreign control; but they were also revolts against types of internal organization associated with foreign control, or against a feudal system of land tenure which was consolidated by foreign control. Independence by itself, therefore, did not satisfy the aspirations of the peoples. We have already outlined the way in which some nationalist movements were frustrated after the war, and how governments sponsored by the former colonial Powers were installed and defended. Subsequently it was these that were characteristically the governments which were under internal threat, and which relied through alliances upon continuing Western support. In the late 'fifties, the question to be determined by Western governments from whom assistance was sought, and which was widely debated in popular journals, was the degree to which internal revolt was inspired from a foreign source, and the degree to which it was a genuine nationalist movement for reform. As it was clearly in the interests of a government which lacked popular support to exaggerate foreign influence, the facts were difficult to ascertain. In a survey of SEATO, Modelski reports: 'Thailand's participation in SEATO's subversion work was closely related to the career, and subsequent fall, of General Phao, who used fear of Communism as a means of securing larger funds for the police, immunity in striking at political dissenters, and increased political stature'.[1] 'The small countries have a propensity for using the Great Powers for their own petty interests, expansionist ambitions, and local preoccupations. They also use Great Power support for strengthening the domestic position of their governments.'[2]

The views of contemporary observers suggest that foreign intervention was not an important influence in the development of nationalist movements in Asia, and that it was only when Western assistance was provided to defend unpopular Asian governments that foreign assistance — Chinese mainly — was sought by rebel factions. When internal revolt first commenced in the newly-created states of Indo-China, foreign intervention was unimportant,[3] though as years passed these internal revolts were officially claimed to be, and popularly regarded as, part of the Cold War and inspired by an aggressive China.

It is still an open question, and must remain so, whether the military pacts made with the United States by small countries on Chinese borders provoked Chinese fear of aggression, and persuaded China to assist revolutionary elements, or whether the pacts were necessary because of justifiable expectations of Chinese aggression. A controlled situation in Europe gives some support to the view that Chinese fear of aggression may have been an important reason for assistance to rebel groups. In Europe, thanks to the 1944 Churchill–Stalin understandings on spheres of influence, foreign intervention by one Power on the side of one local faction did not always lead to intervention by another Power in support of the opposing faction. Because spheres were recognized, British intervention in Greece and Italy, and Russian intervention in Poland and Hungary, did not

---

[1] G. Modelski (ed.), *SEATO: Six Studies*, 1962, p. 101.
[2] *Ibid.* p. 155.
[3] See on Indo-China: J. R. Clementin, 'The Nationalist Dilemma in Vietnam,' *Pacific Affairs*, Sept. 1950; E. J. Hammer, 'The Bao Dai Experiment', *Pacific Affairs*, March 1950; E. L. Katzenbach, 'Indo-China: A Military Political Appreciation', *World Politics*, Jan. 1952; and G. W. Herald, 'Indo-China Uncensored', *United Nations World*, March 1953.

provoke an expectation of further aggression. It was particularly in Asia, in regions which were not declared spheres of influence, that support of weak governments by one Power provoked intervention by another Power on the side of opposing factions.[1]

There were in Asian cases several contributing factors, most importantly the conflict-situation existing between China and the United States of America, which made United States support for an Asian government appear to China as a deliberate aggressive move. The United States stated its policy in terms of 'containing' Communism, and it had its best opportunities to to do this whenever there were unpopular governments calling for support against internal unrest. Burma was of no less strategic value to the United States than Thailand; but it was Thailand which sought assistance, and that was where the United States could readily intervene in Asian political affairs. Syngman Rhee's South Korea was not secure against internal revolt without American help, and there have been those who have suggested that the invasion from North Korea may have been contrived as a means of ensuring American support.[2] Chiang Kai-shek faced bitter hostility and revolt from Formosans and succeeded, thanks to American aid, in quelling it. The privilege-

---

[1] The details of the 'deal', as so many writers have since called it, were not revealed in the official communique released after the Churchill–Stalin talks which took place in Moscow between 9 and 18 October 1944; but in a report to the House of Commons on 27 October Mr Churchill stated, 'On the tangled question of the Balkans, where there are Black Sea and Mediterranean interests to be considered, we were able to reach complete agreement and I do not feel that there is any immediate danger of our combined war effort being weakened by divergencies of policy or doctrine in Greece, Rumania, Bulgaria, Yugoslavia and Hungary. We have reached a very good working agreement about all these countries, singly and in combination, with the object of concentrating all their efforts . . . against the common foe, and of providing so far as possible for a settlement after the war is over.' Further light is thrown upon this far-reaching war-time negotiation in the sixth volume of Churchill's *Second World War*. The 'deal' led to a high degree of tension between Churchill and President Roosevelt and his advisers.

There was no such arrangement for post-war spheres of influence in Asia and the Far East. At Yalta agreements were made with the Soviet Government regarding territories of particular interest to it, such as Mongolia and areas of strategic interest to Russia in relation to Japan. The future of colonial territories in South-East Asia was apparently assumed to be a matter only for the colonial Powers. In any event, the emergence of Communist China after the war would have rendered any agreements irrelevant. The European experience does raise the question whether some understanding of spheres of influence in Asia might not be an appropriate means of stabilizing a continually dangerous Chinese–United States rivalry there.

[2] For instance, I. F. Stone, *The Hidden History of the Korean War*, 1952.

ridden and inefficient governments of Thailand and South Vietnam were willing to align themselves, to provide bases and to co-operate with the West in return for their internal security.

The existence of internal unrest due to feudal land-tenure systems, and to extremes of privilege, does not prove that foreign subversion was absent. All that may be said is that any government which lacks popular support, and whose continuation in office is of strategic value to a major Power, is unlikely to admit that its insecurity is due to internal discontent, and likely to argue that the threat originates with a foreign Power. In so far as the threat to a government is from internal discontent, and in so far as support is given to it by one power bloc, and in so far as this support is interpreted by an opposing power bloc as a threat to it, such a government is a source of a power-conflict.

Clearly there are inter-acting forces which prevent any resolution of a conflict once it is created by the defence of an internal political position. On the one hand the Western hope is that the anti-communist and aligned governments of Asia and Latin America can be persuaded so to change their ways that they might become popular internally; there would then be less danger of a revolutionary change of government, and therefore less danger of the development of nonalignment, or alignment with the Communist Bloc. On the other hand, alignments with military Powers are sought by politically backward countries as a means of defence against internal change; the governments of these countries are anti-communist because they are resisting land-reform and other radical changes which are being popularly demanded. As the small nations are frequently in a good bargaining position due to their strategic value, the delays they can occasion in bringing about the changes demanded are likely to be endless, for they know that there are no acceptable alternatives to them, and that they will be protected against communist-inspired unrest. Thus there is a continuing stalemate relationship between the United States and the unpopular governments of Asia, and a continuing encirclement of China which is not surprisingly interpreted as aggressive.

An expectation of aggression can in this manner lead to seemingly aggressive policies which justify the expectation; this is a situation stemming originally from the defence of governments which lacked popular support by reason of their refusal to institute economic, social and political reform. Expectations of peaceful relations are not possible until there is internal stability unsupported by foreign assistance, and no internal stability is likely until there is a clear expectation that there will be no assistance from outside. The cause of tension and of conflict in these cases traces back, therefore, to the foreign Power which shows its willingness to intervene in the domestic affairs of smaller nations. The alignment is due to a strategic interest of the Great Power concerned which can be made to serve the interests of the insecure government of politically backward countries.

V. REJECTION ALLIANCES

The reluctance of the Great Powers to accept the right of other countries to determine for themselves their form of government, and their readiness to assume that foreign policies can be judged by domestic institutions, has led to many alignments which may otherwise not have occurred. After a revolutionary change leading to the adoption of nonalignment took place in Cuba, the United States pursued commercial and political policies which left this small nation with little option but to seek assistance elsewhere. The status of nonalignment very quickly gave place to a dependence upon China and Russia which could be regarded only as an alignment. No major United States interest would appear to have been threatened (except the private interests directly involved in Cuban investment); had the United States continued to maintain its previous commercial and political policies, a nonaligned status might have been maintained—with Cuba showing cupboard-love leanings toward the United States.

Communist China is another case of rejection alignment. The history and traditions of China, the long-standing commercial and cultural ties with the West, and the earlier tensions between the revolutionary leaders and Russia, give reason to believe that with foresight in the West, China, like Yugoslavia, might have adopted independent policies compatible with co-operation with the West. The deliberate isolation of China by the West, and denial to China of normal trade and opportunities to take part in world affairs, encouraged the revolutionary government to enter an alliance which observers of Chinese affairs at the time regarded as doomed to failure. The alliance with Russia was a rejection alliance, it was a direct result of

Western attitudes, which allowed foreign relations to be determined unduly by prejudice against internal political conditions in another country. If India were to have a communist government, Western reaction would probably be the same. Indian policies of nonalignment would continue; but there would probably be such a rejection by the West that India would have to turn solely to the communist countries for assistance. If Indonesia were to be administered by a communist-dominated government, there would probably be the same Western rejection, which could destroy an independence which is characteristic of the Indonesian communist movement.[1] These are speculative examples given only to suggest that countries can be pushed into hostile alignments by the policies of others designed to prevent this happening.

The causes of alignment are many and varied; they do not always relate to the struggle for power being waged by the leading nations, nor to ideological conflicts associated with that struggle. Alignments arise out of pre-conceived notions regarding the behaviour of nations, out of subjective expectations, out of long-standing enmities and traditional fears, out of internal unrest, and out of policies which isolate nations; in many cases the major power conflict is but a cloak under which other reasons for alignment are disguised.

Nonalignment in the present political circumstances has, therefore, a wider significance than its relation to the Cold War; to be nonaligned is to be free also of the pressures outside the Cold War struggle which lead nations to take advantage of the existence of Cold War alliances. The nonaligned nations do not face, or do not believe they face, threats to their security with which they themselves cannot deal.

[1] See in this connection an article by D. Hindley in *Asian Survey*, Vol. II, No. 2, March 1962.

16

THE DEVELOPMENT OF NONALIGNMENT

Nonalignment cannot adequately be described and explained by the absence of overwhelming pressures away from the 'norm' and toward alignment, such as we have just considered; there are also forces acting in the direction of nonalignment. These latter vary from country to country, and from time to time. There are widespread circumstances such as nationalism, anti-colonialism and economic under-development which influence all African and Asian countries, and therefore aligned and nonaligned nations alike; there are others, which are dominant in nonaligned countries.

I. COMMON INFLUENCES

Post-war nationalism and anti-colonialism, and the pressing problems of economic under-development, are the background circumstances in which *nonalignment* has flourished. These are, however, features shared by all Afro-Asian countries, including those which are *aligned*. While each has a strong influence toward *nonalignment*, clearly each can be more than offset by strong pressures in the direction of *alignment*.

It is an interesting question whether nonalignment now established in a number of countries, at least in part as a result of these background circumstances, will continue to be dependent upon them. Can nonalignment occur in countries which have relatively mature economies and in countries not so intensely affected by post-war nationalism and colonialism, and will nonalignment persist even in Afro-Asian countries once they have achieved economic maturity, and once they are less self-conscious of their new independence? The explanation of nonalignment at which we finally arrive suggests that while the background circumstances have been important in the development of nonalignment, and while they will continue to influence aligned nations in that direction, they are not an essential pre-condition.

(i) *Nationalism*

A highly developed sense of nationalism was the most striking feature of independence movements, and of the newly-created states of Africa, Asia and the Middle East; it was not the traditional nationalism of Europe, which is so much related to language and cultural groups. In many cases the nationalist movements were strong despite the absence of a common language and culture: the former Dutch territories of Indonesia included many different ethnic groups, and very many different languages. In Africa, where national boundaries cut across tribal areas, where similar peoples were separated and peoples with different cultures were thrown together within one administrative unit, nationalism did not rest upon language or culture. It was not a nationalism characterized by devotion to one's country; indeed, after independence frequently it led to sharp divisions within the newly formed nations, threatening their unity and independent existence. Pride in independence, racial dignity, and expectations for the future, rather than traditional nationalism, seemed to be the dominant features. The nationalism of Africa in the post-war period was, in one aspect, Africanism; it was a reaction against the past, a reaction against an inferior status, against racial prejudice, against exploitation, a reaction which extended beyond language, cultural and even racial boundaries. In another aspect it was intensely parochial; it sometimes included unattainable ambitions such as tribal autonomy and economic independence. In both aspects the nationalism was uncalculating. The motto of the Convention People's Party of Ghana was 'We prefer self-government with danger to servitude in tranquillity'.

Immediately after independence from colonial rule, the excitements of freedom for a time suppressed tribal and local loyalties which later were resurgent. Either these local loyalties will develop into a traditional form of nationalism, as they seem to have done in Indonesia and India after earlier rebellion by local groups, or they will erupt and threaten national unity which was precariously based upon newly-found freedom.

The intensity of nationalism in new States varies with the circumstances in which they were created. In the case of India, the voluntary decision to grant independence made in 1947 by the Prime Minister of Britain, Mr Attlee, and the steps previously taken to ensure a smooth transfer of administration, did much to direct popular resentments against a past history and away from the colonial Power, and thus to promote co-operation with Britain, and a less assertive nationalism. In the case of Indonesia, by contrast, freedom was won only after bitter warfare, and even then it was accorded with reservations and conditions which perpetuated antagonisms.

In all cases 'newness' of nationhood is an important consideration in nationalism. Nations which have won independence after decades of struggle against a colonial Power can be assumed to be self-conscious about their new freedom, anxious to preserve it, and over-suspicious of any actions likely to threaten it. Where the leaders of those who struggled for independence were imprisoned, as were President Sukarno, Mr Nehru and many Africans, there is understandably a popular and deeply-felt pride in independence, and a widespread antagonism toward all remaining colonial Powers, accompanied by a widespread sympathy for peoples not yet independent. Because of the recency of colonialism, it is still fresh in the memories of leaders, and each time a new government attributes its difficulties to past colonialism people generally are reminded of it.

There are, however, powerful reasons for nationalism outside the novelty and anxieties of recently-won freedom. Traditional nationalism is a continuing feature of every sovereign State, and newness of independence can only increase the intensity of nationalism which is always present in some degree.

Even though they do not always occur together, the close association between nationalism and nonalignment both in the popular mind of the West, and in official statements of the new nations, is fully justified. The character of Afro-Asian nationalism is perhaps best described by reference to the Bandung Conference at which almost all African and Asian countries were united, despite their deep political differences, in their attitude toward colonialism, and in their affirmation that self-determination and independence were the key to human dignity and to progress. In the view of the nonaligned nations that attended the Belgrade Conference, nonalignment reflected this Afro-Asian nationalism, in particular the desire to take a place in world councils as free and equal members, and the desire to be independent not only in respect of domestic matters but also in making judgements and forming policies in international affairs.

The association between nationalism and nonalignment is close also because nationalism or independence is played upon by leaders to reinforce policies of nonalignment. Mr Nehru once commented that 'A movement must define itself in terms of nationalism if it has to become real to the people. In any Asian country, a movement will succeed or fail in the measure that it associates itself with the deep-seated urge of nationalism.'[1] A lessening of intensity in nationalism can be anticipated in due course as newness and the problems of independence fade. There is no reason, however, for support for nonalignment to become weaker. On the contrary, traditional nationalism is probably a more reliable support for nonalignment than the early reaction against a colonial status.

John Marcus in 'a case study' of *Neutralism and Nationalism in France* shows how what he described as 'neutralism' arose in France during the recent 'fifties, primarily amongst intellectuals and as a reaction against the policies of the United States. In particular there was a reaction against American policies in the Far East which were thought to be dictated by American strategic interests, without sufficient regard for France even when French territories were involved. Neutralism was a reaction of the non-communist left which favoured a speedy settlement in Indo-China. There was a fear, also, that American policies in Europe were disregarding the interests of the peoples concerned. In due course the neutralist 'left' and the nationalist 'right' joined forces to preserve French independence and interests. 'The nationalist concept of an independent France, which in the early post-war years had meant resistance to Communism, then opposition to Germany, now came to mean acting as a bridge between Washington and Moscow.'[2] Marcus asserts that by 1954 neutralism was 'respectable' in France. It developed as a consequence of internal developments and of a reaction against Western policies, and had little to do with Soviet policy. It was associated with the idea that social and economic progress in Europe and in less developed countries was the main defence against Communism, with which co-existence was possible. While the alliance of left and right producing this neutralism proved unstable, it offered a major challenge to Western policies.

[1] *Nehru's Speeches 1949-53*, 1958, p. 163.   [2] Marcus, p. 103.

Having dealt in detail with France, Marcus makes reference to similar developments in both Britain and Germany, each independently inspired by reactions against United States policies. 'It is remarkable that in different countries of Europe, and even among mutually hostile political groups in the same country, strikingly similar reactions to American policies developed and strikingly similar demands for a "different" policy and attitude by the Western powers were evolved.'[1] These observations led Marcus to speculate—without having made any basic study in this instance:

whether the particular combination of ideological leftism with a sense of national pride and with an underlying fear of provocation of war are not also the essential ingredients in the neutralist attitude of, for example, Prime Minister Nehru or President Nasser. . . . That nationalism and social reform, or revolution, should again be joined as twin forces resolving themselves in a neutralist attitude in some of the old countries but new nations of the 'Asia-African' bloc does not appear surprising.[2]

(ii) *Anti-Colonialism*

Anti-colonialism was a basic drive in the nationalist and revolutionary movements which took control in Asia during and after the Japanese occupation, and which dominated African politics. It was the main theme of the Bandung Conference of 1955; it was the common meeting ground of all of Afro-Asian peoples.

In the absence of some strong influences toward alignment, anti-colonialism tends to direct countries toward nonalignment in their foreign policies. In the view of Africans and Asians, the wars of the past have been European wars, many related to winning and preserving colonial interests. Furthermore, the nonaligned nations, and in particular India, Ceylon and Middle East countries, were involved in two European wars as colonial peoples. Their man-power and resources were used, and in some cases their territories were the battle-ground. The issues of the wars were not their direct concern, and the Second World War in particular demonstrated that colonial peoples were expendable. The former European colonial Powers, toward which there was in any event an emotional antagonism, are involved in the

---

[1] Marcus, p. 167.   [2] Marcus, p. 166.

Cold War. This power conflict in which existing international structures are being challenged by Russia and China is, in view of the former colonial peoples, little different from past power conflicts, and not one with which they need to be associated. At the same time the cultural ties, education, law, administration of Afro-Asian nations, and even the personal sentiments of their leaders, are predominantly Western. While there is widespread respect and admiration for the achievements of the powerful nations which have challenged the supremacy of the West, there is no widespread desire to be involved in conflict against the West, even in a Cold War.

While anti-colonialism originally was a powerful influence in the direction of nonalignment, its drive has lost some of its force with the rapid elimination of colonial status and the creation of independent States. At the 1961 Belgrade Conference of nonaligned countries, Mr Nehru declared that 'the era of classic colonialism is gone'. He was attacked by others for saying this especially by Indonesians who were still waging a diplomatic battle for West Irian, but it was equally clear that most delegates understood that his judgement was valid. The end of colonialism was in sight, the remaining areas being those in which administrative and political solutions had still to be found.

A more powerful and continuing influence toward nonalignment is what the Africans in particular term 'neo-colonialism'. African leaders seem preoccupied with threats to the independence of their new nations. B. G. D. Folson, of the Department of Economics at the University of Ghana, was one of many voicing his fears at the Fourth International Conference on World Politics held in Athens in September 1962:

As more and more African territories become independent, the struggle will shift to those subtle and clandestine forms of domination which are grouped under the rubric of neo-colonialism, or, as some, especially in East Africa, prefer to call it, neo-imperialism. . . . Scarcely an African speaks or writes nowadays on imperialism and colonialism without dwelling on neo-colonialism. At African conferences especially neo-colonialism goes in for a lot of flogging. This should not be interpreted as evidence of communist infiltration into African nationalism. The theory of neo-colonialism seems to have been worked out independently, although almost at the same time, by both communist and African nationalists. What is more, in working out the details of the theory too there is a lot that is common between the African approach and the communist. We recognize as true the weapons of neo-colonialism which the communists have enumerated.

The new nations, it must be remembered, have not as yet reached a stage of stability or efficiency in administration which would lead to any confidence in their own abilities to guard against new forms of interference. They are still at the stage of protest. In any event, even stable efficient administration would not be able to offer much protection against the kind of neo-colonialism or imperialism which they fear. For example, the shift in the terms-of-trade in favour of industrial products, and against the types of exports on which underdeveloped countries rely, is seen as deliberate Western policy; or if not deliberate, it seems that no steps are being taken to prevent this shift occurring. The leaders of underdeveloped countries feel themselves powerless to remedy the position, and therefore in the same inferior relationship as they were as colonial peoples when the value of their exports returned to them a similarly reduced benefit. As another example, the leaders of underdeveloped countries feel that economic aid is sometimes so directed as to ensure a trade benefit and a dominant economic position for foreign interests within their boundaries. Again this is a matter with which they are almost powerless to deal as they cannot easily afford to reject aid.

Both sides in the Cold War claim that the other is pursuing policies of imperialism. As far as many underdeveloped countries are concerned, both are suspect. The exclusive European Common Market is regarded as a classic example of neo-colonialism, and the exclusive communist economic bloc permits only those trading opportunities that are agreed as a result of arbitrary decisions. This is a situation conducive to non-alignment. Some of the dangers of neo-colonialism can be avoided, so it is thought, if the indirect restrictions and controls one bloc tries to impose are limited by the competitive influence of the other.

For the same reasons very few economically underdeveloped countries believe it is wise to accept economic aid only from one party in the power conflict, and the reasoning applies as strongly to military aid. The nonaligned countries may sometimes play one side off against the other in order to obtain increased supplies of aid; but they also do this as one means of protecting themselves against the designs of the rival Powers. In other words, nonalignment is in part a response to the pursuit by major Powers of their political and strategic interests: it is seen as one means of self-protection against loss of independence.

(iii) *Underdevelopment*

The poverty of Asia, the urgent need for increasing standards of living, and the consequent importance of industrial growth, are strong motivations for nonalignment, and in particular for endeavours to reduce tensions and to divert arms production in the main industrial countries to more useful purposes.

It is argued that one motive of nonalignment is to play off one Power against the other, and thus to acquire economic and technical assistance not otherwise available. This view is superficial; the aid received by nonaligned States was originally small compared with aid reaching those that were aligned.[1] The former were denied aid, especially during the early 'fifties, as a result of their unwillingness to conform with the trade and political policies of major Powers. Furthermore, had a country such as India been willing to shelter under the SEATO umbrella, its own defence expenditure could probably have been reduced.

The bitter reactions of nonaligned countries to charges that they are indulging in economic blackmail have to be witnessed to be believed. From their point of view the competition in economic aid stems from the rivalry existing between major Powers and is not initiated by the recipients. As far as they are concerned they accept aid not as a gift but see it as a factor in the Cold War. Furthermore, they believe that economic aid is due to them as a right and not as a favour. In *The Charter* drafted in 1962 by President Nasser, it is asserted that nations aspiring to development have a right to part of the national

---

[1] The following table of *per capita* USA aid over the previous ten years was published in the *Far Eastern Economic Review*, 18 Oct. 1962, p. 199.

Iran	$28.80
Pakistan	$15.00
Thailand	$13.10
Ceylon	$7.39
Indonesia	$6.70
India	$6.20
Burma	$4.80
Iraq	$3.30

wealth sapped from them in the past. In serious vein he claims that 'Offering aid is the optional duty of the advanced States. It is a form of tax that must be paid by the States with a colonialist past to compensate those they exploited for so long.'

There are, furthermore, strong psychological responses to the widening gap between Eastern and Western living standards. The nonaligned are amongst the 'have-nots' and freedom is not won, in their view, until equality in social and economic standards is achieved. Expectations have not been realized, so envy and resentment are widespread and are extending as knowledge of world conditions is disseminated. A similar reaction can be expected against Russia as living standards improve there, even though its aid to underdeveloped countries increases.

(iv) *Cultural Ties*

Nonaligned nations are predominantly African and Asian; there is, therefore, a racial and cultural aspect of nonalignment. These are countries which have been made to feel that they live in a world apart from Europe. There is bound to be an element of mutual sympathy amongst nations which have been exploited economically and dominated politically by others.

The fact that nonaligned nations are predominantly non-white is, however, incidental; there are other peoples who have equally been exploited and dominated, and who share political attitudes in common with Asian and African countries because of this. Neutralism generally reflects national reactions against being made use of by major Powers; and this is as true of Sweden, as it is of France, and as it is of the nations of Africa and Asia. The common 'cultural' tie in nonalignment is probably far more related to traditional relations with major Powers than it is to race, though the fact that the nonaligned nations happen to be predominantly non-European, and that major Powers still tend to discriminate against Asian and African peoples, cannot be overlooked as a causal factor in nonalignment.

II. INFLUENCES WHICH ARE PREDOMINANT IN NONALIGNMENT

The special character of nonalignment is more clearly drawn by observation of features which are common to all countries of Africa and Asia, but which are nevertheless predominant amongst nonaligned countries. Broadly these relate to political attitudes, and they are in evidence in types of economic and political organization. The nonaligned nations tend to be those which have followed their struggle for independence with internal reforms of a type the colonial Power was not prepared to institute, and which are inclined more to support the 'revolutionary' movements in world affairs than to defend existing structures. It should be emphasized at the outset that this characteristic does not in any sense conflict with a conception of nonalignment, even in relation to the ideological aspects of the Cold War; in their tendency to support those who challenge existing structures, the nonaligned nations are not thereby adopting attitudes which are favouring the communist bloc more than the West. On the contrary, their challenge to existing structures is of the New Deal, Fabian or Democratic Socialist type which is typically Western, and communists claim that this is so.

(i) *Socialism*

In Europe, neutralism was a 'leftist' sentiment. While neutralism for a European nation could be justified in terms of strategy and national self-interest, the sentiment reflected misgivings about Communism and Capitalism alike, and suggested grave doubts regarding the desirability of a world dominated by either. Neutralism was not indifference to the issues concerned; in European countries, neutralists and socialists represented an over-lapping community group.

In Asia and Africa, and in most underdeveloped countries, there is a similar neutralist–socialist alliance. A high degree of planning, of nationalization, and of government intervention appears to be the only means available by which problems of backwardness can be solved; what little capital is available is concentrated on agriculture, and investment in developmental projects must be on the initiative of a central administration; foreign assistance is best sought and employed through central agencies; land-reform must be nation-wide. Moreover, the new States were conceived in revolution, and the centralized institutions of the revolutionary movement tend to carry over into the life of the new State. Congress in India was a popular front movement created in 1870, and the Indonesian centralized non-party structure was the basis of its successful overthrow of colonialism. Central powers, central direction of planning would tend to be characteristic of any new State which obtained its independence by organized revolt.

In an economy in which there had been widespread private investment, local and foreign, and which was not destroyed in the process of revolt, central direction would operate within the framework of a private enterprise system. In India, the private enterprise basis of the economy persisted after independence, and foreign capital remained. In Indonesia, on the other hand, where there was disruption of production and trade, and administrative breakdowns, especially after the nationalization of much foreign capital, a great measure of planning was necessary.

The philosophical form of socialism in Asia has been influenced by earlier European thinking rather than by later practice; it is a humanistic Socialism which attempts to blend centralization and individual initiative. Many Asian leaders were, like Mr Nehru, steeped in the literature of socialist protest, which, as Robert Heilbroner has said, 'is one of the most moving and morally searching of all chronicles of human hope and despair',[1] and as such would understandably appeal to thoughtful leaders of economically backward countries. In the circumstances of Asia, the alternatives are not Capitalism and Communism, but rather the choices between forms of Socialism. Some nations may follow the Russian way of centralized management of industry and social activity by which that nation was industrialized; some may follow the Chinese course of regional co-operation, induced from the centre by education and persuasion to a degree that subordinates individualism; and others may hope to build a socialist nation by individual participation in decision and action. Most non-aligned nations which have sought Socialism have tended to experiment with this third course, but most have finally moved toward strong leadership.

An Asian Socialist Bureau was formed after a meeting of Asian socialists in Rangoon in 1953. The founder of the Burma Socialist Party, who was then Minister of Industry, reflected a widespread attitude: 'As Socialist leaders we should not do anything that would stifle any freshness of mind, or a new

[1] R. L. Heilbroner, *The Future as History*, 1960, pp. 113-14.

independent ideological approach. It is due to this independent outlook and approach that we could develop this idea of a Third Force—and also the idea of Democratic Socialism.'[1] Such an attitude of mind, flexible, free to adapt, uncommitted to any ideology, but nevertheless favouring some form of planning as a means to an expanding egalitarian economy, places Asian leaders in a world apart from the United States, Russia and China.

It could be anticipated, therefore, that both Western and Communist governments would regard the new Asian nations as unreliable partners in a conflict between the two. Official opinion in the United States, at least until the end of the 'fifties, regarded Socialism as a characteristic which automatically excluded nations from a close alliance with the West. In the American view, Asian Socialism and Communism were one and the same thing.[2] In the Russian and Chinese view, at least until the end of the 'fifties, Asian Socialism was merely a further variation on the theme of the Welfare State; an economic system, retaining many features of private-enterprise, and still associated closely with former colonialists and imperialists, could not come within the communist orbit.

[1] Maung Maung, p. 149.

[2] D. F. Fleming. *The Cold War and Its Origins, 1917–1960*, 1961, p. 1090. Professor Fleming has this to say: 'Throughout the post-war period we gave the breaks to the capitalists and turned thumbs down on the socialists of Europe and Japan. This was done under the slogan that "socialism is just as bad as communism and it leads to communism". This idea was propagated in the United States until it became a hotly held article of faith, and it was acted on abroad until most of the socialist parties were in a state of frustration.

'This was probably the most shortsighted campaign that any group of ruling conservatives ever waged. It was so because the slogan was false. Democratic socialism is the real antithesis of totalitarian communism, and has never in a single recorded case led to it. The one puts personal liberty and democratic self-government first; the other subjects every man to the centralized rule of party and States and puts production above everything. Traditionally, also, there has been deep hatred between the two, the communists scorning the socialists as milk and water bedfellows of the capitalists, and the socialists abhorring the communists as the executioners of freedom.

'This was the gulf which our conservatives failed to widen and make permanent. Instead, both communists and socialists were lumped together and a large part of the non-communist world offended. In 1956 democratic socialism was politically potent in 22 nations of the free world. In 16 countries the socialists were in the governments; in the other 6 they were the strongest opposition party. These 22 nations contain some 725,000,000 people, exclusive of colonial populations.

'A keen British liberal concludes that the great majority of Europeans want something in between regimented communism and unregulated private capitalism. Here, says G. L. Arnold, "is a source of neutralism as potent as any atom bomb".'

Even without this cold-shouldering, any nation which was trying to avoid those features of both systems which it regarded as unacceptable, and was trying to solve its problems within a structure of planning and of personal freedom, would conduct foreign policies which gave it freedom to develop new political and economic institutions. It is a moot question which contributed more to nonalignment in African and Asian foreign policies—the inter-action of internal forces, or the reaction of major Powers to Asian Socialism.

It has to be noted, nevertheless, that types of domestic institutions are not considered by the nonaligned nations to be a test for nonalignment.[1] While Socialism is not a formal prerequisite for nonalignment, it is frequently a response by a new State to the problems of underdevelopment; and Socialism, underdevelopment and nonalignment are likely to be found simultaneously in the one environment.

(ii) *Revolutionary*

Nonalignment and a revolutionary approach to domestic problems tend to appear together. Most of the nonaligned nations had to struggle for independence from colonial rule; independence from colonial rule alone could not satisfy the expectations of the people, who were not less adversely affected by foreign and indigenous institutions associated with colonial rule. Independence as such could satisfy aspirations for freedom; a second revolution was required to satisfy material expectations. In Indonesia foreign estates and capital enterprises were socialized; in Egypt, and in most areas of Asia and the Middle East, land tenure systems were the main objective of attack as they were in China. It was only in countries that were given independence in circumstances which preserved such institutions, as was the case in Malaya and the Philippines, that a second revolution was avoided; and in these cases governments continue to be under pressure to alter these institutions.

No socialist revolutionary government could be aligned with the West, for just at the period in which Asian neutralism was most dynamic, the West, in particular the United States of America, was at the height of its anti-socialist fever. Any government which attempted to overthrow landlordism, and to

[1] See reference to the Belgrade Conference, p. 199 below.

replace it with an economy designed to eliminate feudalism, was in the American view following the pattern of China. Even President Nasser of Egypt was suspect for his views in this regard. Heilbroner, referring to the social changes needed in underdeveloped countries, observed:

Many of these revolutions or near-revolutions will be undemocratic. Most will take the form of a thoroughgoing socialism. All will take its name. This places us on the horns of a tragic dilemma. On the one hand, it holds out the uncongenial prospect of a sharp leftward and collectivist movement as the price of a steep upward economic ascent. On the other hand, it confronts us with the risk of an explosion of proletarian anger if, in the absence of such a movement, the gap between us and the non-communist world continues to widen. In this prospect of bitter alternatives we have hitherto chosen to accept the risks of the second course. We have preferred to let foreign economic development lag, rather than to stir up the brew of social upheaval. In some nations, particularly in the Near East, we have lent support to governments which are anachronistic and corrupt, and which have a vested interest in *preventing* social advance. In others, our contribution to economic development has been grudging or none at all.[1]

United States policy has continued to discourage social and political changes, and reactionary governments continue to be given support, despite more understanding of the economic problems of backward countries. The justification is now that internal political change usually leads to a chaotic period, and even though this might be temporary, it gives opportunities to communist organizers.

Those nations which have undergone their second, internal, revolution, have done this despite Western pressures; apart from any other considerations, they are not likely therefore to be aligned with the West. Where Western pressures have been excessive, countries have tended to look for support to the communist countries, as was the case of Cuba. In the absence of strong Western opposition to internal reform, they have tended toward nonalignment, as is the case with socialist Egypt.

It does not follow that feudal governments cannot be non-aligned; domestic policies and structures do not enter directly into foreign policy attitudes. The Belgrade Conference of nonaligned States recognized this, and included in the gathering

[1] Heilbroner, pp. 164-5.

were heads of governments of countries with feudal economies, such as Iraq. However, either these countries will undergo radical change, or, as is more likely, their nonalignment status will be destroyed; in every feudal system there are strong pressures for internal reform, and the governments under pressure seek the protection of a foreign Power. The result is that nonaligned nations tend to comprise those countries in which rapid social and economic reform has taken or is taking place.

(iii) *Political Outlook*

Leaders of nonaligned nations are basically out of sympathy with the Western notions of power-balances, with alliances, and with the other means of preventing war which are traditional in Western thought. They have little respect for the modern device of nuclear deterrence which endeavours to replace past international institutions such as the balance-of-power. In his Introduction to *Paths to Peace*[1] Mr Nehru supported the arguments of the authors that the wars of the past had not been wars of ideology, but power struggles. He believed that ideology had been employed to good purpose by both sides to justify their aggressions and preparations for war; but that it had been a secondary cause. The struggle between the 'Free World and Atheistic Communism', or the struggle between 'New Democracies and the Western Imperialists' were to Mr Nehru struggles between two power blocs for supremacy and domination. Like Cohn, whose exposition of 'neo-neutrality' we have quoted, exponents of nonalignment devalue war, power, and the claims of each power group. In a letter to a Congress committee in 1954, Mr Nehru wrote, 'Peace can only be preserved by the methods of peace. A warlike approach to peace is a contradiction in terms'. This sounds somewhat trite. But it was a direct contradiction to the Western argument that the only means to peace was to prepare for war, and thus to create a deterrent. In Mr Nehru's view defence in advance, 'sets in motion all the wrong tendencies and prevents the right tendencies from developing'.

The leaders of the nonaligned nations have strong views on all the issues which are part of the Cold War, and on the policies of each group. Indeed it is their strong feelings on these issues

[1] *Paths to Peace* edited by V. H. Wallace, 1957.

which enforce their nonalignment. They see West and East in ways not flattering to either. From their position on the sidelines they are far more aware of the 'double-think' of both sides than either side could be. They have made their own estimate of the validity of the claims that Hungary and East Germany are 'people's democracies', and that Communism is a 'classless society'. They have made their own estimates of situations in South Korea, Formosa, Spain and other centres of repression as 'parts of the Free World'. They are not persuaded that Moscow news is propaganda, that the Voice of America is not, or *vice versa*. They regard espionage and counter-espionage by both sides as subversion. The claims that the Parliamentary system is the only democratic form, and should be adopted by all countries, has as much validity to them as the claim that a 'People's Government' is the last word in representative government. The nonaligned nations see the Great Powers not as they would like to be seen, but as they appear to an outside observer.

This assumed right to make an evaluation, and to pass judgement upon any situation, is the outstanding characteristic of nonalignment policies, and one which prejudices relations between them and members of alliances. In the view of nonaligned nations, both sides are a danger to world peace, and neither side has a monopoly of virtue or of wisdom.

Because Asian leaders are able to look at the Cold War conflict as observers and not as actors in it, and because they are free to make their own evaluations, they are beginning to develop their own notions about peaceful relations. President Sukarno told the Belgrade Conference that:

prevailing world opinion today would have us believe that the real source of international tension and strife is ideological conflict between the Great Powers; I think that this is not true. There is a conflict which cuts deeper into the flesh of man, and this is the conflict between the new, emergent forces for freedom and the old forces of domination. . . . The world must recognize this conflict between the old and the new. . . . Socialist States have emerged. Newly independent states have emerged. . . . All nations must have the freedom to arrange their own national life. . . . All nations must be free to arrange their international relations as they see fit. . . . No Power shall interfere in the struggle of any other nation to change its ideology.[1]

[1] The *Conference of Heads of State or Government of Nonaligned Countries*, Belgrade, pp. 29-30.

The 'five principles' cited by Asian leaders reflect this thinking: mutual respect for territorial integrity and sovereignty,
non-aggression, non-interference in internal affairs, equality
and mutual benefit, and peaceful co-existence. 'These
principles', said Mr Nehru in December 1955 at the time of the
visit of Bulganin and Khrushchev, 'form the basis of our relations
with other nations. If *Panch Shila* were fully and sincerely
accepted by all countries, then peace would be assured to
everyone and co-operation would follow.' Freedom and non-
interference are the key-notes: peace will be achieved finally
'not through alignment with any major Power or group of
Powers but through an independent approach to each controversial or disputed issue, the liberation of subject peoples, the
maintenance of freedom, both national and individual, the
elimination of racial discrimination and elimination of want,
disease, and ignorance, which affect the greater part of the
world's population.'[1]

We have been concerned in this sub-section with the attitudes
and not with the actions of leaders of nonaligned countries;
as is universally the case, actions taken are frequently inconsistent with attitudes and stated policies. For example, President
Sukarno repeatedly declared that he would not employ force
in the settlement of the dispute with the Dutch over West Irian;
but in 1961 he accepted aircraft, naval vessels and munitions
from the Soviet Union, thus seeming to compromise his
nonalignment status, and then moreover used some of this
equipment to land troops in West Irian, even while negotiations were still current. Again, in the case of Goa, the five
principles of *Panch Shila*, which include respect for territorial
integrity and sovereignty, did not prevent the use of forces by
India. In both cases it could be argued that the action was taken
against the remnants of colonialism, and in both cases negotiations had been pressed over many years without the colonial
Powers showing any signs of being willing to change their
position. In both cases it could be claimed that what was done
was merely to win back territory held under colonialism which
rightfully and historically belonged to these newly-created
nations. But if 'aggression' can be justified on these grounds, it
can be justified in other cases in which there are remnants of
colonialism, and in which there are boundaries arbitrarily

[1] Mr Nehru at Columbia University in October 1949.

drawn by colonial rulers taking no account of the separation of kindred peoples, for it could be considered most illogical for new nations to acknowledge the permanency of any such boundaries. For instance, on an analogy with the case of Goa, Indonesia could justify a claim for, and failing negotiation, could justify aggression into Portuguese Timor, and also into Australian New Guinea; for both are separated from Indonesian territory merely by arbitrarily-drawn boundaries, both are populated by peoples already within Indonesian territory, both are still colonies, and neither could survive independently as viable units. Is the principle of anti-colonialism to be joined with *Panch Shila* in a way which makes aggression of this nature against a colony, or liberation of colonial peoples, an exception to 'respect for territorial integrity and sovereignty'?

There will be in the future many other situations in which settlement by bilateral negotiations seems to be impossible, and there will be, especially in Africa, many border disputes arising out of arbitrary and intolerable demarcation lines drawn by European colonial Powers after conflict amongst themselves over colonial territories. Furthermore, it is unlikely that the peoples concerned will for ever wish to remain separated by lines drawn upon a map. If the nonaligned nations justify the use of force by themselves or by others in these post-colonial situations, then their position would seem absurd when they protest against the activities of major Powers to which they take exception. They would also make it easy for a Great Power to argue that nations dominated by another Great Power have a colonial status, and should therefore be freed even by force if circumstances make this possible; this was an argument that was used in the case of Cuba.

The nonaligned countries, unless they manage to clarify their attitudes and the situations in which they regard the use of force as justified, are open to the charge that they do not differ fundamentally from the Great Powers; their objections to Great Power politics and Great Power aggression is that, unlike their own small actions, such aggression endangers world peace and could precipitate nuclear warfare.

(iv) *Attitudes to Possible Aggression*

Many of the larger nonaligned nations, including India, Egypt, Yugoslavia, and Indonesia, are prepared to spend substantial proportions of their national income on defence. Clearly, however, they do not share with aligned nations any expectation of aggression that they cannot deal with by their own national defence forces.

Such differences in expectations as exist between aligned and nonaligned nations seem to stem from differences in beliefs regarding the nature of conflict. The nonaligned nations apparently believe that the removal of fear will remove aggressive policies and actions, whereas aligned nations expect aggression to take place unless fear of retaliation is introduced to deter the potential aggressor. The nonaligned nations seem to have argued that it is not aggressive competition that is responsible for conflict, otherwise nonaligned and other unprotected countries would be more threatened than those which are within some defence alliance. In their view it is fear that is responsible for aggressive acts, and consequently the removal of areas from the power struggle by nonalignment promotes security of the neutralized areas, and at the same time reduces possibilities of conflict between the larger nations. The nonaligned nations would argue that the relative insecurity of Thailand and South Vietnam is due to the existence of foreign bases and forces there, and the suspicion by China of an aggressive policy, whereas the relative security of Burma and Cambodia is due to the neutralization of these countries, and the consequent removal of any possible threat to China. In this view, it is expectation of aggression, and the adoption of seemingly aggressive pacts, that ultimately create a conflict situation.

The nonaligned countries would find support for their emphasis on fear as a cause of aggression from many scientists who have given attention to the place of fear in international relations.

We live in a fear-ridden world. The self-preservative and nation-preservative tendencies are usually associated with fear—fear of our own destruction or fear of losing our wealth or freedom. Fear, however it is stimulated, leads us to view with suspicion the nation that appears to threaten our security. Fear does more than that—it may make us believe that the threatening nation is more evil than it actually may be. . . . It is natural to build up defences against possible attack by non-aggression pacts, by mutual defence pacts and by the accumulation of armaments. The nation or group of nations which has assumed threatening attitudes observes the defensive actions being taken by other groups of nations and it in turn becomes fearful; it makes similar pacts and builds up similar armaments.[1]

The assumption that aggression is the dominating motivation of policy is itself sufficient to create fear of it, and of defensive responses which give the appearances of aggression.

(v) *Leadership*

Outstanding leadership was a characteristic of nonalignment from its inception. The names of Nehru, U Nu, Sukarno, Nasser, Nkrumah, Tito, are names which have dominated post-war Afro-Asian affairs. Leaders of the Afro-Asian countries which retained their alliances with the former colonial Powers seem, with few exceptions, not to be equally outstanding as leaders. It would be a study of its own to determine whether nonalignment was influenced by outstanding leadership, or whether the prominence of this leadership was as a consequence of the struggle for independence and of the policies with which these leaders were associated.

It was argued earlier that the nonaligned countries are for the most part those in which the revolutionary or nationalist movements continued into independence, and whose governments comprised the nationalist administrations; the aligned nations were for the most part those in which, after independence, governments were installed by the outgoing colonial Power. In so far as there is a correlation between nonalignment and continuation into independence of the leadership of the nationalist movements, it could be assumed that the type of leadership would be different from the type to be found in aligned nations. It still does not follow that the outstanding leaders of nonaligned countries were responsible for the non-alignment; the circumstances which enabled them to continue as leaders were responsible. Nevertheless, once installed as the leaders of independent nations, the attributes which won them leadership of the nationalist movement would directly influence the policies they followed.

The nation first to adopt policies of nonalignment was India. Mr Nehru was himself educated into policies of neutralism by

[1] G. H. Stevenson in a contribution entitled 'Canada' in *World Tension*, edited by G. W. Kisker, 1951.

experiences during the struggle for Indian independence. Congress, which was formed originally to ease relations between the colonial government and the peoples of India, led the Nationalist movement. The pattern of neutralism was formed very early. One of the resolutions of Congress at its first annual session in 1885 was a protest against annexation of Upper Burma. In 1904 Congress protested against an expedition in Tibet for fear that it 'threatens to involve India in foreign entanglements'.[1] Congress was continually expressing 'opposition to imperialism and especially to European rule, sympathy with peoples struggling to be free, hatred of war, desire for peace, and antipathy toward foreign entanglements'.[2] In 1907 Gandhi attended Congress and from then on the form of the protest against foreign rule was established: non-violence and non-co-operation. In 1925 Nehru headed the foreign department of Congress. In the 1939 War, Congress opposed British policies to the extent of condoning sabotage; the revolts which took place in India in the summer of 1942 (not publicized at the time) showed a strong nonalignment sentiment. India, frustrated still in its attempts to gain independence, saw the belligerent powers, Britain, Japan and Germany, as equally imperialistic.

It is not surprising that India, from the hour of independence, adopted an independent foreign policy characterized by neutralism, with positive features claimed for it. Mr Nehru explained in 1950:

I have ventured to point out, in this House, that the policy we were pursuing was not merely neutral or passive or negative but that it was a policy which flowed from our historical as well as our recent past, from our national movement and from the various ideals that we have proclaimed from time to time.[3]

The preservation of peace forms the central aim of India's policy. It is in pursuit of this policy that we have chosen the path of non-alignment in any military or like pact or alliance. Nonalignment does not mean passivity of mind or action, lack of faith or conviction. It does not mean submission to what we consider evil. It is a positive and dynamic approach to such problems as confront us.[4]

[1] N. Rajkumar, *The Background of India's Foreign Policy*, 1952.
[2] H. C. Hinton and others, *Major Governments of Asia,* edited by G. McT. Kahin, 1958, p. 103.
[3] *Nehru's Speeches 1949-53*, p. 142.
[4] *Nehru's Speeches*, Vol. III, p. 49.

In the case of India, nonalignment finally emerged because it was Nehru who was the leader of the first government; had the out-going British Government installed some other leader who did not have this same experience in the nationalist movement, different policies may have emerged. Sukarno, Nasser, Tito, and Nkrumah were personalities equally associated with many years of leadership in the revolt and struggle for independence; their continued leadership was a force in the direction of nonalignment. However, subject to a more exacting analysis and a better perspective of Asian and African developments, one is led to conclude that the leadership aspect of nonalignment may not be as casually significant as might at first appear. Rather, conditions which created nonalignment created the leaders. The nonaligned nations have tended to be those which had won independence, had undergone social revolution, and which had substituted some form of strong leadership for Western forms of government. The conditions were conducive for the appearance of leaders whose activities and responsibilities would bring them to world attention. Whatever the reason, strong leadership is associated with nonalignment.

Nonalignment, then, is a condition which tends to occur whenever the pressures of circumstances are not sufficiently strong to justify alignments; but nonalignment cannot be explained just as a 'norm' which occurs in some natural fashion. There are many and varied influences which attract nations toward it. Some of the strongest influences operate on aligned and nonaligned nations alike, and some seem to be unique to nonalignment. While nonalignment is popularly thought of in terms of nationalism and anti-colonialism, these are not the distinctive influences which finally determine the foreign policies of a nation.

17

THE ZONE OF ACCEPTANCE

I. THE NON-UNIVERSALITY OF ALLIANCES

After the Second World War, British, French and other colonial empires quickly disintegrated. The same political circumstances which caused this disintegration prevented the further extension of Great Power alliances; independence having been finally won, there was a resistance in new countries to involvement in any power alignments. Furthermore, the high degree of international tension, the great risks of involvement in nuclear war, and evaluations of policies unfavourable to both sides, reinforced a strong trend away from power blocs, and toward independent foreign policies. Russia and the United States failed to organize world affairs into two military or political blocs; while their own military power daily increased, their support decreased as new sovereign States emerged, and as some of the established States of the Middle East and Latin America re-appraised their interests.

The Great Powers failed to maintain even the military alliances that were initially formed. 'Polycentrism' is a term now widely used in connection with communist developments; rather than a continuous growth of Communism taking its direction from one centre, there have developed breakaways, as in the case of Yugoslavia; struggles between communist countries, as between Russia and China; and revisions of Communism as in the cases of Indonesia and India. Reviewing the tensions within the communist area in an article entitled 'The End of the Monolith'[1] Walter Laqueur comments:

Political scientists undertaking some form of qualitative analysis will have a hard job to establish the exact composition of the mixture and the character of each regime, and whether it belongs to the bloc or not. As the bloc is transformed into a polycentric system, and that system itself endangered by sudden shifts of political allegiance, it

[1] *Foreign Affairs*, an American quarterly review, April 1962.

will be exceedingly difficult to determine who belongs where, especially as those directly concerned may not always know the answer themselves.

What Laqueur says of Communism applies with no less force to the other bloc; the Asian and African economic and political structures are now so mixed that classification is most difficult in terms of either Western or Eastern systems.

This process of disintegration is likely to continue in the circumstances of world politics dominated by nuclear deterrence. From the point of view of smaller nations, the strategic significance of political and military power blocs is greatly reduced when each of two Great Powers has a deterrent force not dependent upon the military contribution of others. If there were a power conflict between communist and other countries with only conventional weapons available, far tighter military arrangements would be in the interests of the main contestants, and also of those dependent upon them. Furthermore, the longer the stale-mate nuclear position continues, the more opportunities there are for the development of 'polycentrism' and actual break-aways from the two power blocs.

Nonalignment feeds on this disintegration. Any nation reacting against the restraints imposed on it by membership of a bloc, is unlikely to join the opposing bloc; it is far more likely to adopt a nonaligned attitude, as was the case of Yugoslavia. The number of nonaligned nations can grow indefinitely, for nonalignment, not being an organization of States dominated from one centre, cannot be defeated by the separatist forces which in the past have finally destroyed imperialism, and weakened power blocs. Nonalignment, by definition, is the creation of these separatist forces—it is an attempt to break away, and to stay away from all power blocs. Nonalignment is a reaction against British, French, Dutch and other imperialism, and against American and Soviet attempts to create imperialism. It is also against a third alliance of nonaligned States.

II. THE OPEN-DOOR POLICY OF NONALIGNED NATIONS

While this desire for independence cannot be regarded as new, after the Second World War there was a revolution in international relations which increased both this desire and the opportunities for fulfilling it. A revolution in the international system was brought about by the creation of many small but independent States, the widespread acceptance of their sovereign role, and the provision of a forum at the United Nations where all nations, even the smallest, had an equal opportunity to express themselves on all issues. This revolution provided the conditions which made independent foreign policies practical.

Independence in foreign policies was an attraction to the Afro-Asian States which had formerly been colonies, but it was not confined to them. Josip Djerdja of Yugoslavia has observed:

It would be wrong to conclude from the present stage of the policy of nonalignment that in its future development and manifestations it will be a matter only for countries which broke off, or demand the breaking off of dependent relations with countries which dominate them. The immediate perspectives of the development of this policy are such, as shown by the tendencies in Asia, Africa and Latin America, that it will probably manifest itself in other countries as well, so that it will be impossible to say that the policy of nonalignment is only a specific outgrowth of particular circumstances in which certain countries develop. There were, of course, weighty reasons why at a certain time the policy and practice of nonalignment spread and consolidated in newly independent countries, but this policy is founded on aspirations common to all nations to proceed with development and construction in peace and on the basis of equality.[1]

Because they appreciated the widespread appeal of nonalignment, the leaders of the nonaligned countries were most insistent that they should not form a closed society. In Mr Nehru's words,

Mention has been made of a 'third force'. I have not been able to understand quite what it means. If by the term is meant a power bloc, military or other, I am afraid I do not consider it desirable, apart from the fact that it is not feasible either. The biggest countries today are small compared with the two giants. It would be absurd for a number of countries in Asia to come together and call themselves a third force or a third power in a military sense. It may, however, have a meaning in another sense. Instead of calling it a third force or a third bloc, it can be called a third area, an area which—let us put it negatively first—does not want war, works for peace in a positive way and believes in co-operation. I should like my country to work for that.[2]

[1] An article by Josip Djerdja in *Krsto Bulajic,* translated from Serbo-Croatian by C. Kiriloff of the Australian National University.

[2] *Nehru's Speeches 1949-53,* p. 236.

When eventually a conference of nonaligned countries was being called on the initiative of President Tito and President Nasser, it was clear that Mr Nehru was not enthusiastic, but asked that there be included a wide group of nations from Latin America, Europe and Africa. In June 1960, President Nasser opposed the formation of a neutralist bloc because 'we then would have to apply our policy of nonalignment to all three blocs'.

While the immediate purposes of rejecting the formation of a nonaligned bloc and resisting formal organization were to avoid national commitments and the appearence of a bloc activity, there have been important and perhaps unintended side-effects which have added greatly to the influence of nonalignment in Asia and Africa. The nonaligned countries, not being a bloc, not having any relationships amongst themselves which prevent close relationships with others, have been in a good position to promote Asian and African nonalignment. The leaders of the new nations, the 'Colombo Powers', comprising India, Pakistan, Burma, Ceylon and Indonesia, had continued associations and personal contacts established amongst themselves before independence. They were in a position to take the initiative in bringing together Asian and African countries on a regional basis, regardless of ideology or alignment. No government was excluded from their society (with the exception of South Africa), except by its own refusal to participate, as was the case with Australia and New Zealand.[1] The Conference of Asian and African nations held at Bandung, Indonesia, in 1955, which was convened by the Colombo Powers, created a community of nations which cut across alignments, and even included China.

The African and Asian States at Bandung were all opposed to any form of colonialism and imperialism, even though some were still under the controlling influence of a Western power. The nonaligned nations had in these circumstances a prestige and standing which was envied by the leaders of aligned countries. It was difficult for a politician from the Philippines to champion the cause of freedom from colonialism or foreign influence, when it was the nonaligned nations that had finally won their complete freedom and independence.

---

[1] Mr Nehru at Bandung went out of his way in a final speech to make this clear. He expressed the hope that Australia and New Zealand would find it possible to attend consultations amongst Asian and African nations.

Open and frequent contact between aligned and nonaligned countries, which is apparently the aim of nonaligned leaders, must in these circumstances favour nonalignment. At Bandung the influence of the nonaligned leaders on the policies of others was a matter for comment. Bandung seemed to be a turning point in the policies of the United Arab Republic, it greatly influenced Cambodian foreign policies, and it encouraged African leaders still seeking independence for their countries. The effect of the Bandung Conference merely brought to attention what had been taking place through less formal contacts; and since then the large number of meetings which have taken place each year in the Afro-Asian region, each of which has been attended by big delegations, has brought these nations into contact on an unprecedented scale.

Over seventy official or semi-official meetings took place within the region during 1961. Even these do not wholly reflect the extent of personal contact in the region, for there were in addition many private conferences, small committees and informal meetings, and there were conferences held outside the region attended by Asian and African representatives. The twenty-five nonaligned nations were usually prominent, and they were provided with a ready-made forum from which to explain their position. Of some significance also is the publicity which each of these gatherings was given in the Afro-Asian newspapers. The participation of leaders of newly independent states as principals, advancing their own views, was a new experience, and therefore an item of news value. At each of these conferences delegates were speaking to an audience comprising peoples from almost all underdeveloped countries in Africa, Asia, the Middle East, and even Latin America.

The nonaligned nations have not only maintained an open door, they have also effectively dissuaded against groupings which would draw a barrier between them and other States in the region. SEATO, which in the view of the nonaligned countries is undesirable and which would have provoked a serious reaction from China if it had been strongly backed by Asian countries, has been rendered relatively ineffective by the policies of the nonaligned nations. Attempts by aligned States to form economic and political organizations with an anti-communist flavour have received no assistance from India and Indonesia, and have in consequence failed. Indonesia has given a cold response to Malaya, the Philippines and Thailand each time they have attempted to organize a restricted association. Indonesia rejected in 1961 a Japanese proposal for the setting up of an Asian Inter-Parliamentary Union, insisting that any such union should include African States also.

III. THE PRESENT POSITION

The table on page 214 shows the alignment-status of each of the one hundred and thirteen members of the United Nations (as at December 1963), and six other countries not members of the United Nations. It will be seen that there are some twenty-seven nations with a declared nonalignment status. Within the 'Casablanca' group, which comprise the African component of the nonaligned Powers, there are some whose status might be in doubt, for example, Ethiopia and Tunisia. There are four neutrals, including Laos which must be included in this neutralist group by reason of agreements entered into at the Geneva Conference of 1961-2.

There are, in addition, twenty-three African States whose foreign policy attitudes are not as yet clearly defined. Eleven of these are members of the Brazzaville group of French-speaking countries. Five belong to the Monrovia bloc within which there are those, such as Nigeria, that declare themselves to be 'independent' and not 'neutral'. Libya joined with the nonaligned nations in sponsoring the Cairo Economic Conference.

It would be as erroneous to group these nations on the basis of identical foreign policies as it would be misleading so to group the members of NATO or of the Warsaw group. However, in the same sense and for purposes of classification, it is reasonable to speak of a nonaligned group, and separately of these other African groups. All may fairly be described as being nonaligned or as progressing toward independent policies. Dr Blyden of the University of Nigeria stated the position to the Fourth International Conference on World Politics in September 1962 in the following terms:

Whether couched in the moderate and carefully-guarded language of the Brazzaville/UAM group, the bold and self-assertive pronouncements of the Casablanca/UAS powers, or the cautious and

TABLE 1. MEMBERS OF THE UNITED NATIONS as at December 1963, showing *alignment status* (Bracketed countries are not members of the United Nations)

NEUTRALIST		African States not formally nonaligned	COMMUNIST		WESTERN		
Nonaligned (Belgrade Conference) (1961)	*Neutrals*		*Warsaw*	*Other*	*NATO, SEATO, CENTO, Alliances*	*OAS*	*Other*
Afghanistan	Austria	Burundi	Albania	Byelorussia	Australia	Argentina	China—Formosa
Algeria	Finland	Cameroun*	Bulgaria	(China)	Belgium	Bolivia†	Ireland
Burma	Laos	Central African Republic*	Czechoslovakia	Mongolia	Canada	Brazil†	Israel
Cambodia	Sweden	Chad*	(East Germany)	(North Korea)	Denmark	Chile‡	Jamaica
Ceylon	(Switzerland)	Congo—Leopoldville	Hungary	Ukraine	France	Colombia	Japan
Congo—Brazzaville		Dahomey*	Poland		Greece	Costa Rica	Jordan
Cuba		Gabon*	Rumania		Iceland	Dom. Rep.	Malaysia
Cyprus		Ivory Coast*	U.S.S.R.		Iran	Ecuador †‡	(South Korea)
Ethiopia		Kenya			Italy	El Salvador	Spain
Ghana		Kuwait			Luxemburg	Guatemala	South Africa
Guinea		Liberia			Netherlands	Haiti	Trinidad & Tobago
India		Libya			New Zealand	Honduras	
Indonesia		Madagascar*			Norway	Mexico†	
Iraq		Mauritania*			Pakistan	Nicaragua	
Lebanon		Niger*			Philippines	Panama	
Mali		Nigeria			Portugal	Paraguay	
Morocco		Rwanda			Thailand	Peru	
Nepal		Senegal*			Turkey	Uruguay‡	
Saudi Arabia		Sierra Leone			United Kingdom	Venezuela‡	
Somalia		Togo			U.S.A.		
Sudan		Uganda			(West Germany)		
Tunisia		Upper Volta*					
U. Arab R.		Zanzibar					
Yemen							
Yugoslavia							
Since declared nonaligned:							
Syria							
Tanganyika							
Total: 27	4(1)	23	10(3)	10(1)	20(1)	19	10(1) / 113(6)

*Members of the Brazzaville group of French-speaking countries. †Observer at Belgrade. ‡Observer at Cairo.

diffident policies and practices of the Monrovia 'bloc', there is general agreement among students of current African politics that all of these various groups are dedicated to the basic principles underlying their common goals and objectives: 'African Unity' and 'Independence'; the withdrawal of alien rule from the continent (whether styled 'liquidation of imperialism, colonialism, neo-colonialism etc.' or 'total liberation', or merely, the achievement of the right of self-determination); the elimination of racial discrimination and segregation against the black man throughout the continent; and finally, the promotion of peaceful co-existence in the world community. Even the Brazzaville/UAM group of States, their strong and unwavering loyalty to France notwithstanding, are on record as espousing a policy of neutralism (if not of nonalignment)— a policy mildly expressed as that of 'not taking sides', but to invite both sides to a dialogue from which only can emerge a solution which constitutes a positive progress for international peace and co-operation.

There are, in addition, a number of African countries which are not yet sovereign States, but whose membership of the United Nations must be anticipated. It would be reasonable to assume that their foreign policy attitudes will be similar to those of the present States of Africa.

The table shows the members of the Communist bloc and the members of the Western alliances. Warsaw and NATO alliances comprise governments whose status is in no doubt. SEATO includes some governments, particularly Pakistan and to a more limited extent the Philippines and Thailand, which have from time to time expressed dissatisfaction with the support they obtain from the alliance. These are countries in an area in which the nonalignment sentiment is strong, and there are both internal and regional pressures in this direction.

The Organization of American States includes four countries which had observer status at the Cairo Conference of Developing Countries which took place in July 1962, and which was sponsored by nonaligned countries. Economic considerations are attracting many of these and other small countries toward a non-bloc status. Latin America has many of the features encouraging nonalignment; underdevelopment, political backwardness, foreign domination. Any social or political changes which enabled valuations to be made freely of the nature of the power conflict could lead these countries away from the

Organization of American States as a military adjunct of the West, to a nonaligned status.

This leaves a handful of countries not classified, including Formosa, South Korea, Spain and a number of others whose position in the Western bloc is well known; it also includes Malaya whose status is, as we have already seen, complicated by its Chinese population.

In summary, world relationships are based on three groupings: thirteen Communist countries, most of which can be regarded as having a 'middle power' status in industrial and population terms though still underdeveloped; secondly, a Western group of fifty-one nations, including nine or so developed nations having a similar 'middle power' status, another twenty-two small or undeveloped countries, and nineteen Latin American states; thirdly, a group of some forty-five, and potentially more, small and large nations which are in neither power bloc, and most of which are more underdeveloped than the majority of the countries of the alliances.

The changes in alignment-status that are likely to take place are in respect of those underdeveloped nations of Africa, Asia and Latin America which are being attracted by the political status of independence and by the economic advantages of nonalignment. Any other changes are less likely as they would have to occur in developed nations, closely associated with military alliances for reasons of their security within and outside the Cold War conflict.

IV. DEGREES OF NONALIGNMENT

It will be at once clear that classifications of this nature cannot be interpreted as giving an equal status to every nation within each group. Mr Tugbiyele, also of Nigeria and also expressing himself at the Fourth International Conference on World Politics, asks:

How nonaligned could professing nonaligned Afro-Asian countries be? In their relationships with countries of the East and West, some hard facts can hardly be dismissed: many of the countries under reference have their legacies of foreign rule—educational, economic, cultural, and even occasionally religious. Most of them now use foreign languages as their lingua franca—such languages being those of the former imperial Powers, almost invariably Western

Powers. Partly on account of hang-overs and stereotypes, and partly on account of sound practical logic, most of them still carry on major parts of their dealings with their former imperial masters. They are also mostly divided into the sterling bloc and franc zone areas. Some of them are members of the British Commonwealth while others are members of the French Community. It may make news to say that Ghana is 'going red'. But the truth is that most of Ghana's trading, economic, military and educational affairs are still conducted with the West. Guinea's unsuccessful experiment in employing large-scale Russian personnel in preference to French, and India's recent quibbling over the purchase of fighters are typical eye-openers with regard to the impacts of what can be regarded as regulating factors of nonalignment.

It is not only in Africa that traditional economic and cultural ties have an influence, but throughout Asia and certainly in Latin America. Blyden, however, notes in the paper to which reference has just been made, that the leaders of these countries have a habit of visiting both Moscow and Washington, and of endeavouring to maintain contacts and to learn the points of view of both sides.

The traditional neutrals, such as Sweden and Switzerland, have in addition to their neutrality status a high degree of nonalignment in their policies, and this seems to be increasing as a result of the role they must now play along with nonaligned countries in a continuing Cold War. If it is assumed that there is a continuing nuclear stale-mate, then traditional neutrality associated with actual hostilities between major Powers becomes an anachronism. It is to be expected that the neutrals will play a more active part in the spirit of nonaligned countries in the resolution of major conflict.

While considering degrees of nonalignment it is appropriate to mention in passing the neutralist sentiments which have found expression not only in Britain and other European countries, but also in Canada and elsewhere throughout the Western alliances. In Japan 'neutralism' is of a 'fanatic cast', according to one observer, and is a factor no politician can afford to ignore. The expression of these sentiments, however, should not be regarded as necessarily influencing the continuing alignment policies of these countries.

18

THE RIGHTS AND OBLIGATIONS OF NONALIGNMENT

Nonalignment confers a distinctive status on the countries adopting it as a policy. Once this status is generally recognized as a continuing one (and this stage is now being reached), it will carry with it equally distinctive rights and duties. By implication other countries will have reciprocal rights and obligations arising out of nonalignment.

It is the conventionalization of rights and duties that establishes a recognized and orderly relationship amongst States. In the absence of such conventions, frustrations and tensions occur, and this has been the case between nonaligned and other nations. An understanding of the essential features of nonalignment, and an analysis of its motivations and objectives, such as we have already attempted, could be a basis on which rights and obligations are gradually built. The converse is also true: an awareness of rights and obligations as they emerge could help to clarify the nature of nonalignment.

Despite the long history of neutrality, despite legal clarifications and general acceptance of agreed procedures that have taken place, and despite deliberate and conscientious attempts by neutrals to remain neutral, there has always been controversy regarding neutrality. The conventionalization of nonalignment promises to be an even more difficult process. One special reason is that the major Powers still expect the nonaligned nations to act as neutrals: any additional or different rights that are claimed, or any neutral obligations not accepted by the nonaligned States, seem to provoke unfriendly responses from the major Powers.

I. THE RIGHT NOT TO BE INDIFFERENT

Nonalignment includes the right not to be indifferent to issues in dispute between the Great Powers. The question of recognition of a government involved in Cold War diplomacy is a useful example in this regard. The position of the traditional neutral would be that recognition is accorded only after a substantial number of governments has accorded it, and only provided that this number includes at least the main contestants or their allies in any power-conflict which might be current. If there were two rival claimants for recognition, each supported by one of the two rival Powers, then the neutral government would refrain from the recognition of either. The nonaligned nations, on the other hand, accord recognition wherever in their view the government is in undeniable control of the political institutions of the country concerned. They have been prepared to act, regardless of the views of any great Power, and entirely on their own judgement, as to the status of a new government.

Most foreign policy decisions that nonaligned governments take impinge directly upon the Cold War, and many may be even more 'unneutral' than decisions regarding recognition which can be justified on the formal and non-political ground of effective control. Most decisions of necessity reflect an assessment, an evaluation, touching upon the nature of the conflict, and on the merits of the issues being debated. Policy decisions in relation to nuclear testing, disarmament, fighting in Korea, disputes over Formosa, the future of Laos, all seem to reveal political attitudes, and even sympathies. The traditional neutral government would endeavour to remain strictly neutral in a dispute touching upon the Cold War. If it did not deliberately remain outside international organization, as does Switzerland, it would even refrain from casting a vote at the United Nations. But the nonaligned claim the right not to be indifferent in respect of any issue: far from being indifferent, the nonaligned nations feel strongly about the issues at stake, and claim the right and duty to express themselves, and to intervene with proposals for the settlement of disputes.

Furthermore, the right not to be indifferent is exercised by nonaligned States in relation to the fundamental assumptions of power-conflict. The nonaligned nations do not accept the proposition that possession of power makes its use legitimate; they do not accept that rights to employ power, to threaten the use of force, or to exercise economic pressures, are created merely by the possession of superior military or economic strength. They are not against the use of force by an international organization or even by a nation; but they do not agree that possession of power confers any special rights. Unlike neutrals, they claim a status that does not rest upon the existence of a power rivalry. They claim that nonalignment should be the basis of an international structure. They are, therefore, not merely claiming the right to attack the day-by-day policies of other countries; they are also refusing to recognize the rights which the great nations have always assumed to be theirs as an integral part of their sovereignty.[1]

In these ways the nonaligned nations act in ways regarded by the main contestants as prejudicial to their conduct of the Cold War. Sometimes they affect adversely one side more than another, and for this reason their policies have given rise to hostile responses. Nevertheless, there can be no legitimate objection by the main contestants to free expression of views, or to the commercial and other relations that nonaligned nations might have with each of the rival blocs. While the merits of the dispute are still being discussed, and while negotiations are still directed to resolving conflict, and before a decision is taken to resolve the conflict by resort to force, any embarrassment that either side might suffer as a result of the policies of the non-aligned countries has to be accepted.

The position would clearly be different if there were open warfare. Nonalignment is a status of peace-time relationships; it relates to acts and attitudes of nations involved in a power conflict short of war. In the event of open warfare between the main power blocs, nonaligned countries would be obliged, as all countries are, to declare themselves either as neutral or at war. Those that choose neutrality would immediately be subject to the restraints of, and have the rights and duties associated with, neutrality. These would over-ride rights claimed under non-alignment, for at that stage even the expression of judgements made on the merits of the dispute could be interpreted by one side as prejudicial to the conduct of the war, and therefore as an act of war.

II. THE OBLIGATIONS OF IMPARTIALITY

The right to pass judgement, according to an assessment made on the facts of a particular situation, is one of the main character-

[1] In this connection the observations of W. Friedmann in *The Changing Structure of International Law* (1964) are of great interest and an important bridge between Western and Eastern thinking.

istics of nonalignment which distinguishes it from neutrality. It is the one which most provokes reactions from nations participating in the Cold War. If in the exercise of this right there is partiality, prejudice, inconsistency or an absence of reasoning and knowledge of the facts, then nonalignment is not respected by other nations, nor by world public opinion, and its status is reduced in consequence.

The impartiality required is not the passive indifference associated with traditional neutrality: it is impartiality associated with active participation in world councils, and therefore an attitude which is based on the facts and on an objective interpretation of them by the nonaligned governments. It is the non-passive impartiality of a judge who first makes a judgement, and second supports his judgement by reference to precedents, considerations of justice, and the interests of the community, which in the case of nations is the world community. The nonaligned countries, to maintain their status, are obliged to consider each case or aspect of a dispute between other nations on its merits, and in its historic perspective.

If they are to take part and to be impartial in international organizations in which disputes are discussed, nonaligned nations have an obligation to insist upon the adoption of impartial procedures. For example, in order to make an objective judgement in any dispute, it is necessary for the Security Council first to ascertain the facts. This is a procedure usually strongly resisted by those directly involved in the dispute, so much so that an Australian Foreign Minister at one stage felt the need to make the finding of facts before decisions were made a cardinal point of policy. At a stage before Australia was caught up in the Cold War, and when it was a member of the Security Council soon after the United Nations Charter was drafted, and while the Charter objectives were fresh in the minds of statesmen concerned, the Foreign Minister, Dr H. V. Evatt, declared in the Parliament:

We are conscious that Australia was not elected (to the Security Council) to represent merely Australian interests. It was elected as a Power to advocate democratic procedures as well as democratic objectives, and to stand by the principles of the United Nations Charter . . . In the case of the Persian and Spanish situations (these were the two tests before the Security Council at that stage), Australia has been emphatic, first, that the Security Council, once its jurisdiction has been invoked, should not be side-tracked from performing its functions under the Charter, and, second, that the Council should not deal with a dispute or a situation *until it has impartially and fearlessly ascertained the relevant facts on which a just judgement can be made.*[1]

III. NONALIGNMENT TAKES PRECEDENCE OVER UNITED NATIONS RESPONSIBILITIES

The obligations of nonaligned countries could cut across their United Nations responsibilities, or at least across the formal acceptance of these responsibilities. The United Nations is an organization in which the veto provision alone ensures co-operation between the Great Powers. If, as happened in the case of the Korea dispute, and to some extent in the case of the Congo dispute, voting circumstances and administrative procedures enable one bloc to act despite the wishes of the other, the non-aligned nation has no option but to assess the situation and make its own judgement, despite any formal Assembly or Security Council resolution, or despite any act by the Secretary-General. It would have been wholly inconsistent with nonalignment had India automatically joined the United Nations force in Korea and supported United Nations military action there, a decision which was made by the Security Council in the absence of Russia. Having examined the facts, India took some part in a humanitarian way, and concentrated in bringing the fighting to an end.

So far conflict between the obligations of United Nations membership, and the obligations of nonalignment, has not been important. The nonaligned nations have not been in situations which obliged them to act in defiance of a majority decision of the United Nations. Their voting strength in the Assembly is now sufficient to ensure that no major decision is taken without their support. No decision by the Security Council is usually possible without the agreement of the Great Powers, and the nonaligned nations are not likely to object to a decision agreed to in the Security Council. There are, however, two cases in which formal United Nations obligations and obligations of impartiality could be in conflict.

The first such case is one in which the Great Powers are in agreement over action to be taken against a small State. For instance, some boundary or tribal dispute in Africa could find the Great Powers agreeing to impose law and order in ways not

[1] H. V. Evatt, *Australia in World Affairs*, 1946, p. 192.

acceptable to the nations of Africa, many of which are non-aligned. The second case is more important. This is the one in which the Secretary-General, acting without precise United Nations authority, and perhaps after consultation with some of the Permanent Members of the Security Council, initiates some move in the settlement of a dispute. This is a likely eventuality especially in circumstances in which the Secretary-General acts as mediator after a failure to reach agreement in the Security Council, and in circumstances in which the Great Powers agree some action is required in a particular situation, but in respect of which they do not wish to have to declare their hands. It would be open to the nonaligned nations to oppose the Secretary-General on the formal grounds that he had exceeded his powers; but should they fail in this, they would be inclined to take more direct steps if their rights or obligations as non-aligned nations seemed to be challenged.

The opportunities for conflict between United Nations and nonaligned obligations are limited, especially now that there are so many nonaligned nations within the United Nations. It is useful to observe the possibility of conflict only because this underlines the position of the nonaligned countries in world affairs. The principle of impartiality is likely to be held by them to over-ride any obligations occurring merely as a result of the procedures of an international organization.

By tradition and through local custom the nations that are nonaligned are far more concerned with the resolution of conflict than with the settlement of a dispute by direction or enforcement; they are more concerned with resolving the Cold War struggle than with a victory for either side. The judicial procedure of finding one side guilty and the other innocent is in many cases foreign to them, and in their view this is not an effective means of promoting stable International Relations. It is unlikely, just on these grounds, that they could be persuaded to give strong support to a Security Council or a Secretary-General's direction which in their view had not exhausted possibilities of peaceful settlement, and which in their view did not take fully into account the facts of the case.

IV. NATIONAL APPLICATION OF IMPARTIALITY

We have argued that nonaligned nations, in theory, are impartial in assessing the value of Great-Power actions, and seek procedures which lead international councils to impartial decisions. If tensions with major Powers are to be avoided, and if the nonaligned countries are to maintain their status, no less important is a studied impartiality in respect of their own policies.

Clearly nonalignment carries with it a duty not to enter into the strategic planning of any major Power, and not to allow any foreign Power the use of nonaligned territories. This was the basis of the invitation to Belgrade. If a nonaligned government were to invite the forces of another Power into its territories, or were to enter into any agreements under which it could receive protection from another nation, its nonalignment would automatically be destroyed, and there would be no obligations on other Powers to respect a nonaligned status. Neither can a nonaligned nation support any intervention in the internal affairs of any other country; any revolt or political change or change in policy is a matter for the peoples concerned.[1]

In many matters the nonaligned countries have a duty to be neutral, in the traditional sense. For instance, in commercial dealings, in the receipt and purchase of defence equipment, and in any action which touches upon relations with Great Powers, a strict avoidance of power-bloc involvement is required. Mr Nehru caused anxiety in Western circles in June of 1962 by purchasing certain fighter aircraft from Russia, instead of maintaining traditional Western sources of supply. He did this in part for certain technical reasons connected with the supply of the equipment then required; but this consideration apart, from a nonaligned point of view, he acted wholly correctly: a commercial offer was made by Russia for the sale of certain aircraft on terms better than could be obtained elsewhere, and non-acceptance of this offer would have been interpreted quite justly as an unneutral act. Any rejection of the offer would have had to be based upon firm evidence that Indian security would be prejudiced in some way; for instance, that there was some intent to withhold spare parts in certain circumstances. No such evidence was apparent.

The need to be neutral in all matters associated with economic aid and technical assistance poses very great problems. Non-

---

[1] Friedmann would argue that this is in accord with International Law. See *The Changing Structure of International Law*, pp. 264 ff.

aligned nations clearly must be prepared to accept such assistance from any quarter, without discrimination. However, they have the right to reject any proposal which they consider would prejudice their nonaligned status. Furthermore, nonaligned countries have a duty to other nations not to accept economic and technical aid from any source, if the conditions are such as to affect the independence of their policies. The status of a nonaligned country, and therefore of nonalignment itself, rests upon each nonaligned nation taking whatever internal measures are necessary to prevent any foreign government from interfering in matters of domestic jurisdiction. The obligation is on the nonaligned nation to ensure that the traditional 'rights' of stronger Powers are not exercised. At the same time, all such measures must be non-discriminatory; the same rules, procedures and restraints must be imposed in all cases.

V. THE RIGHT OF PARTIALITY

This does not mean that a nonaligned country cannot discriminate internally in favour of one political theory against another. All nations have an unquestioned right to determine for themselves what institutions they shall have. Furthermore, in guarding their own security and their own institutions, all nations, including nonaligned nations, have the right to discriminate in favour of propaganda and activities of one party in an ideological conflict; if it upholds Communism, a nonaligned nation may accept no obligation to prevent its advocacy, and if it is endeavouring to preserve another type of system, it may discriminate in favour of that system.

It is in this respect that the conduct of nonalignment is far more difficult, and likely to create far more international tensions, than neutrality. A neutral nation is an isolated one; its political institutions are of no importance to either power bloc, provided its neutrality is complete. But the nonaligned nations are not isolated; they are active in international relations, and they are amongst the nations which both sides in the power rivalry hope to win to their side. The leaders and the peoples of these countries may have personal sympathies with one power group or the other. Sometimes the sympathies are clear, sometimes they are disguised. In every case a consistent nonalignment in relation to the major struggle has to be maintained, whether the country concerned is socialist, communist, capitalist or feudal. The separation of internal policies and prejudices from foreign policies which touch upon the main rivalry, can be achieved only if a set of generally acceptable rules is observed.

VI. RIGHTS AND OBLIGATIONS IN RESPECT OF BLOC ACTIVITIES

In principle, nonalignment is opposed to any military or political alliances. These are dissociative arrangements, and therefore tend to promote, and not to resolve, conflict. The same is true of economic blocs, and India in particular has been opposed to Afro-Asian Common Market ideas. Moreover, it is not possible to separate politics and economics, and if the right of bloc activity is conceded in economic matters, there is an implication that political bloc activities designed to achieve economic ends may be pursued, and this may lead to general political activity. By forming a third bloc the nonaligned nations would be acting contrary to their objectives, and any influence that they had on the other two blocs would be through power balances and bargaining, and not through processes designed to break down blocs and to resolve conflict. It may be that this is the way nonalignment will finally develop under pressure of economic circumstances; but if it does the concept of nonalignment will be destroyed, and there would be a return to traditional forms of balances-of-power.

A third economic bloc or Afro-Asian–Latin American Common Market is so unlikely that the question of principle may not be important. A more likely development is the co-ordinated activity of the nonaligned nations in respect of each of the specialized economic agencies of the United Nations, and in respect of other international economic organizations, as there has been in respect to their political work at the United Nations. Nor is there anything to prevent the new nations directing world attention to those domestic policies of the industrial nations which prejudice the economic development of underdeveloped countries. In the immediate post-war period attention was directed by Australia to unemployment in the main consuming areas as being prejudicial to countries exporting primary products. The new nations are likely to direct similar attention to the terms of trade, as post-war shifts in the terms of trade have seriously prejudiced their living standards and economic development—some scholars have argued that the underdeveloped countries have lost more in this way than thay have gained through economic aid. The inclusion of the full employment obligation in the United Nations Charter could be regarded as a precedent for discussion in the Assembly of other domestic economic policies.

19

THE THEORY OF NONALIGNMENT

I. THE LIMITED ROLE OF THE NEW NATIONS

So far the only constructive role which the new nations themselves have suggested that they can play is one of mediation. They took part in the 1962 Geneva Conference on Disarmament as a result of a General Assembly resolution, and their appearance there seemed to be welcomed by the Powers more directly concerned. Their main function seemed to be to impress upon the major Powers the need for negotiating in good faith, and to suggest compromise proposals.

In the role of mediator the nonaligned countries have an advantage in that they are not committed in the Cold War dispute. From their point of view decisions may be based on considerations of world interest. They do not feel impelled to arbitrate in favour of one side or the other. They seek to resolve the power conflict and not to assist either side to win it. Bertrand Russell has underlined this:

I should wish to see a greatly strengthened neutral bloc studying the questions at issue between East and West, offering solutions which should leave the balance of power unchanged and could therefore be accepted by both parties without loss of face. I should wish my own country as a neutral to take a vigorous part in this work. The work of neutrals should consist not only in suggesting diplomatic agreements but in finding ways of dispelling the melodramatic picture of evil which at present dominates each side's conception of the other. Some people think that, if Britain became neutral, it would mean sacrificing any influence for good that it might have in world affairs. The exact opposite is the truth. It is the neutrals who can best do the work which is necessary for saving the world from disaster, and this is true not only of nations but of individuals. Whatever preferences an individual may feel for Capitalism or Communism, as the case may be, he can best serve mankind by remembering that the conflict between the two is much worse than either, and that in the service of humanity, the best thing that any of us can do is to mitigate the acerbity of the conflict, first in his own mind, and then wherever he has influence. Some think Communism evil, some think Capitalism evil, but neither is as evil as the belief of each that the other is evil.[1]

The fact that the nonaligned countries have themselves insignificant military power is a strength rather than a weakness in this context. Emmanuel Tugbiyele of Nigeria has commented:

The nonaligned nations are specially qualified to restore a balance of trust among the big Powers in either bloc; they can urge the destructiveness and futility of war without incurring the odium of seeming to advocate cowardly submission, and they can speak to governments on both sides without being thought to be actuated merely by bias. They cannot be suspected of being concerned with promoting the success of either side. In finding solutions to the grave problems of peace and war, nonaligned nations have an immense power for good—the power of the weak. Even the two major Powers themselves have pointed out that the contributions of the nonaligned and uncommitted nations in the seventeen nation Geneva disarmaments talks were 'very valuable'.[2]

The smaller nations cannot in any circumstances achieve a balance between the major Powers. Their activities must be confined to meditation, arbitration, and suggestions of alternative means of bringing about peaceful relations. It follows that in any particular dispute they are powerless unless the Great Powers wish the conflict to be resolved. For example, local disputes such as existed in Korea, Vietnam and other areas of tension, could be resolved with the help of the intervention of the smaller countries only if the Great Powers agreed that the areas concerned are to be treated as nonaligned. In this way the local factions become the party principals, and the conflict is taken out of its previous Cold War context. In Laos the major Powers concerned took an active part in the negotiations, and in the creation of a neutral State, and they undertook to withdraw forces if negotiations were successful. The nonaligned countries were able to play some part in these circumstances, even though the discussions continued to be within the general framework of the major Power rivalry.

The role of mediator is a traditional one in international relations. Arbitration, on the other hand, has usually not been

[1] B. Russell, *Bulletin of the Atomic Scientists*, March 1962.
[2] Paper contributed to the *Fourth International Conference on World Politics*, 1962.

acceptable when sovereign States are concerned. However, the level of distrust between major Powers, and the acute bitterness which is a feature of any dispute between them, limit the possibilities of mediation. It could also open up the way for arbitration by independent persons or nations. It may be politically convenient in local situations in which the major Powers consider a settlement is in their mutual interests, and in which there are two rival factions, for them to rest upon arbitration. In this way they would be relieved from any responsibility to advance the case of a local faction, or to take responsibility for any decisions finally made.[1]

The new nations have already made a major contribution to discussion at the United Nations, and their presence there has markedly altered the nature of the world organization. The United Nations was based on the assumption that unless major Powers could work together in peaceful relationships, no international organization was possible. It was decided at San Francisco, therefore, to give each of the Great Powers a veto on decisions taken in the Security Council which was the only organ which could make a decision involving enforcement. The United Nations was in effect an organization designed to enforce decisions against one or more small nations, but not in any way to act in restraint of a major Power.

The nonaligned nations regard the United Nations in quite a different way, and their numbers enable them to give effect to a changed approach. The dangers of major war are not primarily disputes between smaller Powers. They are related to the conflict taking place between major Powers even though the occasion might be a dispute amongst smaller Powers. The nonaligned nations have helped to transform the United Nations from an organization to maintain peace amongst small nations,

---

[1] In Australia arbitration has been developed in the industrial field to a high degree. Industrial disputes which have an important sociological or political aspect, and which could not possibly be settled by negotiation between the parties concerned, are frequently handed over to independent men or institutions who are required to arbitrate. The acceptance of the decision is an implied pre-condition of submission to arbitration. Many Australian historians have noted that the refusal of one side to attribute any good faith to the other is the main feature of the struggles which have led to the development of the system of arbitration. They point out that it is precisely this mutual mistrust which has led to the acceptance of independent statutory tribunals, and to the demand for independent men who can act as arbitrators. In the international field the nonaligned countries could be required to act as arbitrators, rather than mediators, for the same reasons.

to an organization in which smaller nations exercise some restraints on major Powers. The Security Council, originally conceived as the most important organ of the United Nations, takes second place to the 'People's Forum', to use Senator Vandenberg's description of the Assembly. There are consequential constitutional changes that appear to be required so that the independent nations may be represented in the Security Council on a basis justified by their numbers, and so that they can play their full part in the organization as a whole. Even without these changes occurring they have been able, through the work of nationals on the Secretariat and through Assembly action, to break down the power alignments within the United Nations, and to remove some of the objections to an organization which would otherwise be Western dominated.

Without detracting from the practical value of these forms of intervention, it needs to be stressed that they can be marginal only. It would be misleading to suggest that the nonaligned nations have a role in world affairs that could be immediately significant in reducing tensions between the major groups or in preventing conflict. The mediation and arbitration function of the nonaligned countries depends upon the parties involved finding it acceptable. If there is any hope being entertained that the smaller countries can play some positive role which will resolve the disarmament stale-mate, there will be disappointment. The nonaligned countries have helped to clarify issues; they have helped to stabilize the independence of smaller countries; they have helped to break down bi-polarization of the major conflict; and they have usefully intervened in situations like Laos and in discussions such as have taken place over proposals for banning tests of nuclear weapons. These are all important contributions; but equally they are all marginal. At best they can accomplish no more than reduced tensions at a particular time or in respect of a particular place.

The important role of nonaligned countries is a longer-term one, and one which involves the final development of an international structure in which all sovereign States regardless of size can live together in a competitive, but not an aggressive, relationship. There is understandably no clear realization of this role by the nonaligned nations. The development of an international system of nonalignment is an unintended effect of nonalignment policies; nonalignment is creating a system, not as a deliberate objective of national policy, but as a result of the nonaligned nations each pursuing its own policies. Each of them is quite unwittingly helping to create an international structure and a system of relationships which can ultimately make a far greater contribution to international relations than any of the planned activities described above. In short, the role of the new nations is that of a model, or more accurately, the presentation of an alternative model to the orthodox power image which has so greatly dominated and constrained thought on International Relations. If the model is a useful one it should help to explain relations between States generally, and help to predict future trends. For this reason it is relevant to construct a theory of nonalignment, and to relate it to other theories in the field of politics and sociology.

II. THE THEORY OF NONALIGNMENT

The relations amongst nonaligned States, and their own relations with others, cannot be explained by reference only to a power model. True it is that they are commonly explained as a resultant of the conflict between the two super-States; but this explanation does not account for the influence—however limited—of small nonaligned States on world politics, it does not explain satisfactorily why a great nation risked nuclear warfare over the independence of one small State, and it too readily leads to the prediction that nonalignment as a guide to policy has no relevance outside the context of a bipolarized power struggle. The common image of nonalignment is a creation of our preoccupation with power theories; we have attempted to fit this new phenomenon into the orthodox power-balance model. It would be scientific to use nonalignment to test the value of our power model rather than to adopt an image of nonalignment which conveniently fits into it.

The term itself has lent support to a power interpretation—'nonalignment' carries with it a special connotation, suggesting that it is a policy based merely upon avoidance of any involvement in two existing power alliances. The earlier term 'neutrals' was even more closely related to the orthodox power-model. Nonalignment emerged in the Cold War context; but it was incipient even before World War II, and certainly before the commencement of Cold War alignments which appeared in 1946 or 1947—a year or so after the United Nations Charter Conference. It was the current circumstances which gave nonalignment its name; but these are not an important part of its explanation. On the contrary, the end of the Cold War, some tacit understanding between the two thermonuclear Powers, the breakdown of economic blocs and military alliances, would create an environment conducive to nonalignment, and it would almost by definition extend universally in the absence of a power rivalry and of accompanying alliances. In this sense nonalignment is a necessary accompaniment or even pre-condition of the end of the Cold War and of disarmament.

Active hostilities could force some nonaligned nations to side with one alliance or the other; but the effects of another world war are so unpredictable that it is pointless to speculate whether nonalignment would be destroyed by it. If one were forced to a judgement it would probably be that nonalignment would be the one type of international system which could survive; certainly no universal collective security system could result, except one temporarily imposed by the victors. What, then, is the theoretical basis of nonalignment?

(i) *Cybernetic Basis*

In so far as the nonaligned States form a bloc or give expression to a community of interest, this is entirely on the basis of communication. The organizing pressures are not related to power. The British Commonwealth is an organization which grew out of an imperialist empire acquired by power; it finally evolved into a system which is communication-based. The nonaligned States have as their starting-point a community of interest without even a history of power.

In any association of nations which is voluntary, and in which each member acts independently and avoids alliances, communication is the only associative influence. This is as true of federations as it is of the British Commonwealth, the nonaligned nations, and the United Nations. The structures and procedures can be predicted: *ad hoc* arrangements for consultation, central organization with limited powers conferred by consent, and unanimity as a principle of decision-making in any matter regarded by a member as being vital to it.

Under the influence of these States the United Nations has undergone substantial changes: except in form, it is no longer a collective security organization. The Security Council—once the main focus of attention—is a reminder of a past era, and if in the future it is enlarged, it will function only as a small executive of the Assembly, with effective powers no greater than those already possessed by the Assembly, which today is the more influential organ. What is evolving is an international organization, which can deal with any matter of international concern—including matters that some States might claim to be matters of domestic jurisdiction under Article 2.9 of the Charter—with no enforcement powers other than those that rest upon recommendation, and which require an overwhelming consensus of world opinion before they can become effective.

The goal to which international co-operation is currently directed appears, on analysis, to be no longer a world government with enforcement potential against a member State on the analogy of provincial government dealing with lawbreakers; but a universal international system in which communication, knowledge of consequences, feed-back, awareness of revisionist demands which a consensus views as legitimate, can lead to change and adjustment to change—a process not possible in conventional systems of alliances and collective security dominated by alliances. In so far as the world organization retains and exercises force, it will be employed only with a limited police function, supervising conflict situations where local communication between States or rival factions has broken down, until such time as contact is restored and negotiation becomes practical.

The full explanation of this development in world organization is not the presence of nonaligned nations; the same political realism which led to communication-based nonalignment has induced these trends in relations between States at the United Nations. The explanation cannot be found just in a power-model.

(ii) *Adjustment and Power*

This movement away from collective security and toward discussion of conflicting interests blurs what would otherwise be clearly defined conflicts between revisionist and *status quo*

States. An international structure necessarily becomes less rigid and more responsive to demands for change once there is open discussion of conflicting interests; how, otherwise, can we explain the virtual elimination of colonial administration? In so far as the international system accords to a cybernetic model, policies of States can be re-directed in the pursuit of national interests; and in so far as each State acts independently and is subject to the pressures of dialogue, a clash between the relatively satisfied and the relatively dissatisfied is theoretically avoidable. Adjustment can be substituted for the use of power.

Nonalignment theory provides some insight into these relations between States. The nonaligned States have no effective military power with which they could induce or deter the major nations; implicit in their nonalignment is the belief that power-politics is relevant only to acquiring, maintaining or breaking a privileged position too valuable to be negotiated. Thus the options of adjustment and the use of power are dramatically featured; nonaligned States cannot rely upon power and must adjust, while the major States have a technical capacity of power sufficient not to have to accept the course of adjustment. The relative value attached to adjustment and to power is thus shown to be an important feature in decision-making: few adjustments are too great to negotiate if there is no power, and few are acceptable if adequate power is available to make them unnecessary. Examples range from tariff bargaining in the 'thirties, and the maintenance of the 'closed door' in colonies, to compromise on Cuba, and to the pursuit of self-defeating policies such as the United States has pursued in relation to China.

Availability of adjustment and of power cannot be measured in terms only of technical possibilities; availability also depends upon domestic and international political pressures. Technically the means of economic adjustment to disarmament are available, but in practice they might not be. Technically the power to suppress and even to eliminate the opposition in Vietnam has always been available, but in practice it has not. The nuclear weapon may have increased the availability of adjustment, and decreased the availability of power: and the forum provided by the General Assembly has also had this effect.

In the view of the nonaligned States the absence of alliances throws the balance in favour of peaceful adjustment and against power; States which are committed to act independently cannot rely upon the military or economic might of an alliance, and must therefore rely upon goal changing and adjustment, and not upon the threat or the use of power. Governments which lack popular support must, in these circumstances, adjust to survive, and States involved in international conflict are forced to negotiate.

If nonalignment described in these terms has a utopian flavour, this may be at least in part because Western thinking has for such a long time been expressed by reference to power analogies; if Deutsch's model were better known and were part of our thinking processes, even the devaluation of power in nonalignment would probably be more credible.

(iii) *Negotiation and Justice*

There are obviously many nuclear implications inherent in this concept of nonalignment. The devaluation of power in favour of communication as the integration factor in social organization seems to imply that conflict of interests can be negotiated. This, in turn, implies that conflict is either subjective or that the interests involved are not objectively vital, and are therefore subject to negotiation. In the nuclear age it could be argued that almost any national interests are subordinate to the national interest in preserving peace; but the subjective elements of nationalism persist even in the nuclear age. The difficulty is removed only if certain principles of justice are universally acceptable, and these include self-determination, independence, the avoidance of power-pressures—in short, the absence of power politics.

The argument would appear to be circular; but here again our difficulty traces back to our power concepts, and a great reluctance to entertain 'justice' as a meaningful and relevant influence in relations between States. As was pointed out earlier there are certain universally acceptable rules of behaviour which justify some regard for the effective influence of 'justice': economic and racial discrimination, restrictions on access to raw materials, certain economic inequalities, foreign political dominance of peoples, are prevalent but nevertheless usually considered to be 'unjust'.

It is here that we can note the reasons why nonaligned States do not regard the East–West conflict in black-and-white terms— as many Western and Communist leaders have seemed in the past to expect. In a power-politics system any action by an alliance which is designed to uphold peace, freedom and 'right', is justified and is deserving of support. More than one party to a dispute can act on the basis of 'right', and open conflict is therefore invited. The nonaligned States attempt to judge each issue on its merits, and refuse to take an over-all view, or to balance 'right' and 'wrong'; the merits that they take into account include the avoidance of war as a goal (for which reason they saw only danger in supporting continued Western protests over Hungary), and the merits relate to independence and anti-colonialism (for which reason they attack Western policies in Asia, Africa and Latin America). To do other than treat every issue on its merits would be to imperil their independent position and policies, and to lead them into alliances.

Their attitude has been described by those writing about nonalignment as reflecting 'an exclusive monopoly of rectitude' and it is alleged that some neutralists 'assert a moral neutralism'. Sometimes their attitude is regarded as a moral indifference— 'a plague on both your houses'.[1] There is little if any evidence of this. The claim made is only that each nonaligned State reserves the right to make an independent decision in respect of any and every matter of policy of the major nations, and to order its own policies accordingly. In Nehru's own terms, 'We have to do our thinking, profiting by the example of others, but essentially trying to find a path for ourselves suited to our own conditions'. Certainly the nonaligned nations, in making their independent judgements regarding aspects of the Cold War, do not entertain the moral rectitude which each party to the Cold War claims for itself.

(iv) *Non-alliance and Unrestricted Communication*

An alliance is a symptom of a break-down in communication: it also contributes to a further deterioration in perception, reception, feed-back and other parts of a flexible international system. Only through power can a State afford to maintain an

[1] Lyon, p. 67.

inefficient communications system, and the nonaligned States have limited power. Easy contact with East and West is essential to the pursuit of their national interests. Unlike 'neutrals', which are content to stand aloof, the nonaligned States are, for pressing economic, strategic and political reasons, obliged to maintain open communications with all leading nations. A visit to Moscow is usually balanced by a visit to Washington; but the balancing is mere diplomatic discretion, the important aspect is the contact.

It is probably true to say that nowhere is a more informed and mature appreciation of the issue of the Cold War to be found than amongst the leaders of the nonaligned countries. From time to time, and usually quietly, their insights have been at the disposal of the major nations; the dispatches of the United States and Soviet Ambassadors from Belgrade and Cairo probably contain more wisdom than can be readily absorbed by any government committed to an alliance—as United States Ambassador Kennan discovered. These States are important points of contact for the major Powers. The nonaligned leaders believe that they have helped to maintain communication between East and West by maintaining their own communications, and have a role to play in disarmament negotiations, in the future of territories such as Laos, in reaching agreement over China, and in all such Cold War matters on which direct communication is inhibited.

How useful a function the nonaligned States have in this respect cannot readily be determined. It is clear, however, that by being not committed they have an ability to adapt and to adjust which is important in the playing of any such role. Commitment and learning are incompatible; this is probably as true of States as it is of students. The rigid Western economic and political systems, and the rigid communist systems, not merely impede their own economic and social progress, but endanger international relationships. The new States, by comparison, are flexible; the constant experimentation and changes in Yugoslavia, Egypt and Indonesia, for example, may be evidence of adaptability rather than failure or lack of direction. Nonalignment as a foreign policy is in any event dictated by the need to remain uncommitted to those economic and political institutions inherited from the West, which may or may not prove suited to the needs of the new nations as they develop. It may be neither Capitalism nor Communism which is required and which ultimately emerges, and commitment to either would introduce rigidities which could prejudice development.

(v) *Internal Organization*

It is in these terms that it is possible to explain the apparent failure of Western political institutions in the new States. Formal oppositions, like power, are a luxury which only developed and affluent States can afford; an opposition is an obstruction in any input–output electronic model. It is a resistance within the process of decision-making. It need not necessarily add to the quality of decision-making because it is a foreign body, an incompatible part of the total communications mechanism. Opposition is related to the power model of society, and to orthodox concepts of politics, and is not easily incorporated within a model of society which rests upon communication for cohesive operation. Re-education (emotionally termed 'brain-washing'), nationalism, guided democracy and strong leadership, are all aspects of social organization which can reasonably be explained in communication terms in a society which seeks ultimately to avoid power struggles. Equally, of course, re-education, propaganda and commitment to an ideology, and the severing of perception and avoidance of feed-back, can be demonstrated by reference to a communications model to be destructive of adjustment processes, and to threaten the integration of society. There is here a wide field of research and study which has not been sufficiently cultivated due to re-occupation with orthodox power explanations of social organization.

(vi) *Associative Arrangements*

The avoidance of alignments is merely the negative aspect of nonalignment; alignments are regarded as disassociative, capable of creating barriers and of separating States. Positively nonalignment favours associative regional and functional arrangements. It is not accidental that the post-war period has been characterized by the growth of regional and functional international organization.[1] Both nonalignment and this type

[1] See in particular Claude, *Swords into Plowshares*.

of organization are relevant to the political and strategic circumstances of the nuclear and communications age.

The approach of nonalignment is basically non-discriminatory; alliances and economic blocs are a form of discrimination, and independent judgement on issues as they arise is an exercise of non-discrimination. Non-discrimination in the pursuit of national objectives is perhaps the most appropriate description of nonalignment. Referring again to the communications model, the screening and priority given input stimuli and their use in decision-making is related directly to interpretations of national interest, and not directly to ideology, power, moral judgements or other forms of discriminatory screening which render a communication system less efficient in making decisions designed to further the national interest.

Here one must observe the close relationship between nonalignment and the concept to which reference has already been made, that of 'nationalist universalism'. Nonalignment employs basically the same concepts. Nonalignment is a theory or policy which is applicable to any society, primitive or mature, armed or unarmed. It focuses attention upon aspects of social organization never satisfactorily explained by power. It was a philosophic approach before atomic weapons were added to the military power of nations, and expounded first in a complicated social environment in which a class and caste structure was maintained on a basis of rights and obligations, and which did not rest upon the exercise of power.

PART VI
THE EVOLVING SYSTEM

20

THE EVOLVING SYSTEM

In Part II, some of the inadequacies of orthodox theory and practice were examined; in Part III, attention was drawn to altered features in the world environment which have accentuated these inadequacies; in Part IV we were concerned with the models needed to take into account these altered circumstances, including certain evidence of an evolving world community; and in Part V, nonalignment was described as an emerging system which gave some insight into the behaviour of States generally.

In this sixth part the intention is to describe the international system which appears to be evolving, and to describe it in terms of the models that have been introduced. At the outset, in a review of trends in theory, it was suggested that there has been in recent years a shift of interest from descriptions of non-war situations, such as balance-of-power and collective security, to a consideration of a condition of peace which requires no enforcement support. In the current international system there are both aspects: power politics as a theory and description of international relations has drawn attention to the former. The models and terminology employed in this study are designed to bring into focus those aspects of international society which are relevant to self-supporting stability or a condition of peace.

I. THE REQUIREMENTS OF POLITICAL REALISM

In describing the evolving system (especially when drawing attention to aspects which relate to a condition of peace and may for this reason smack of idealism), it is only those trends which are historically in evidence that can be regarded as relevant. No system, however positive in the sense that it might be designed to secure a non-war or a peace condition, can be imposed or organized on a universal scale; the most ingenious devices and idealistic policies are not necessarily acceptable or politically practical. The characteristic which distinguishes the politically practical from the impractical is not the importance or the magnitude of the objective, but the procedures which are required to attain it; an unimportant improvement in international relations may be much more difficult to achieve if it depends upon procedures of negotiation and agreement which pre-suppose good-will and the absence of acute tensions, than a far-reaching revolution in international relations which can be brought about by no more than the pursuit of national interest by States acting independently. In a condition of acute power rivalry, the attainment of any agreed objective is impractical if agreements and co-operative planning are required. This has been demonstrated in the case of disarmament negotiations— the success of which could reasonably be regarded as vital—in which it has been found impossible to reach even a preliminary stage of agreement. A change in the system of international relations evolves as the nuclear deterrent itself developed, through the unilateral and unco-ordinated policies of the States within it, and of the Great Powers in particular.

Furthermore, in the absence of agreements and co-operative planning, no system can replace another, and no system can evolve into another, unless the new one first develops alongside, becomes part of, and finally dominates the existing one. If a new system evolves in the existing Cold War pattern of strategic and political relationships, it must initially be an addition relevant to, and compatible with, the existing system of nuclear deterrence. Put in different words, an altered system must develop out of existing structures, and cannot be superimposed by negotiation of agreements.

Furthermore, the evolution of a system cannot be by supranational planning or by pressure. Experience is that sovereign States, and especially major rivals in a power conflict, will accept only those controls on their freedom of action which are objectively imposed, that is, imposed by environmental factors, and not by particular nations, by organized groups of nations, or even by an international organization. It is this consideration which destroys the practicability of most proposals put forward for world government, or systems involving the supervision by a super-State.

These conditions are all difficult ones to meet. When they are met it is by accident rather than by design; they are the types of conditions which can be attributed only to those evolutionary changes which take place in social organization. The nuclear deterrent does not provide a condition of peace; but it does provide a good example of a system which developed as an emergent, an unplanned development consequent upon the invention and possession of nuclear weapons by both parties to the Cold War. It has subsequently deliberately been improved upon by devices such as the 'hot line'. It is by the discernment of controls and trends as they are emerging, by fostering and by improving them, that the most effective contribution can be made to a developing social or political organization.

Nonalignment also has these characteristics of a politically viable international system which has developed out of the circumstances of the time. It appeared spontaneously as an international institution, and, after initial rejection by other Powers, won acceptance. No negotiation or formal agreement brought it about and none are required for its extension. Unlike the nuclear deterrent it has no enforcement capability; it is relevant to a condition of peace. It provides an environment in which restraints on Great Powers arising from it cannot be attributed to a particular State or to the deliberate decisions of any group of States.

Nuclear deterrents and nonalignments are but two of the institutions which have—unexpectedly—evolved since World War II. It is they which dominate international society, and are primarily responsible for its present structure. Regionalism, functionalism, sub-systems of power balances, also help to determine this structure, some contributing to non-war stability, some to a condition of peace, but all being integral features of the system. If political realism is meaningful, it refers to policies which are relative to real conditions, and not to the imagery of policy makers.

In the approach here adopted the importance of power in world politics is not in question; the value to be placed on power may or may not be as overwhelmingly important as power theorists assert. The approach is designed to enable assessments of all influences including power, and to describe how they operate to bring about the situations with which we are familiar.

The purpose of studies of International Relations is to evolve general theories which suggest policies by which peace and security may be achieved. A power approach is relevant to policies seeking security in non-war conditions; in a sense a study of power politics is one limited to this particular objective. If it is held that non-war conditions are as much as we can reasonably hope to achieve, then the devices of power politics are those upon which a 'realist' should concentrate. There is reason to believe, however, first, that policies of power politics are ultimately destructive of security, and second, that they are self-creating in that they create the conditions which demand them.

Hence, without arguing against the realism of power, the existence of force, the willingness of States to risk force, non-passive responses to change and other features of power politics and power politics in disguise, and without excluding them from consideration, we have employed a model which nevertheless does not exclude consideration of features of the international system which contribute to a condition of peace.

II. A CONDITION OF PEACE

A system in a condition of peace—as distinct from the absence of war—is one in which States compete without experiencing the need to engage in competitive armament, one in which continued stability is ensured by means of continuous and smooth change and adjustment to change within the system, and one which ultimately makes existing major weapons irrelevant to the conditions it establishes. It is one which does not rest upon sanctions, but is self-supporting through the interests and policies of each member.

There have always been some features of international society which were positive in the sense that they contributed to such a condition of peace; but their significance has not been sufficient even to attract the attention of observers, and the persistence of power concepts and non-war structures is evidence of this. The international system which is evolving under pressure of nuclear strategy and world consensus does however contain features which attract attention to a condition of peace. Acknowledgment of the right of sovereign independence, respect for territoriality, observance of non-discrimination in most-favoured-nation treatment, widespread international organization designed to improve living conditions, provision of a world forum, and altering environmental conditions in the fields of communications and education have contributed to the foundations of an egalitarian international system. Non-war devices, such as collective security under the Security Council, were deliberately introduced; while they have faded into insignificance, other controls, nuclear and political, have emerged and led to a system of relationship never envisaged at San Francisco in 1945.

It will have been observed that the policies being forced upon nuclear States by reason of nuclear strategy (as described in Part III), and the policies of nonalignment, are both directed toward the exercise of sovereign independence, and the avoidance of involvement in the political affairs of other States. The interests of all States are becoming more and more in the direction of independent defence policies, the avoidance of blocs and alliances which limit their freedom of action, and which could involve them in a nuclear war of no direct concern to them. The deterrent system, by reason of its inherent defects and complications, imposes on nuclear Powers certain rules, the essential one of which, in the words of Walter Lippmann, is that 'the paramount rule of policy in this age is that, as between nuclear Powers, there can be no important change in the *status quo* by the threat of force or by the use of force'.[1] The basic tenet of nonalignment is similar: no nation by reason of its power may interfere in the internal affairs of another nation, no matter what the possible loss in strategic interests; internal political developments must be allowed to run their course, and no nation may underwrite the internal position of any other nation. The nonaligned nations merely generalize and extend the principles which nuclear Powers find by experience that they must observe.

This interplay and complementary existence of the two systems is of greater significance in world affairs than could be deduced from an explanation of nonalignment in the terms of power politics such as are used to explain neutrality. Far from nonalignment being the creature of the bi-polarized conflict, it has contributed to the stability of the relations of the thermonuclear States by removing areas from their competition, by contributing to political restraints exercised upon them, and by

[1] W. Lippmann, *The New Diplomacy of the Nuclear Age*. Speech delivered to the Anglo-American Press Association, Paris, 1962.

creating a system of relationships outside alliances into which aligned States can enter. In short, nonalignment could be a relevant response not only for small nations, but in one form or another also for others whose nuclear capability makes it vital that there should be no involvements in situations which are not vital to them.

Sub-systems of nuclear deterrence, and the further extension of the system of nonalignment, are likely to develop side-by-side and to overlap. Nonalignment has extended so far by reason of the creation of new States or by reason of internal revolutions within old States; and the possibilities of these developments are not yet exhausted. It has as yet made little progress in breaking into alliances, though some possibilities exist in Latin America, in the Middle East, and perhaps in Eastern Europe. It is likely to extend even to middle Powers such as France, Britain and China once they face realistically the alternatives of independent nuclear deterrence, on the one hand, and on the other, a non-voting membership of an alliance with a thermonuclear Power. Both the circumstances in which it developed and its nature give strong support to the view that nonalignment was a response to circumstances, a relevant development, a growth as spontaneous and as inevitable in the circumstances as was the emergence of the system of deterrence once both Great Powers possessed nuclear weapons. As such it can continue to develop alongside the nuclear system, gradually including within its scope more and more countries, large and small, and offering an alternative system by becoming a dominant feature of international politics.

III. OBSERVANCE OF SOVEREIGN INDEPENDENCE

In order that the rule of non-interference may realistically be applied inside and outside Great Power relationships, it is necessary that non-military as well as military means of interference be eliminated, and this includes the elimination of all forms of economic and political pressures, subversion and discrimination. The main responsibility for the internal stability for a nation rests finally with that nation, and it is for it to determine what is interference, and to deal with it accordingly. Calvocoressi has observed that 'the principal Powers have found themselves compelled to compete for the favour of third parties, as the weight of the uncommitted has grown in international politics and the domination of the giants has been neutralized by their mutual frustration. And it is not possible to get this favour by interfering in other peoples' affairs. Force in international politics has become to some extent self-defeating.'[1] In this context Lippmann has called for 'more modest estimates of what the West can do and far greater imagination in shaping foreign policies'.[2] Kaplan summarizes, 'The uncommitted nations have an interest in supporting the established norms concerning non-interfering in internal affairs in order to protect their independence; and the blocs, in order to obtain the support of the uncommitted nations, at least have to act circumspectly with respect to these norms'.[3]

Nonalignment as the policy of a nation is primarily the avoidance of involvement in any power bloc, either in military, in political or in economic affairs. It has, therefore, a basic element of non-discrimination in the treatment of parties to the Cold War. This is not a neutral attitude; in all activities, including direct intervention into the affairs of the Great Powers, the nonaligned nations in theory at least act non-discriminatorily, applying the same judgements and tests to both sides, pursuing their relations with both sides on the same basis. It is this non-discrimination which led to the unintended effect of creating a system of relationships. It commenced in relation to the Great Powers, but it was soon apparent that the same attitude was relevant to situations outside the Cold War, and to all relationships.

If nonalignment policies were to be generalized so as to have an application outside the specific Cold War conflict, and were to be given general application in all relationships, then there would be an approximation to the theoretical ideal of basing international relations on complete non-discrimination. As such nonalignment is of interest in academic studies concerned with the theory of peaceful International Relations. In their pure form, as distinct from their policy application, neutrality, the neutralism described by Marcus, the neo-neutrality described by Cohn, nonalignment and non-discrimination represent stages in world organization, commencing with a world structure

[1] P. Calvocoressi, *World Order and New States*, 1962, p. 25.
[2] K. W. Thompson, p. 47.
[3] Kaplan, p. 252.

dominated by power rivalries in which power balances and a war were the instruments of national policy, and leading to a Utopian condition of peaceful relations created and made stable by nothing outside the policies of sovereign States. It is this continuum which is of special interest in the twentieth-century nuclear age. A cybernetic model is an appropriate one for its initial study; the relations between States which avoid alliances, which have no means other than decision-making and steering to preserve their interests in their relations with Great Powers, provide a system which can be idealized so as to be useful as an analytical model. Acquaintance with the idealized model could also, obviously, help decision-making in nonaligned States in the conduct of their policies.

IV. DIPLOMACY

The evolving international system, and the communications aspect of it, is well exemplified by twentieth-century changes in diplomacy. In the traditional view, and one expounded by Morgenthau, the objectives of diplomacy are defined in terms of national interest, and are supported by power.[1] The area of discretion is limited to the possibilities of sacrifice of worthless rights for real advantage. Negotiation from strength was the aim. A 'good', that is, successful, diplomat was one who was aware of the view-point of others, not so as to accommodate them, but so as to frustrate them. Diplomatic victory was the achievement of a goal by skilful bargaining supported by power, or alternatively, the skilful employment of the threat of power. Diplomacy was rather narrowly defined as symbolic, legal or political representation of one State at the courts of another.

It is acknowledged that this form of diplomacy has now largely vanished, and the reasons given for 'the decline in diplomacy' is the introduction of new forms of communication, and greater ease of travel which decreases the value of local representation and increases the importance of diplomacy at a high political level and at centres such as the United Nations.[2]

This, however, is an over-simplification—and one which is inevitable in a power approach. For practical purposes, modern diplomacy is now far more, and not less important in relations between States; it includes the total process of decision-making.

---

[1] Morgenthau, *Politics among Nations*, 1960, Part Ten.   [2] *Ibid.*

In a power-model—and perhaps in past centuries—diplomacy was the means by which decisions already taken were implemented. In the twentieth century decision-making is a process which is not separable from the feed-back of negotiation, which is usually taking place simultaneously at very many centres. A decision over the future of Berlin, or a particular crisis situation in respect of Berlin, is tied up with negotiation in a number of capitals, at the United Nations, and with information being received from a number of other capitals where leaders are likely to react. The operative decisions tend to follow, and not to precede negotiation. While foreign-offices are still given added prestige by physical security precautions, in practice diplomacy is in this sense open; in so far as there are secrets this is largely because governments fear their own oppositions and public opinion, and wish to avoid the inflexibility in negotiation which a preliminary declaration of policy might induce.

The efficient diplomat in a power system is one who has a healthy scorn for the government and people of the State to which he is accredited, and who is not diverted from the pursuit of his nation's goals; in this system many a diplomat who understands well the others' view point, has been recalled. In a communications system the diplomat at a post or in the foreign office who understands the responses of foreign governments, who can anticipate their responses, who can judge the subjective estimation of just claims, is valuable in supplying the feed-back which leads to altered national goals and policies. The diplomat who pursues faithfully his instructions, and does not feed-back likely responses, or the foreign office official or minister who is not emotionally or intellectually capable of interpreting feed-back and changing goals, is capable of bringing about a breakdown in communication, and policy will be directed toward goals attainable only by force.

In a power system the glamorous spy has a vital function; on the one hand information about policies and responses must be secret, and on the other the intent of the enemy or potential enemy must be known so as to frustrate his designs. In the communications system, espionage is so important that it becomes an integral part of the system, the glamorous spy giving place to attachés and others who seek out and give information and make sure the enemy or potential enemy does not have designs based upon ignorance. It is now generally

agreed between East and West that the Soviet secrecy in the late
'fifties over their missile programme led to a United States
assumption that there was a missile gap, and led the United
States unnecessarily into an extensive military programme.
Mystery over the Australian–British rocket range has led to spy
charges; and it could lead to Soviet defence responses in that
area which might not occur if the facts were known. In a
communication-based model, espionage is valuable; in practice
it could give place to organized information services once there
is a full appreciation of the vital necessity to supply information
to other States.

In a power system the strongest diplomatic missions are
accredited to friendly States, those with which there are
alliances, and the least experienced are accredited to others.
The British Commonwealth countries and the United States send
strong missions to the capitals of each other. They are poorly
represented in the Socialist countries. Where there is a high
level of tension there is withdrawal or 'non-recognition' of the
government. In a communication-based system, the strongest
missions are accredited to States with which relations are
strained, or at centres such as the United Nations where there
are opportunities for negotiation with all States.

It is clear that the power or the communication approach is
likely to depend not merely upon the circumstances of the day,
but upon personalities, attitudes, and abilities to approach other
governments and peoples without racial, cultural or ideological
inhibitions. If one assumes the power model to be relevant
analogy, there will be one kind of approach to relations between
States, and if one assumes the communications model to be
relevant analogy, there will be another; in each case the
approach is to a degree self-fulfilling. Closed diplomacy
invites suspicion, espionage and aggressive policies, and open
diplomacy established communication. This is no new observation; what is novel is the realization that the ultimate employment of power in war cannot achieve national goals, and the
realization therefore that the power-politics approach to
negotiation may lead to threats which are not credible.
Consequently negotiation on this power basis fails.

However, it is an evolving system rather than any altered
personal approach which has altered diplomacy. Regional and
functional organizations, many of which are highly technical,

have spread the decision-making function within each State. A foreign office usually claims final policy responsibility, but there are today few departments of government not concerned with international organization: health, agriculture, tele-communications, shipping, science, trade, all enter into foreign policy. It is no longer possible to determine policy and relation-ships on a political—far less a power—basis. Disease knows no political boundaries, and no nation can sensibly be excluded from an international health scheme. There is developing a wide area of international co-operation on a specialized, technical and non-political basis, and the relationship thus established provides part of the network of information which is involved in decision-making. The test-ban agreement was greatly assisted by negotiation or exchanges of view-points between scientists both informally and officially. In none of these technical negotiations is power important; nations small and large co-operate on a basis of equality, an equality which is in practice undeniable when health, transport and such matters are the subject of international co-operation.

Furthermore, to achieve a 'diplomatic victory' by power, or even by subtlety, is of no great value if, as a result, a nationalist sentiment has been aroused through the accompanying diplo-matic defeat. The art of diplomacy is that of making the greatest possible use of all information obtainable, and therefore rests, not upon power, but upon the efficiency of the information and communication system that the State possesses. The United States relations with China, United States policy in Vietnam, British policy in Suez, United States attitudes to Cuba and responses to information coming from Latin America, Soviet policy in Hungary, and earlier failures in relation to Yugoslavia—all these were failings due to the employment of power and disregard for facts. World War I has been regarded by some scholars as inevitable once the break-down in commun-ication occurred, but avoidable had each government been fully informed of all relevant information regarding the intentions and responses of others. Diplomacy as an instrument of power to carry out a decision is different in kind from diplomacy as a means toward decision-making. Both are employed and probably always will be; but it is being politically unrealistic to assume that diplomacy is always an instrument of power. In the evolving nuclear international system it is only exceptionally such an instrument. Its use as an instrument of power is an open confession, either that the decision-making process has been affected by domestic pressures, ideological commitments, break-downs in information and interpretation services, or that the State is not capable of alteration in goals and adjustment to change and has no option but to employ force. Power diplomacy forces upon another State an intolerable option, and reflects an inability to adapt to circumstances; communications diplomacy is designed never to create an intolerable option, and reflects an ability to balance national interests, including interests in avoiding conflict. Neither is possible in an absolute form; the existence together of the two types of diplomacy indicate the two types of relationship which exist simultaneously between States, those based upon power and those based upon communication. Their co-existence is a competitive one, and the use of power only is no longer either politically or militarily efficient.

V. PRESTIGE AND POWER

Morgenthau regards prestige as being worthy of special attention in his power approach to international politics. The image a State has of another is an image of its power, and according to Morgenthau displays of power, and pomp and ceremony are an important part of power politics.[1]

From our point of view, prestige policy is not important when it is merely a means of convincing other States of one's power, for deceptions of this nature are not for long possible. Prestige is of significance when it contributes to irrationality in decision-making in relation to nuclear strategy. The Soviet Union gave the government of Cuba certain undertakings in respect of security from United States attack, and later was required to implement these. The crisis which followed in 1962 was one which involved the prestige of the Soviet Union in the eyes of Asia, Africa and Latin America. The United States has given certain undertakings in respect of the security of West Berlin, and if any threat to that security were perceived, the United States would be faced with a prestige policy decision. In neither case would it be rational to engage in nuclear warfare, even

---

[1] Morgenthau, *Politics among Nations*, 1960, Chapter 6.

limited nuclear warfare; but in both cases nuclear warfare could be brought about by prestige policy.

While thermonuclear States are aware of their own vital interests in avoiding confronting each other in situations not vital to their interests, this is not to say that they are aware of avoiding prestige policies which could in the future lead to such confrontation. The United States Government's position in South Vietnam in 1963-4 was a prestige one, involving both its domestic and international status; it was one of long-standing, making withdrawal difficult. Presumably, care would be taken in the future not to become involved in a situation of this kind. However, the interplay of politics at the domestic and international level is such in all States as to make highly probable the repetition of such situations. It is in this sense that ideological arguments, popular strategic fears, and pressures of military and industrial groups are relevant to foreign policy.

To those who were intimately associated with the development of weapons of mass destruction, the atomic bomb represented a discontinuity in relations between States; the literature of post-war protest reflected this. In the perspective of International Relations, the thermonuclear weapon and means of its delivery are related to the consequences of conflict, not to its sources. Realization of these consequences has hastened already existing trends toward independence in the policies of States, but the danger of war is not thereby removed. The rationality of limited nuclear warfare has already been argued;[1] prestige diplomacy and policy remain a likely cause of such warfare. It is the assessment of prestige values that is the incalculable factor in strategic policy. If the prestige policy is not credible to others, deterrence may not operate, and conflict could ensue. Accurate assessment of prestige policy requires accurate assessment of public opinion, leadership and other influences on the decision-making process, and this is rarely possible. It would seem that if a prestige policy is required for domestic reasons, its international significance needs to be communicated to other States. An encouraging feature of world politics is the growing realization that it is important to communicate accurate information about policies, and interpretation of policy statements, rather than to mislead and endeavour to disguise intentions. Responsible governments

[1] See pp. 153 ff. above.

today are inclined to ensure that statements made for domestic consumption are re-interpreted for foreign consumption. Even the realization that this is important is an indication of an increasing understanding of the way the international system functions.

VI. SMALL WARS AND PEACE-KEEPING

We have so far observed those trends within the evolving international system which relate to a condition of peace; they are a consequence of nuclear strategy and world consensus. They affect primarily the thermonuclear and major Powers. The world system, however, includes a large number of States whose relations with each other are not subject to overwhelming strategic restraints, and less and less subject to them the more the more powerful nations contract out of non-vital obligations. Furthermore, they are States facing problems which are a legacy of the past, and which are likely to be resolved only after political and military conflict.

The terms 'nation' and 'State' have been used almost interchangeably and for purposes of variation; the difference is important in this context. More exactly, the term 'nation' refers to groups of peoples with common languages and cultures, or peoples who are unified for some other reason. The term 'State' refers more to the existence of a government, as distinct from the peoples governed. It is possible, therefore, for a State to include a number of national groups, for a national group to extend beyond the boundaries of a State and to include more than one State, and thirdly, for States and nations to overlap geographically without any common boundaries whatsoever. In Africa and Asia it is only rarely that the boundaries of a nation and a State coincide, and when they do it is frequently not because of common culture or language but merely because of the exercise over a long period of the powers of the colonial authority upon the peoples under its jurisdiction. In the existing situation it is only rarely that States represent national groups. In this sense it is confusing to speak of nationalism in relation to support for State Governments, and more usually the nationalism is related to an ethnic group or to Africa as a whole.

In these circumstances, one would expect to find tensions

existing between the national group and the State, between nationalism and the objectives of the State. The primary aim of the State would be to create a nation within its boundaries; but on the other hand, the nationalism of the groups might seek either the creation of independent States or amalgamation with other States. As yet sociologists have had little to say as to the factors which produce the nation, though they can point to some evidence regarding relationships between groups, and the integration which takes place between similar peoples. While it would be going too far to suggest that peaceful relations will exist only when, by one means or another, the boundaries of the State and the boundaries of the nation coincide, clearly nationalism in this sense has an important bearing upon principles of self-determination. The conflict between nation and State throws some light upon the use by the State of self-determination in some cases, and the avoidance of this principle in others.

Lucy Mair has observed

. . . of the new African States only the two smallest, Rwanda and Burundi, were political units in the period before colonial rule; the only other examples, as it happens, are territories which at the time of writing are not yet independent—Swaziland and Basutoland, each of which recognizes a single paramount chief. In all the others there are numbers of peoples speaking different languages, and very commonly those who do have a common language are divided into groups which a century ago were politically autonomous[1]

Boundaries, race, experiments with administrative systems, are bound to lead to numerous and serious conflicts in Asia and Africa. No world authority or super-Power can impose stability, nor would it be in the interests of the peoples concerned, for it is change which is required. The States of Asia and Africa are evolving their own means of settlement of disputes. The continuing economic and strategic interests of major Powers hamper them in their endeavours, and accompanying regional disputes will be increased resistance to all forms of Western influence.

The peace-keeping function of the United Nations was not taken seriously once it was found that Member States would not make the necessary agreements with the Security Council for

[1] L. Mair, *New Nations*, 1963, p. 96.

the allocation of forces. Furthermore, there was prejudice against the idea that a Security Council decision against a small State could be enforced while a veto protected from any enforcement action those States which are the main danger to world peace. However, the idea of a United Nations peace-keeping force, invited to act by the parties to a dispute, has an attraction in the circumstances in which new and developing States find themselves.

The United Nations has now had some experience in its police or peace-keeping role in which it aims to hold the ring while disputes are settled. Its success is limited, and no clear principles seem to have been agreed. The objectives of United Nations intervention are firstly to remove the possibility of outside intervention, especially to avoid a local situation becoming a Cold War one, and secondly to facilitate agreement between disputing parties. In respect of the latter, its objectives are cease-fire, mediation and supervision of a settlement until stability is reached.

Two courses are open. The United Nations can be a force in the background to prevent any fighting that might occur, and to ensure the continuation of administration and legal forms unless changed by agreement. Alternatively, it can insist as a prior condition of intervention and include in its directive to its Commanding Officer, the disarming of all factions except legitimate police forces. The first course ensures a power solution to the dispute, with the United Nations intervening frequently after fighting commences, any minorities being at a disadvantage. The second course may be more prolonged but ensures no solution other than one agreed between the factions. At the time of writing, the United Nations is involved in Cyprus; the Commander may not disarm the two factions. No peaceful solution is in prospect.

Vietnam, Korea, Germany are examples of divided peoples not likely to resolve their differences while each side is supported by other Powers. In each case United Nations peace-keeping would enable settlement, provided there was disarmament in the first instance. The barrier to such intervention is the reluctance of the Great Powers interested to allow settlement by this procedure.

It is to be noted that this peace-keeping or police function of the United Nations does not imply enforcement or collective security. The action is taken under Articles of the Charter dealing with peaceful settlement of disputes. Intervention is by consent, and is not concerned with the nature of settlement, which is entirely a matter for the parties concerned, with the help possibly of mediation by the United Nations or another agent.

VII. EVOLVING FOREIGN POLICIES

Conflicts of interest are both inevitable and desirable; resolving them by means which are not destructive of life and valued property is the central problem of social organization civilized Man has faced. We have argued here that war between States cannot be prevented by the creation of supra-national bodies, by agreements collectively to prevent the use of force; the only games that States are able to play—however much their leaders and peoples may desire to enter others—are those which occur spontaneously in their relationships, and which are relevant to their environment. By understanding these, the nature of the game, and the rules which are observed, the Political Scientist and the Statesman may from time to time be able to suggest and effect increased orderliness, may be able to foresee the need to alter rules and penalties before the game itself is brought to an end, and even to suggest new games which can be played simultaneously to which a smooth transfer can be made in due course.

For this reason, it is the evolving system which is of interest— it is the future and not the past which is of concern. It is prediction, and not wisdom after the event which is of value, and which is the ultimate test of science.

In this chapter it has been observed that nuclear deterrence and nonalignment are two important emergent features of world society. The appearance of each was initially abhorrent to many observers—nonalignment was once described as 'immoral'. For the Political Scientist, as for the Historian, they are nothing other than phases in an evolving world society, to be understood, so that policies can adjust to them, and if possible adjust them. There is reason to believe that of these two features nonalignment, which reflects the historically persistent desire of men to be independent, may be more stable than nuclear deterrence, which is threatened by the historically persistent fear of men of loss of independence through the superior power of others. The two games have independence as the goal, the one an independence that is mutual by definition, and can therefore be attained by all, and the other an independence which if finally attained by one is a threat to all others.

The evolving system is the merging of the two, deterrence remaining as a back-stop, a reserve defence against any opponent, and nondiscrimination or nonalignment being the forward game in which all players have an equal role, if not an equal ability.

Evidence that this is the trend is in the altering nature of diplomacy, and more generally in the more far-sighted approach to decision-making which has been forced upon major States by the political and strategic circumstances of the twentieth century. However, while the great and powerful industrial States have no longer to face conflict of interest over competition in acquisition of new resources, and in exploitation of un-developed areas, the smaller States are in the throes of consolida-tion and adjustment after centuries of overlordship. It is they which face the greater, if not the more dangerous, national situations.

This is a conclusion arrived at by analysing strategic and political trends, and by reference to behavioural aspects of relations between States; these are conclusions based on deduc-tive reasoning. Traditionally International Relations has been inductive, and the study of the foreign policies of States has been an important part of it. A study of recent trends in the policies of the United States, the Soviet Union and the major States, on the one hand, and of the new States of Africa and Asia, on the other, should lead to the same conclusions. The interplay of deterrence and nonalignment should be in evidence in each case.

Foreign policy can be predicted in more detail than merely the interplay of deterrence and independence, and it is in this way that more insight into the evolving system can be obtained. If foreign policy is regarded as the pursuit of national interest by promoting or resisting change and adjusting to change, then the presence or absence of certain conditions will determine policy. For example, the type of economy, whether planned or unplanned, welfare or profit oriented, the level of employment, and the machinery for internal adjustment to change are governing factors. The type of political institutions are also important, whether pursuit of national interest as perceived dominates sectional interests (this could determine, for example, attitudes toward arms control proposals), whether internal instability requires the distraction of foreign excursions or the requested intervention of other States. The degree of dependence upon foreign markets and sources of raw materials could determine to some degree the economic and political bargaining position of States. The level of development of the economy influences dependence on aid and foreign capital, and the level of arms reflects ability and willingness to adjust to altered circumstances. The likely support from others through alliances and common regional ties influences willingness to accommodate and ability to resist adjustment to new conditions. The social system, the means of 'mass' propaganda, the educational system, have a bearing upon change and adjustment to change. History and culture influence attitudes toward law, toward imperialism, and toward race.

The evolving international system is characteristized by an increased dependence upon all these national factors—the ability of a State to adjust to altering conditions—and a decreasing dependence upon international structures such as alliances and collective security designed to maintain the system against change. The foreign policy of States is in the twentieth century an important study, not as part of history or as a means of predicting on the basis of past performance, but as the basis of an analysis of the world system of Sovereign States to ascertain to what extent it is capable of meeting the demands of peaceful change.

21

THEORY AND POLICIES

Policies of power politics are policies of escape from negotiation, and particularly from adjustment. The definition commonly given to power, the ability to ensure other parties adopt certain policies, implies a refusal to adopt theirs, to negotiate compromises, or to adjust to theirs. In power politics what cannot be obtained by reference to morality, law and political consensus is obtained by power where power is available.

Under pressure of nuclear strategy and world consensus even great Powers can less frequently and less easily adopt this escape, and are forced to consider negotiation and adjustment. The degree to which policies and political attitudes have changed since 1945 is in any judgement remarkable—acceptance of claims to independence, and adjustment to altered institutions in other States. Governments give indications that they understand that there are reasons to doubt the value of alliances to peace and security, the wisdom of the policy of not recognizing States on grounds of their ideology or policies, the usefulness of discriminatory treatment of States thought to be hostile, the use of restraints on travel and communications, the benefits of certain types of propaganda that distort decision-making processes, and generally the pay-off thought previously to be obtained from policies that have been regarded as traditional national policies of power politics. At least some doubt is entertained also regarding the international aspects of national power politics, collective security and international organization designed to exercise enforcement powers, and the other traditional international procedures for maintaining peace and security. Indeed, decision-makers in States with experience in international affairs have an understanding of the adjustment in foreign policies required now that power-policies cannot be pursued with certainty, for example, increased and improved, and not decreased and impaired processes of communication, in situations of increased tension. They have had experience showing that ineffective use of influence is self-defeating; aid which discriminates is likely to produce more enemies than friends, power leadership is likely to weaken alliances, the export of ideologies and of political and economic institutions is likely to produce resistance to the ideas and structures it is intended to spread.

I. IMPACT ON NATIONAL POLICIES

The full impact of the altered strategic and political environment is, however, not perceived even yet. Even when perceived and acknowledged intellectually, it will continue to be ignored politically for as long as circumstances permit—and probably even to a point of fatal consequences—because it goes to the roots of established society.

Foreign and strategic policies are to promote and to protect national interests. These national interests relate to properties held by nationals overseas, investments nationally which compete with foreign investments, the sale and purchase of goods under conditions which benefit the economy, the economic institutions on which the economy rests, the distribution of income to be maintained, the balance between agriculture and industry thought to be desirable, the political and social institutions to which value is attached, security, prestige, independence, and, in developing States, the acquisition and accumulation of capital, terms of trade, and freedom from any form of foreign influence which would prejudice economic and political development.

All of these national interests are affected by a continuous flow of events both within and outside the State. They may be promoted and protected by acts regarded as domestic, and others regarded as foreign. In fact, no line divides the two; a subsidy to agriculture affects directly the interests of agricultural producers in other States. In the pursuit of national interest the means adopted understandably tend to place the greatest burden of adjustment on those outside the boundaries of the State. A device in the days of colonialism was to reserve the markets of colonial areas for the exports of the colonial Power, a device which in the 'thirties threw the burden of adjustment of the British textile industry on to Japan. The British Commonwealth reserved the markets of each other for a mutual benefit by a system of preferences. Tariffs, quotas and embargoes are other examples of government domestic intervention to make adjustment within an economy unnecessary, or less politically difficult to manage.

These are examples from economics and commerce. Of more significance frequently are similar procedures which touch upon social and cultural adjustments. Censorship and repressive legislation are means of avoiding adaptation at a national level to changes taking place elsewhere. Educational systems and vehicles of mass propaganda can give some protection against foreign influence by creating false images of competing systems, and ultimately this is effective in reducing cultural and commercial competition.

The traditional role of government in the power-model is to accept power-input (the resources made available to it by the community), and to allocate power-output in ways best calculated to further national interest. The allocation of power-output is related to the defence of power-input. In the modern State, the government has more and more intervened in the economic and political life of the community, not merely to protect existing power-input, but also to increase it. Armaments and legislation to ensure political conformity, are some of the processes. Even intervention by the Federal Government in the United States into racial disputes within States was justified on the grounds that otherwise the foreign negotiating power of the United States would be impaired.

Yet a role of government in the nuclear age, and the role in the communications model, is to ensure the least imcompatibility between the interests of the community, and the interests of other States as perceived by them. This involves negotiation and bargaining whenever possible, and attempts to persuade other States that their interests lie in certain directions; basically, however, the government is required to ensure internal adjustment to changes taking place in other States. This requires, in many instances, a reversal of traditional policy— far from making change unnecessary, the government of a State is required to facilitate change and adjustment to change as part of the endeavour to attain peace and security.

Thus it is that foreign policy in the twentieth century has become turned inward; peace and security is a function of domestic policies and not of international structures. This is no new observation. Marxists have argued that peace will be secure when all States are communist States, and the Western democratic leaders argue that the cause of peace will be promoted by all States adopting Western political institutions. The agreed proposition is that peace and security are a function of *domestic* pressures and policies. The precise nature of the way in which these pressures and policies must be re-directed has been far from clear; the cybernetic model helps to make it clear. The State, whether communist or free-enterprise, is required, if the goal of peace and security is to be achieved, to intervene constructively and not restrictively, that is, to facilitate adjustment to change, and not to afford protection against it.

Thus it is that in the nuclear age governments have less opportunity to avoid their universal responsibilities, and are forced to face the unpleasant task of ordering the national life of their peoples to conform with the requirements of a changing international environment. Governments are required, in the interests of peace and security, to contract out of the traditional role of government in the modern State—protection of interests threatened by foreign changes—and actively to engage in promoting adjustment. This is the political impact of nuclear strategy and world consensus—an impact which democratic States in particular will find difficult to accept, for in democratic States sectional interests often have sufficient political influence to offset national interests.

We already have some understanding of the need for economic adjustment. The *laissez-faire* school of the nineteenth century, and modern economic theory generally, point to the need to weigh short-term welfare against values attaching to prestige, nationalism, defence, industrial-cultural development and other non-economic objectives. One of the most significant international developments, after the twenty years crisis between the two wars, was a mature recognition of the need to separate commercial policy from political ambitions. Economic non-discrimination is now a universally accepted principle; the exceptions permitted by GATT for the defence of industries against change must be first argued and justified. That there are many exceptions made is undeniable; but undeniable also is the acceptance in principle of non-discrimination and of orderly alterations in tariff policies designed not to damage other economies.

Adjustment in political and social thought and institutions, on the other hand, is the central problem yet to be tackled. There is no political GATT to control political discrimination, nor is there any felt need for one. On the contrary, the preservation of political institutions has been featured as the main purpose of the Cold War. One means is to discriminate strategically and politically, and economically in so far as this is possible, in favour of States with approved institutions, and against those possessing the institutions of the opposing party. Interference in the political life of other States has been an important aspect of Cold War diplomacy and strategy. The concept of 'co-existence' is an acknowledgment that commercial competition can be handled without political friction; but it implies also that outside this contact, States with different systems merely exist side-by-side with the least possible inter-play of ideas.

The demands made upon sovereign States in a world society cannot, in the nuclear-world consensus era, be avoided by reliance upon national power, alliances or international institutions; a world society, whether it comprises independent sovereign States or is a unified world community, is integrated and harmonious only to the extent that each of its parts is adapting to the requirements of the whole. The issue, Sovereign States or World Government, side-steps the basic problem; the pressing issue is whether localities—be they States or other organized groups—acting separately or within a world organization, are capable of responding to the demands made upon them by altering circumstances. If so, then the construction of the world community is unimportant; if not, then local resistances to change will require the support of local defences, and of international organizations in which localities can unite against the demands made upon them by others. In these terms world government could be the negation of a world community.

II. LAW OF RESPONSIBILITY

A system of sovereign States, each independently evolving policies designed to pursue its interests within the framework of a world community, rests upon the recognition of sovereign equality by all. While this has been the legal position, in the power model some States are 'more equal' than others. In the altered political environment of the nuclear era, sovereign equality is more widely observed. In order that such a system can operate, each State is obliged to assume that each other State is acting or believes it is acting in its own best interests. An exercise in role-reversal is required of decision-making in interpreting the policies and likely responses of other States.

To operate the communications or decision-making model, not only must there be an assumption of rationality, but furthermore, an endeavour to understand the national decision-making process which is assumed to exist. In the absence of relevant information, faulty information and distorted images may be determining policy. Each State has the opportunity to convince others that their perception is faulty; each State must, however, finally accept the policies of others as being designed to achieve their interests. An assumption in the communication or decision-making model is that the policies of other States are perceived as the most rewarding for them in the given circumstances and with given knowledge. This could be termed the Law of Responsibility. In the Cuba crisis, the United States took the position that missiles in Cuba were perceived as a threat to the United States and had to be removed by force if necessary. The Soviet took the stand that any attack on Cuba was a matter of vital concern—whether for reasons of prestige, internal politics, or idealism is of no relevance—to the Soviet. Each had to accept the judgement of the other, no matter how irrational it might have appeared. Only when each was accepted was settlement possible. Confrontation between Malaysia and Indonesia, India and China, or any other conflict is negotiable or not according to whether there is or is not this role-reversal acceptance of the position of the other side. It is when communication in this matter breaks down that one side endeavours to impose its policy upon the other.

III. ADJUSTMENT AND APPEASEMENT

The option States have always faced is that of restraint and adjustment, or, the use of force or power to resist change. In the twentieth century this option no longer favours the most powerful States. Acceptance of change and adjustment is now the lot of all States in a world society in which nuclear weapons and political consensus have created some egalitarian conditions. Nevertheless, the option still exists, even though adjustment or compromise is chosen in most cases. To what extent will Great

Powers be prepared to adjust, and to what extent will dissatisfied States be prepared to accommodate to 'neo-colonialism'—
where is the line to be drawn between adjustment and appeasement? In a border dispute at what point are vital national
interests threatened? In a racial conflict, where is the line to be
drawn between accommodation and sacrificing the integrity of
the established society?

There are no accepted laws in respect of these matters; in
any event, each dispute is a separate case, and judgement of
national interest transcends observation of law. There is no
court of reference, whose opinion can be enforced. A relevant
influence is a world consensus, which along with the nuclear
deterrent is the important feature of modern world society.

However, the final decision is with the State. How much
change is acceptable in the economic, social and political
areas of the national society? One central value is survival of the
group, and of the essential character of the group. There have
been inroads made into the sanctity of commercial interests;
but the image each nation has of itself has so far not allowed
major change. It is this which is nationalism. Political conflict,
and even war, is still entertained as necessary in the protection
of some values.

The 'Just War' thinking is still widespread; at least super-
ficially, it now relates to political rather than to commercial
interests. A clear distinction exists in the minds of the Soviet
citizen and of the United States citizen of a 'just war'. 'In
substance, the just war is the war fought either in self-defence
or in collective defence against an armed attack. Conversely,
the unjust—and, of course, the unlawful—war is the war
initiated in circumstances other than those of self- or collective-
defence against armed aggression.'[1] The American prosecutor
stated before the International Military Tribunal at Nuremberg,
'Our position is that whatever grievances a nation may have,
however objectionable it finds that *status quo*, aggressive warfare
is an illegal means for settling those grievances or for altering
those conditions'.

It is not an accident that the doctrine of the just war is
advanced by academics and representatives from a powerful
nation; the doctrine is, in practice if not in exposition, little
more than the argument that any attack on the *status quo* is

[1] Tucker, pp. 16 and 31.

unjust and illegal; change can be brought about legally only with willing consent of dominant powers. When Dulles said 'we know that our enemies do not have moral scruples' he was logically correct on the assumptions of the doctrine; our enemies are by definition those who wish to change the *status quo*. Mr Dulles recognized the need for peace to be based on justice, and observed, 'If you have a world in which force is not used, you must also have a world in which a just solution of problems of this sort can be achieved'. The occasion was the Suez Canal crisis. A fair interpretation is that it is for the State with the predominance of power to determine what are or are not just solutions to problems. It is necessary only to undertake role-reversal exercises in relation to Suez and Panama, South Vietnam and Cuba, Greece and Hungary, to show how subjective is this doctrine of 'just war'. The 'just war' doctrine is a power-politics doctrine. If there is just or legal war, then, in a system in which there are no peaceful means of change, there must also be just and legal aggression.

It is impossible, however, to separate value-judgements from the operations which establish them; it is precisely because the power model has been the accepted one, because of policies based upon it, that the values that exist do exist. A different value-judgement exists in nonaligned States, and the goal of survival in the nuclear age is forcing upon States an alteration of popular value-judgements which they helped, in different circumstances to instil. This was one of the problems President Kennedy faced during the Cuban crisis. Economic adjustment to disarmament, economic adjustment to growth in developing economies, sociological adjustment to the impact of new philosophies and ideas, all relate to important aspects of peace and security, and are possible only by deliberate State leadership and action, designed to ensure adjustment.

IV. THE UNITED STATES

We have already observed that internal adjustment will be especially difficult for democracies. Of all States, the United States of America will have most difficulty in adjusting to the changed world environment. The changes that are taking place in the world environment require an acceptance of economic and political policies and institutions in foreign States which are unacceptable within the United States. When change occurs in neighbouring regions, as in the case of Cuba, it is interpreted as a challenge to the institutions of the United States. Even when further away, United States action is directed to preserve institutions which may not be relevant. Kaplan has observed:

The United States is not always aware of its role as the gendarme of the *status quo*, although the character of the regimes which the United States has supported in the past and at the present time—together with its well-known aversion to socio-economic reforms which transgress the sanctity of private property relationships (no matter where it exists, how it was acquired in the first place, and how venal and corruptive its impact on a given country)—ineluctably stamps the United States as the main bulwark of the *status quo* in a revolutionary world.[1]

In South Vietnam the United States 'permitted capital equipment to be imported under the program only for privately owned and operated enterprises'.[2] The inability to accept and to adapt internally to altered conditions in other States inevitably leads the United States to act defensively in its external relations, and to interfere in the domestic policies of other States. United States relations with Communist China have had an irrational aspect, and have been justified by distortion of fact and circumstances which have made progressively more difficult any alteration in attitudes. The power approach, the ability not to have to adjust, has so dominated United States policies, that future full adjustment to the nuclear era is likely to be politically impossible. Where pressures can be brought to bear safely, as perhaps in Latin America, United States institutions will be preserved there for as long as possible; where pressures cannot safely be brought to bear the United States will tend to isolate itself, as has been the case with Cuba.

As Asia and Africa turn to socialism in one form or another, and as the welfare State develops elsewhere, and as intervention, for example by economic and technical aid, becomes less effective in influencing trends, the United States will tend to isolate itself from world developments. Tensions within the United States are inevitable; United States' commitment to its institutions is not only a political reality in terms of popular attitude, but is also founded upon and backed by interests

[1] Kaplan, p. 219.
[2] J. D. Montgomery, *The Politics of Foreign Aid*, 1962.

which must be judged to be as influential as any likely political leadership. On the other hand, it is United States' diplomats and scholars that have made the most outstanding contributions to International Relations in the last five years; it is they who have detected the nuclear dilemmas, and pointed to the need for communication, goal-changing, and adjustment to altered conditions.

V. POWER AND COMMUNICATION

Technological developments, improved international planning, and consultation, have greatly reduced the political incidence of economic relations between States; in a sense, success in this field has aggravated political tension. The more closely States are tied commercially, geographically and by communication, the more threatening appears to be the influence of foreign political ideas. The power which will win the Cold War is the one which is first able to expose its institutions to competition, and therefore the first to make adjustments which are relevant to it and which make of it a politically relevant system in terms of the needs and ambitions of its people. It is not clear that Western Democracies are destined to win, and the cybernetic model provides a clear warning in this respect. Defence of certain political institutions, which in any event needed protection against internal pressures, by the employment of force against another State, may qualify as a 'just war' within a power-model, but as an unnecessary suicide within a communications model.

Power and communication models both have a relevance once there is a power situation already in existence. Take the example of Australia. Australia, located in Asia, will be required by international pressures to employ its resources in the interests of Asian peoples, and to work out a mutually satisfactory resource-exploitation relationship, if not to accept major modifications in migration policy. But the power situation already dominates policy; there is isolation from Asia, non-participation in Asian conferences, reliance on United States defence pacts. The fear-power approach is incompatible with an adjustment, goal-changing approach. Current Australian foreign, migration and economic policies will ultimately bring about the situation they seek to prevent, and while this might even be understood by political leaders, the fear-power approach will continue without major modification and lead to ultimate confrontation with Asia.

South Africa, Australia, the United States are amongst many States that are already committed to a power-politics approach to their relations with many other States. Any alternative approach may be impossible to adopt, at least in the absence of an understanding by others of this fear-power involvement, and deliberate steps taken by others to allow adjustment over an extended period of time. The balance between pressures upon *status quo* States, and giving necessary time for adjustment, is a delicate one to maintain by those that are dissatisfied with the existing international structure. Furthermore, it is politically an impossible policy to follow for any length of time, as was demonstrated in the case of Japan in the 'thirties. Any government intent upon giving other States time to adjust, as the earlier Japanese government did, is likely to fall in favour of a more determined and aggressive one.

Once foreign policy is perceived as a function of domestic planning, the scope for adjustment is widened. The options are not merely the give and take in international negotiation, but also the give and take in domestic planning. In a border dispute, there are prestige and perhaps strategic options relating to where a line is to be drawn, but there are also others which are domestic in character and will not appear at the conference table, such as re-settlement and re-employment of displaced persons, altered strategy, altered trading patterns if resources are affected. In an ideological conflict there are prestige and strategic bargaining positions, as in Korea, Vietnam and Berlin; there are also options affecting political institutions, degrees of independence of foreign control, the interests of governing elites. The power-model provides no alternatives to conflict, or power politics in one form or another; a communications model at least points to the possibilities within decision-making processes of weighing both the international bargaining options and the internal adjustments.

It is for this reason that mediation is an increasingly important international institution. No Asian government believed that the Sino-Indian border dispute was one which had only a power motivation or outcome; all were aware of domestic political factors, especially in India. It is mediation, rather than negotiation, which is the instrument suitable where unilateral internal adjustment is required as part of a settlement. The conflict situations which have developed in Asia and Africa, since new States were created there, are ones which are likely to become even more numerous as border and related disputes occur. They will relate to prestige, leadership, tribal custom, irrational resource distribution consequent upon colonial demarcations; the processes toward settlement will necessitate internal accommodation to change, face-saving, sometimes population movements, and other steps which are not encouraged by outside decision and enforcement, but are made possible by internal processes of adjustment.

VI. POLITICAL SCIENCE AND POLICY

Because it is beginning to observe these features of world society, and to explain them, the study of International Relations is entering upon a phase which will bring it into sharp conflict, not only with orthodox studies, but also with orthodox policies. The Political Scientist is not concerned with solutions or goals, but an analysis of processes of relations between States is as challenging to foreign policy now as Keynsian theories were to traditional fiscal policy in the 'thirties. In that case reversal of accepted policy was required if governments were to achieve their goal of economic stability—expansion instead of contraction of credit was required in periods of recession. In this case, reversal of many accepted policies is required if governments are to achieve their goal of peace and security.

We arrive at these conclusions:
Orthodox power theory is based on several assumptions that cannot be substantiated; it has led to policy conclusions that are both self-perpetuating and self-defeating in terms of peace and security; the altered strategic and political conditions of the nuclear age have imposed significant restraints on the employment of force, and on the exercise of economic and political power; States are being obliged to break from reliance upon alliance and forms of collective security, and to pursue their own independent strategic and political policies; these trends which seem to be strengthened by current strategic and political conditions are part of a long-term continuum toward increased

nationalism associated with the growth of the modern State; the world society is one in which there is an increasing independence of each of its units, each co-operating in regional and functional arrangements, and in an international organization that no longer rests upon enforcement;

Accompanying the decrease in the role of force and of power, there is an increase in the role of decision-making, which implies an increased interest in each State in the responses of other States to its policies, in processes of change, in goal-changing, and in national adjustment to change elsewhere; to understand these aspects of relations between States, concepts, systems and models are required which relate to steering, to communication, to feed-back and to other aspects of decision-making.

Nonalignment, looked at in this perspective, is a relevant response to the conditions of the nuclear age; and there are trends in relations between other States toward a world society of independent States that do not rest on, however much they are influenced by, power relations; these trends can be explained by reference to the theory of nonalignment; under pressure of nuclear and political circumstances a system not dependent upon power is emerging, comprising independent States, each pursuing policies designed to avoid involvement in the affairs of others; and the theoretical basis of this system is non-discrimination in political as well as economic relations.

BIBLIOGRAPHY

WORKS CITED IN THE TEXT

Accra Conference. Official Reports.

BAADE, F. *The Race to the Year 2000.* Camelot Press, 1962.

BARWICK, Sir Garfield. Roy Milne Lecture reported in *Current Notes on International Affairs.* Australian Department of External Affairs, Canberra, July 1962.

BAYLEY, David H. 'The Indian Experience with Preventive Detention', *Pacific Affairs,* Vol. XXXV, No. 2. University of California, Summer 1962.

Belgrade Conference. Proceedings of the *Conference of Heads of State or Government of Nonaligned Countries,* Belgrade, 1-6 September 1961.

BLYDEN, Edward W. 'African "Neutralism" and "Nonalignment"'. Paper presented to the *Fourth International Conference on World Politics,* 1962.

BOASSON, C. H. *Approaches to the Study of International Relations.* Van Gorcum, 1963.

BOULDING, K. E. *Conflict and Defence: A General Theory.* Harper and Row, 1962.

BURNS, E. M. *Ideas in Conflict.* Methuen, 1963.

BURTON, John W. *Peace Theory: Preconditions of Disarmament.* Knopf, 1962.

——.'Regionalism and Functionalism', *Australian Outlook,* Vol. 15, No. 1, April 1961.

BUTZ, Otto. *Of Man and Politics.* Holt, Rinehart and Winston, 1961.

Cairo Conference. Official Reports.

CALLARD, Keith. *Pakistan: A Political Study.* Macmillan (New York), 1957.

——. 'Pakistan's Foreign Policy'. Paper presented to the Thirteenth Conference of the *Institute of Pacific Relations,* New York, 1957.

CALVOCORESSI, P. *World Order and New States.* Chatto and Windus, for the Institute of Strategic Studies, 1962.

CARTHY, J. D. and F. J. Ebling (eds.). *The Natural History of Aggression.* Academic Press, 1964.

CHILDERS, Erskine. *Common Sense about the Arab World.* Gollancz, 1960.

CHURCHILL, Sir Winston. *The Second World War, Vol. VI: Triumph and Tragedy.* Cassell, 1954.

——. House of Commons Speech on independent deterrent, quoted in *The New York Times,* March 1955.

CLARK, G. and L. Sohn. *World Peace through World Law.* Harvard University Press, 1960.

CLAUDE, I. *Power and International Relations*. Random House, 1962.
——. *Swords into Plowshares: The Problems and Progress of International Organization*. Random House, 2nd ed., 1959.
CLEMENTIN, J. R. 'The Nationalist Dilemma in Vietnam', *Pacific Affairs*, Vol. XXIII, No. 3, September 1950.
COHN, George. *Neo-Neutrality*. Translated from Danish by A. S. Keller and E. Jensen. Columbia University Press, 1939.
Conference. *See under* Accra, Belgrade, Cairo, Fourth.
CRNOBRNJA, Bogdan. Article in *Krsto Bulajic* (Belgrade).
DAVIES, Chief H. O. 'The New African Profile', *Foreign Affairs*, Vol. 40, No. 2. January 1962.
DEAY, S. K. *Panchayat-i-Raj: A Synthesis*. Asia Publishing House, 1962.
DEUTSCH, K. *The Nerves of Government*. Free Press, 1963.
DJERDJA, Josip. Article in *Krsto Bulajic* (Belgrade). Translated by C. Kiriloff.
DOUGLAS, William O. *North of Malaya*. Gollancz, 1954.
EDWARDES, Michael. *Asia in the Balance*. Penguin, 1962.
EMERSON, Rupert. *Representative Government in Southeast Asia*. Cambridge, Mass., 1955.
EVATT, H. V. *Australia in World Affairs*. Angus and Robertson, 1946.
FLEMING, D. Frank. *The Cold War and its Origins, 1917-1960*. Allen and Unwin, 1961.
FOLSON, B. G. D. 'The Communist View of Colonialism—an African View'. Paper presented to the *Fourth International Conference on World Politics*, 1962.
Fourth International Conference on World Politics. Athens, September 1962.
FOX, W. T. R. (ed.). *Theoretical Aspects of International Relations*. University of Notre Dame Press, 1959.
FRANKEL, J. *The Making of Foreign Policy*. Oxford University Press, 1963.
FRIEDMANN, W. *The Changing Structure of International Law*. Stevens, 1964.
FROMM, Erich. *May Man Prevail?* Doubleday, 1961.
GALBRAITH, Kenneth. Address on economic development reported in *The Hindu*, July 1961.
HAMMER, E. J. 'The Bao Dai Experiment', *Pacific Affairs*, Vol. XXIII, No. 1, March 1950.
HARTMANN, F. H. *The Relations of Nations*. Macmillan (New York), 2nd ed., 1962.
HEILBRONER, Robert L. *The Future as History*. Harper, 1960.
HERALD, G. W. 'Indo-China, Uncensored', *United Nations World*, Vol. VII, No. 3, March 1953.
HERZ, John H. *International Politics in the Atomic Age*. Columbia University Press, 1959.

HINDLEY, Donald. 'The Indonesian Communists and the C. P. S. U. Twenty-Second Congress', *Asian Survey*, Vol. II, No. 2. University of California (Institute of International Studies), March 1962.

HINSLEY, F. H. *Power and the Pursuit of Peace.* Cambridge University Press, 1963.

HINTON, H. C. In *Major Governments of Asia* (ed. G. McT. Kahin). Cornell University Press, 1958.

HOFFMAN, George and Frederick Neal. *Yugoslavia and the New Communism.* Twentieth Century Fund, New York, 1962.

HOFFMANN, S. (ed.). *Contemporary Theory in International Relations.* Prentice-Hall, 1960.

JOHNSON, Paul. Article in the *New Statesman*. London, 1 June, 1962.

KAHIN, G. McT. (ed.). *Major Governments of Asia.* Cornell University Press, 1958.

KAPLAN, M. (ed.). *The Revolution in World Politics.* Wiley, 1963.

KATZENBACH, E. L. 'Indo-China: A Military Political Appreciation', *World Politics*, Vol. IV, No. 2, January 1952.

KELMAN, H. C. Article in *Journal of Social Issues*, Vol. XI, No. 1, 1955.

KENNAN, George F. *Soviet Foreign Policy, 1917-1941.* Van Nostrand, 1960.

——. *Russia, the Atom and the West.* Oxford University Press, 1958.

KENNEDY, Senator John F. Statement in Congress, quoted in *Royal Institute of International Affairs*, Vol. 37, No. 4, p. 458. Oxford University Press, October 1961.

KISKER, George W. *World Tension.* Prentice-Hall, 1951.

KLERRUU, Wilbert. Statement on Preventive Detention in *Manchester Guardian Weekly*, 11 October 1962.

KRAUS, Wolfgang. 'Political Development in a time of Crisis: Notes on Democracy and Leadership in the New Afro-Asian States'. Paper presented to the *Fourth International Conference on World Politics*, 1962.

KUMARAPPA, Dr B. *Capitalism, Socialism or Villagism?* Shakti Karyalayam, Madras, 1946.

LANGROD, G. *The International Civil Service.* Sythoff-Leyden, 1963.

LAQUEUR, Walter. 'The End of the Monolith', *Foreign Affairs*, Vol. XL, No. 3, April 1962.

LASSWELL, H. D. 'The Scientific Study of International Relations', *The Year Book of World Affairs*. Stevens, 1958.

LEIFER, Michael. *Cambodia and Neutrality*, Working paper, No. 1, Department of International Relations, Australian National University, 1962.

LIPPMANN, Walter. *The New Diplomacy of the Nuclear Age.* Speech delivered to the Anglo-American Press Association, Paris, 1962.

LYON, P. *Neutralism*. Leicester University Press, 1963.

McLELLAN, D. S., W. C. Olson, and F. A. Sondermann (eds.). *The Theory and Practice of International Relations*. Prentice-Hall, 1960.

MAIR, L. *New Nations*. Wiedenfeld and Nicolson, 1963.

MANNING, C. A. W. *The University Teaching of Social Sciences: International Relations*. UNESCO, 1954.

MARCUS, John T. *Neutralism and Nationalism in France*. Bookman Associates, New York, 1958.

MARTIN, L. W. (ed.). *Neutralism and Nonalignment*. Praeger, 1962.

MAUNG MAUNG, Dr U. *Burma in the Family of Nations*. (Revised 2nd ed., Amsterdam, Djambatan, 1957.) Published also in the United States and Canada by the Institute of Pacific Relations (New York, 1957).

MILL, L. A. *British Malaya 1824-1867*. Methodist Publishing House, Singapore, 1925.

MILLS, C. Wright. *The Sociological Imagination*. Grove Press, 1961.

MODELSKI, George (ed.). *SEATO: Six Studies*. F. W. Cheshire for the Australian National University, Melbourne, 1962.

——. *A Theory of Foreign Policy*. Pall Mall Press, 1962.

MONTGOMERY, J. D. *The Politics of Foreign Aid*. Praeger, 1962.

MORGENTHAU, Hans J. *Politics among Nations: The Struggle for Power and Peace*. 3rd ed., 1960.

——. 'A Political Theory of Foreign Aid', *American Political Science Review*, Vol. LVI, No. 2, June 1962.

NASSER, Gamal Abdel. *The Charter*.

NEHRU, Jawaharlal. *Nehru's Speeches 1949-53, Vol. I, II, III*. The Publications Division, Ministry of Information, Government of India, 1958.

——. Introduction to *Paths to Peace* (ed. V. H. Wallace), Melbourne University Press, 1957.

NIEMEYER, G. *Law Without Force*. Princeton University Press, 1941.

NKRUMAH, Kwame. Speech at the *Belgrade Conference*.

PARKINSON, F. 'Social Dynamics of Underdeveloped Countries', in the *Fourteenth Year Book of World Affairs*. Stevens, 1960.

PARTRIDGE, P. H. 'Images of the International Order', in *The Australian Journal of Politics and History*, Vol. IX, No. 1. University of Queensland Press, May 1963.

PAUL, J. and J. Laulicht. *In Your Opinion*. Canadian Peace Research Institute, 1963.

PURCELL, Victor. *Malaya: Communist or Free?* 1954.

RABINOWITCH, Eugene. 'The Failure at Geneva', *Bulletin of the Atomic Scientists*, Vol. XVI, No. 2, February 1960.

RADAKAMAL, Mukerjee and H. J. Dey. *Economic Problems of India*. Macmillan, 1941.

RAJKUMAR, N. *The Background of India's Foreign Policy*. Foreword by Lal Bahadur Shastri. All Indian Congress Committee, 1952.

RIVKIN, Arnold. 'Principal Elements of U.S. Policy towards Under-developed Countries'. Lecture to *Royal Institute of International Affairs*, Vol. XXXVII, No. 4, Oxford University Press, October 1961.

ROSENAU, G. N. (ed.), *International Politics and Foreign Policy*. Free Press, 1961.

ROSS, David. The Belgrade Conference article in *New Left Review* (London) No. 12.

RUSSELL, Bertrand. *Common Sense and Nuclear Warfare*. Allen and Unwin, 1959.

——. 'The Case for British Nuclear Disarmament', *Bulletin of the Atomic Scientists*, Vol. XVII, No. 3, March 1962.

SALISBURY, R. F. *From Stone to Steel*. Melbourne University Press, 1962.

SANDFORD, F. H. *Psychology—A Scientific Study of Man*. Wadsworth Publishing Co., 1961.

SCHUMAN, Frederick L. *International Politics: The Western State System in Transition*. McGraw-Hill, 3rd ed., 1941.

SCHWARZENBERGER, G. *Power Politics: A Study of World Society*. Stevens, 3rd ed., 1964.

SETON-WATSON, Professor. 'Nationalism and Imperialism—Old and New'. Paper presented to the *Fourth International Conference on World Politics*, 1962.

SHERWANI, Latif Ahmed. 'The basis of Nationalism in the new Afro-Asian States'. Paper presented to the *Fourth International Conference on World Politics*, 1962.

SNYDER, R. C., H. W. Bruck, and B. Sapin. *Foreign Policy Decision-Making: An Approach to the Study of International Politics*. Free Press, 1962.

SPANIER, J. W. and J. L. Nogee. *The Politics of Disarmament*. Praeger, 1962.

SPATE, Oskar. Article in *The Asiatic Review*, Vol. XLIV, London, January 1948.

SPIRO, Herbert J. 'New Constitutional Forms in Africa', *World Politics*, Vol. XIII, October 1960.

SPYKMAN, N. *America's Strategy in World Politics*. Harcourt, Brace, 1942.

STALEY, Eugene. *The Future of Under-developed Countries: Political Implications of Economic Development*, published by the Council of Foreign Relations. Harper, 1961.

STANOVNIK, Janez. 'The Economics of Nonalignment', *Krsto Bulajic* (Belgrade).

STEVENSON, George H. 'Canada' in *World Tension* (ed. George W. Kisker), Prentice-Hall, 1951.

STONE, Isador F. *The Hidden History of the Korean War*. Turnstile Press, 1952.

SUKARNO, Dr Ahmed. Belgrade Conference, 1961.

Survey of International Affairs, 1930.

THOMPSON, Kenneth W. *Political Realism and the Crisis of World Politics*. Princeton University Press, 1960.

THOMPSON, Virginia McLean and R. Adloff. *The Left Wing in Southeast Asia*. Published under the auspices of International Secretariat, Institute of Pacific Relations. William Sloane Associates, New York, 1950.

TÖRNUDD, K. *Soviet Attitudes towards Non-Military Regional Co-operation*. Helsingfors, 2nd ed., 1963.

TUCKER, R. W. *The Just War*. Johns Hopkins University Press, 1960.

TUGBIYELE, Emmanuel A. 'What Contribution can the Nonaligned Afro-Asian Countries make toward World Peace and Development?' Paper presented to the *Fourth International Conference on World Politics*, 1962.

WADIA, P. A. and K. T. Merchant. *Our Economic Problem*. New Book Company, Bombay, 1954.

WALLACE, V. H. (ed.). *Paths to Peace*. Melbourne University Press, 1957.

WALTZ, K. N. *Man, the State and War*. Columbia University Press, 1959.

WIENER, N. *The Human Use of Human Beings*. Eyre and Spottiswoode, 1950.

WIGHTMAN, D. *Toward Economic Co-operation in Asia*. Yale University Press, 1963.

WILLIAMS, W. A. *The Tragedy of American Diplomacy*. World Publishing Co., Cleveland, 1959.

WOLFERS, A. *Discord and Collaboration*. Johns Hopkins University Press, 1962.

WRIGHT, Q. *The Study of International Relations*. Appleton-Century-Crofts, 1955.

INDEX